ROGER STEVENSON
MARCH, 1993

**A New Diversity
in Contemporary
Southern Rhetoric**

A New Diversity in Contemporary Southern Rhetoric

Edited by
Calvin M. Logue
and Howard Dorgan

Louisiana State University Press
Baton Rouge and London

Designer: Christopher Wilcox
Typeface: Palatino
Typesetter: G & S Typesetters, Inc.
Printer: Thomson-Shore, Inc.
Binder: John Dekker and Sons, Inc.

10 9 8 7 6 5 4 3 2 1

Library of Congress Cataloging-in-Publication Data

A New diversity in contemporary Southern rhetoric.

  Includes bibliographical references and index.
  1. Political oratory—Southern States.   2. Speeches,
addresses, etc., American—Southern States—History
and criticism.   3. United States—Politics and government—1945–   .   I. Logue, Cal M. (Cal McLeod),
1935–   II. Dorgan, Howard.
PN4193.P6N48   1987   815'.01'08975   86-21152
ISBN 0-8071-1312-3

Contents

Acknowledgments

With this collection of original essays on public discourse in the contemporary South, the inquiry into southern public address continues. Waldo W. Braden edited *Oratory in the Old South* and *Oratory in the New South*, and Cal M. Logue and Howard Dorgan edited *The Oratory of Southern Demagogues*. In addition, the LSU Press published Braden's *Oral Tradition in the South* (1983), which, among other things, examines the nature of the southern orator.

All of these books, including the present one, carry forward an area of scholarly investigation first promoted by the late Dallas C. Dickey of the University of Florida. By directing several graduate studies in southern public address and by presenting to the Speech Association of America (now the Speech Communication Association) the idea for the first volume in this series, Dickey gave a strong impetus to the early interest in southern oratory. When Dickey died, Waldo W. Braden, Boyd Professor Emeritus of Speech, Louisiana State University, became the scholar who would promote and direct much of the recent study of public discourse in the South. Indeed, it was Braden who, in delivering the keynote address at the 1974 Conference on the Rhetoric of the Contemporary South, Boone, North Carolina, inspired this collection of essays.

Therefore, the editors wish to express our indebtedness to him for his research in the area of southern public address and for his encouragement during our work on this study. In addition, we note the contributions of Carl Kell, Western Kentucky University, and Stuart Towns, University of West Florida, who along with Howard Dorgan cosponsored six summer conferences on the rhetoric of the contemporary South. Finally, we recognize the support and advice provided by the editors at the Louisiana State University Press.

A New Diversity
in Contemporary
Southern Rhetoric

INTRODUCTION

Public Discourse
in a Changing South

Calvin M. Logue
Howard Dorgan

With the close of World War II, the South entered a period of radical economic and social change. Many southerners' wartime experiences had included a move from farm to town as war-related industries and services demanded manpower. Then the immediate postwar period continued to be marked by accelerated industrialization and urbanization, which were generated by the rush to supply goods-hungry Americans with merchandise denied them during the war. Although this postwar South remained "rural in outlook," notes Numan V. Bartley, "almost half" of the 1950 southern population was residing in cities, and "income from industry and services dwarfed that from cotton and tobacco."[1]

More significant, however, was a change occurring in the South's social structure. In the 1940s, southern blacks and whites began the initial struggles that ultimately resulted in a major postwar realignment in the region's race relations. Numerous young southern blacks returned to civilian life after having served in areas where the color line was less obvious and less restrictive. Furthermore, those who returned probably knew many of those who did

1. Numan V. Bartley, *The Rise of Massive Resistance: Race and Politics in the South During the 1950s* (Baton Rouge, 1969), 10.

1

not, but who joined a swelling tide of minorities migrating to industrial centers in the Northeast and Midwest, where chances for economic and social advancement appeared more promising.

In addition, southern blacks began to hear civil rights demands from "brothers" and "sisters" outside the region. By 1942 the Congress of Racial Equality (CORE) had been formed and had staged sit-ins in some public accommodations in northern and border states, and in 1947, members of CORE made the first "freedom ride" into the upper South. The following year, President Harry Truman issued an executive order racially integrating the nation's armed forces, and the United States Supreme Court ordered the University of Oklahoma Law School to admit a black, Mrs. Ada Lois Sipuel. Indeed, between 1948 and 1952, federal and state courts handed down a series of decisions in Kentucky, Oklahoma, Tennessee, North Carolina, Texas, and Virginia that forced state-supported graduate and professional schools to admit blacks.[2] By the time the Supreme Court made its reexamination of the old "separate but equal" principle of the 1896 *Plessy* v. *Ferguson* decision, the South had begun to feel surrounded by an integration-of-public-higher-education movement that threatened to sweep across the border states and into the Deep South.

Then came 1954 and the Supreme Court's decision in *Brown* v. *Board of Education*. What followed was the nation's second great assault against Dixie, and what eventually resulted was a significantly altered South. As a consequence of *Brown* and other rulings, which successfully challenged and significantly dismantled the long-established caste system of racial segregation, southern blacks and whites became caught in strong crosscurrents of commercial, industrial, social, religious, educational, and political change. The decision provided impetus for more than two decades of civil rights struggles that began over public education but soon touched all areas of southern social and economic life. The South was to change and to change irrevocably. Therefore, it seems appropriate to speak of the "contemporary South" as that South developing after the *Brown* decision. It is this South and the

2. August Meier and Elliott Rudwick, *CORE: A Study in the Civil Rights Movement, 1942–1968* (Urbana, 1975), 3–39; *Sipuel* v. *Board of Regents of the University of Oklahoma,* 332 U.S. 631 (1948); see Willard Alva Underwood, *The Rhetoric of Black Orators: Perspectives for Contemporary Analysis* (Ann Arbor, 1973), 107–10.

public discourse of the region that the authors in this volume study.

A Brief Overview of the Contemporary South

Several students of southern history have noted parallels between the South of 1954 to the present and the South of 1861 to just after the turn of the century.[3] Succinctly stated, the modern side of these parallels suggests that in 1954 the nation launched its second great war against a dissident South. With the full force of numerous political and social institutions—national legislative bodies, the courts, the mass media, organized religion, education, and even the arts—a massive assault was launched against forced segregation in the South. By the mid-1960s, following ugly racial disturbances in Little Rock, Montgomery, Selma, and Birmingham and the 1963 March on Washington with the "I Have a Dream" speech by Martin Luther King, Jr., a solid national consensus had emerged against Dixie's segregationist policies, and the South had once again been defeated.

Then came the last half of the 1960s and the Second Reconstruction. The Civil Rights Act of 1964 desegregated public accommodations; the Voting Rights Act of 1965 opened polls to blacks; and the Civil Rights Act of 1968 declared discrimination in housing illegal. Coinciding with passage of these acts was an outpouring of state and federal court decisions implementing the *Brown* mandate. Like it or not, the South was being reconstructed.

By the early 1970s the South had entered what H. Brandt Ayers suggests was a period of neo-progressivism, or what might have been labeled the "new New South." Led by a cadre of moderate state governors—Linwood Holton of Virginia, Reubin Askew of Florida, Dale Bumpers of Arkansas, and Jimmy Carter of Georgia—and perhaps inspired by the optimistic pronouncements of the L. Q. C. Lamar Society, the South rushed headlong toward the modernizing moods, values, and programs of the emerging south-

3. See, for example, John Egerton, *The Americanization of Dixie; The Southernization of America* (New York, 1974), 23; C. Vann Woodward, *The Burden of Southern History* (Rev. ed.; Baton Rouge, 1968), 107. Woodward, however, expressed caution about this tendency to draw parallels between Reconstruction and the Second Reconstruction (168–71).

ern Sun Belt. Mirroring the experiences of the original New South, southern states were now promoted as having solved their racial problems and as having rejoined the Union. During the 1880s and 1890s, Henry W. Grady and John B. Gordon, among others, had suggested that the South could be trusted as a stable area for capital investments and as a dedicated partner in the nation's new imperialistic endeavors.[4] Likewise, some southerners of the 1970s lauded the region as fertile soil for every seed of social and economic progress, even claiming that the time had come for Dixie to assume a position of national leadership. "The freshest, most helpful, most energetic section of the country," argued Terry Sanford, "is the South. . . . The South's time has come, after a century of being the whipping boy and backward child. The South can lead the nation . . . and all the better, because the nation has never been in greater need of leadership."[5]

The fearful, defensive, self-isolated South that less than a decade earlier had retreated behind the slogans "It's all because of outside agitation" and "Leave us to settle our own problems" seemed to have disappeared. Also less visible was the one-issue, one-minded political environment that had bred the extremes of Orval Faubus, Lester Maddox, and George Wallace. The constant marches and demonstrations usually climaxing in violence had subsided. Furthermore, that somewhat sanctimonious image of the rest of the nation was tarnished. Violent episodes in Watts, Chicago, and Newark proved that racial animosities were not limited to the South. Indeed, the 1970s saw a beleaguered Boston send representatives to Charlotte, North Carolina, to study how that southern city had integrated its public schools.[6]

The 1970s witnessed the exuberance of southerners rediscover-

4. H. Brandt Ayers, "You Can't Eat Magnolias," in Ayers and Thomas H. Naylor (eds.), *You Can't Eat Magnolias* (New York, 1972), 16–18; "Could It Be the South's Turn to Save the Union?" Atlanta *Journal*, April 16, 1972; Henry W. Grady, "The New South," in A. Craig Baird (ed.), *American Public Address, 1740–1952* (New York, 1956), 187; Cal M. Logue, "Restoration Strategies in Georgia, 1865–1880," in Waldo W. Braden (ed.), *Oratory in the New South* (Baton Rouge, 1979), 38–73; see Howard Dorgan, "A Case Study in Reconciliation: General John B. Gordon and 'The Last Days of the Confederacy,'" *Quarterly Journal of Speech*, LX (1974), 90–91.

5. Sanford quoted in Atlanta *Journal*, April 16, 1972.

6. "Lesson in the South: Boston Students Observing Results of Busing in Charlotte, N.C.," *Time*, November 4, 1974, p. 88.

ing their own southernness. Numerous educated, middle- and upper-class individuals, for example, dared to reveal their enthusiastic appreciation for the "pickin' and singin'" Nashville sound. Equally large numbers of the region's professionals now lauded the virtues of southern speech, southern small-town life, southern arts and crafts, southern folklore and folkways, southern religious practices, and southern social values. Perhaps most significant, however, were the general migration *toward* the South and the increased numbers of northern blacks who now began to say, "We can go home again." Finally, there were even the in-migrants to the region who started praising the South as an example for the nation. "I believe," wrote Richard Goodwin, "that despite the adversities of the South and the wrongs of which the South can justly be accused, there are powerful elements of Southern life which can serve to liberate the entire nation. There is a sense that life is more than the accumulation of material goods; a belief in the individual, not as a solitary wanderer, but as a person whose place among his fellows is to be secured and respected; and, above all, a fierce desire that people be able to shape their own destiny in their own way." [7]

But had the South of the 1970s really begun to solve its racial problems? Was the optimistic rhetoric of the new wave of southern governors primarily wishful thinking or the expected public relations clack? Had these more recent New South promoters, as one Democratic committeewoman of Mississippi charged, merely "learned the new lingo"? [8] Were changes on the surface rather than substantive?

Unfortunately, there were enough scattered racial conflicts throughout the 1970s to cast at least a thin shadow on this new image of a harmonious, progressive South. There was a 1971 race riot in Memphis, Tennessee; there was the lengthy controversy over the Wilmington 10, nine black men and one white woman who were said to have received unfair trials and unjust sentences for actions they were accused of taking during a 1971 racial distur-

7. Richard N. Goodwin, "The End of Reconstruction," in Ayers and Naylor (eds.), *You Can't Eat Magnolias*, 66. Goodwin represents himself as a "native New Englander."

8. "Is There a New South?" *Atlanta Journal and Constitution Magazine*, February 20, 1972, p. 16.

bance in Wilmington, North Carolina; there were fights over a busing plan in Richmond, Virginia; there were racial clashes in Miami, Florida; and there were the disturbing reactivations of the Ku Klux Klan, highlighted by the Greensboro, North Carolina, bloody confrontation between the Klan and the Socialist Workers' party. All these incidents demonstrated that southerners had not created any utopia for black/white relations. In addition, as Jerry Himelstein suggested in his study of a 1979 referendum in Hattiesburg, Mississippi, some white southerners may have found new, more subtle ways to express their racism in the political process.[9]

There is one final comparison that might be drawn between the contemporary South and the South of 1861 to just after the turn of the century. In *Origins of the New South* and *The Strange Career of Jim Crow*, C. Vann Woodward established that in the last decade of the nineteenth century the South and the rest of the nation turned away from earlier reform moods and policies and entered a period during which Jim Crowism became firmly institutionalized.[10] As the United States shouldered the "white man's burden" in Cuba, Hawaii, and the Philippines some citizens conveniently forgot the lofty principles of racial justice that had inspired the Fourteenth and Fifteenth amendments to the Constitution.[11] Is it possible that a similar turning away from civil rights and equal opportunity has been demonstrated throughout the nation, as well as in the South, during the first half of the 1980s?

It is perhaps too early to answer this question definitively. Nevertheless, representatives for various minority groups have charged that in this decade they have not seen their civil rights and economic opportunities protected to the fullest possible extent. The defeat of the Equal Rights Amendment, the rise in Klan activity, the growth of such right-wing forces as the Moral Major-

9. See Robert A. Francesconi, "James Hunt, the Wilmington 10, and Institutional Legitimacy," *Quarterly Journal of Speech*, LXVIII (1982), 47–59; "Bad Days in Memphis," *Nation*, December 20, 1971, pp. 653–54; "Busing in an Angry Glare," *Life*, March 3, 1972, pp. 26–31; and *Time*, November 12, 1979, p. 20. Jerry Himelstein, "Rhetorical Continuities in the Politics of Race: The Closed Society Revisited," *Southern Speech Communication Journal*, XLVIII (1983), 153–66.

10. C. Vann Woodward, *Origins of the New South, 1877–1913* (Baton Rouge, 1951), 215–16, and *The Strange Career of Jim Crow* (New York, 1955), 69–74.

11. Woodward, *Origins of the New South*, 325.

ity and Senator Jesse Helms's Congressional Club, the critical re-examinations and the curtailing of the multitudinous social programs begun during the 1960s and 1970s, and the general policies of a more conservative national administration have been cited as evidence of the nation's abandoning that spirit of reform that dominated the American scene for almost thirty years.

Regional Change and Regional Discourse

The years between 1954 and 1984, therefore, have witnessed numerous social, economic, and political changes in the South. As George Tindall observed in 1972, "The old landmarks have fallen in rapid succession: the one-crop agriculture, the one-crop industry, the one-party system, the white primary, the poll tax, racial segregation—indeed so many foundations of the old order." [12] Furthermore, as each element of the old order was challenged a new round of regional debate ensued. Thus candid dialogues, *in the South by southerners*, developed around questions of how citizens should react to the new judicial, legislative, and social decisions affecting the region.

This new discourse emerged, in part, because for the first time in the South both white and black integrationists and segregationists were provided opportunities to express opinions. Not since Reconstruction had whites been forced to share the public forum with blacks. [13] But now, as more blacks spoke out for civil rights, registered to vote, campaigned for public office, and competed for grades and jobs, whites were required to communicate directly about and with this newly vocal minority.

In addition, southern whites were provided a broader range for participation in this public forum. Prior to 1954, most whites—at least when speaking publicly—defended the white supremacy rationales that had existed since slavery days. Whites with different views had been ostracized, smothered by popular appeals to racism, or heard only by a few who met in private. As Morton Sosna has noted, "Jim Crow ruled, and all classes of white Southerners either defended this arrangement or recognized it as a reality of

12. Tindall quoted in "Is There a New South?," 16.
13. Cal M. Logue, "The Rhetorical Appeals of Whites to Blacks During Reconstruction," *Communication Monographs*, XLIV (1977), 241–51.

the New South."[14] Now these barriers to a freer ideological expression for whites and blacks began to fall in the South, first in black churches, then on university campuses, next in some white pulpits, and finally in chambers of commerce, civic clubs, and legislative councils.

Indeed, the ensuing debate touched all the South's public and private institutions, enveloping them in a profusion of moral, ethical, legal, and practical questions. None of these institutions, however, faced a greater quandry than did southern churches. Dedicated as they supposedly were to the dignity and brotherhood of mankind, they were forced to decide whether issues of racial equality and social justice came within their purview. Black churches, of course, saw this as beyond question and quickly became the centers of minority protest. But for southern white churches—and particularly for Protestant denominations—the situation was different. Thus a regional debate developed, one that dealt specifically with the subissue of church involvement in all the disputes *Brown* had generated.

As a direct result of all these pockets of regional debate, a new diversity of public expression emerged, and it was significantly different from the narrow range of white rhetoric heard prior to 1954. Responses to court-mandated changes in the social status of blacks tended to fall into at least three general categories. First, there was the response of southern blacks, represented for example by Rosa Parks's 1955 refusal to move to the back of a bus, by the subsequent Montgomery bus boycott, by the nonviolent strategies of Martin Luther King, Jr., by the multitude of protest marches, demonstrations, freedom rides, sit-ins, kneel-ins, wade-ins, and stand-ins, and by the tremendous volume of black religious civil rights discourse. Many blacks abandoned their accommodating postures and developed more candid and assertive language, strategies, topics, and arguments. Newly won freedoms encouraged these blacks to communicate publicly the feelings, convictions, and aspirations often previously suppressed. The result was a direct black/white rhetorical confrontation over the morality, expediency, economy, and legality of racial discrimination.

14. Morton Sosna, *Southern Liberals and the Race Issue: In Search of the Silent South* (New York, 1977), 302.

A second response came from states' rights and white supremacy advocates, often in the South's demagogic tradition. Included here were the intimidation by the white Citizens' Councils, the violent reactions of such southern law enforcement stereotypes as Bull Connor, the strident voices of the Ku Klux Klan, the demagoguery of Orval Faubus, Ross Barnett, Lester Maddox, George Wallace, and similar state and local politicians, and the many racist "hate tracts" circulated throughout the South. In opposition to social change mandated by judicial and legislative action, most southern whites employed defensive rhetorical strategies built not only on traditional states' rights arguments but on biblical authority, principles of free enterprise, economic cost-effectiveness, scientific racism, education theory, and charges of Communist influence.

Finally, there was the response of white liberals and moderates. With a few notable exceptions, such as in the case of Ralph McGill and Hodding Carter II, the discourse of this group of citizens constituted a rather late rhetorical movement, since prior to the early 1970s the southern climate had often been far too hostile to whites who advocated moderate or liberal racial attitudes. But with the arrival of the late 1960s and early 1970s, there came a greater regional tolerance for integrationist principles, and thus prominent southerners such as Charles Morgan, LeRoy Collins, Reubin Askew, Dale Bumpers, and Jimmy Carter established appreciative audiences for their more progressive social doctrines. Indeed, John D. Saxon has labeled southern discourse of the early 1970s a "rhetoric of optimism," arguing that the region was then experiencing "a spirit of renewal, of change, of departure from the past, a recognition that the South [would] no longer frustrate itself with lost or negative causes." In his gubernatorial inaugural address, for example, Jimmy Carter proclaimed, "No poor, rural, weak, or black person should ever have to bear the additional burden of being deprived of the opportunity of an education, a job, or simple justice." [15]

Before the 1970s, however, there had been a sprinkling of young white southerners—mostly university students and liberal clerics

15. John D. Saxon, "Contemporary Southern Oratory: A Rhetoric of Hope, Not Desperation," *Southern Speech Communication Journal*, XL (1975), 268; Carter quoted in Ayers and Naylor (eds.), *You Can't Eat Magnolias*, 364.

or social workers—who had bravely joined the protesting blacks, who had clasped hands and sung "We Shall Overcome," and who had even participated in the marches, sit-ins, and freedom rides. Usually labeled "outside agitators," these few southern white "radicals" violated many of the region's written and unwritten laws of racial segregation. In the process, they often engendered more intense animosities among the segregationists than did their black partners in protest.

In summary, the immense social, economic, and political changes wrought in the South between 1954 and the early 1980s stimulated a diversity of public discourse. What were the various southern responses to the social changes and upheavals? What was said by the South's blacks, by conservative whites, by moderate or liberal whites, by southern governors, by national political figures from the South, by southern women fighting for or against the Equal Rights Amendment, and by southern clergymen addressing racial issues? The contributors to this volume seek answers to these questions.

The Essays

Each of the eight essays focuses on a separate subdivision of the South's rhetorical experience from approximately 1954 to 1980. The first is Howard Dorgan's "Response of the Main-line Southern White Protestant Pulpit to *Brown v. Board of Education*, 1954–1965." Dorgan finds that although early pronouncements by state and regional church conferences tended either to support *Brown* or to call for "peaceful acquiescence to its mandate," the vast majority of local clerics fell victim to the intimidating influences of traditional southern racial attitudes and to the pressures of white Citizens' Councils. In his essay he examines the discourse of the following subgroups of southern Protestant ministers: those who took a position in support of integration or of peaceful compliance with the spirit of *Brown;* those who spoke against the decision or in support of traditional southern racial attitudes; and those who remained silent on the issue. Even though his final judgment on the southern Protestant pulpit is mixed, Dorgan is generally critical of the South's spiritual leaders for their inability to assume a significant leadership role during this moral crisis.

The second essay, G. Jack Gravlee's "Black Rhetoric of Social Revolution," focuses primarily on the role of southern black religious rhetoric, particularly the contributions of Martin Luther King, Jr., in the civil rights protests. However, the essay also looks at the influence in the South of the more radical black voices of the period. Gravlee contrasts the instructional function of rhetoric and music—as these evolved from the black church and particularly from King's erudition—with the inciting but reactionary function of the strident militancy of Malcolm X and Stokely Carmichael. For the most part, Gravlee credits the progress made by southern blacks after 1954 to their rhetorical adaptation during situations of intense social conflict.

In the third essay, "Ralph McGill's Moderate Campaign for Racial Reform," Calvin M. Logue examines this influential Georgia journalist's public campaign on behalf of black southerners. After considering what motivated McGill to take his unpopular moderate stance, Logue analyzes the strategy of "public instruction" that recurred in a variety of forms in the journalist's public communication from 1946 to 1969. Logue concludes that McGill was "a crusader with common sense" and suggests that this Georgian's moderate approach to race questions provided southerners an alternative to racial conflict.

In "Fulbright and Ervin: Southern Senators with National Appeal," David Zarefsky appraises the public argumentation of J. William Fulbright and Sam Ervin. He explains how Fulbright's faith in education governed the Arkansan's stated views on civil rights and foreign policy, and how Ervin's preference for strict constitutional interpretations guided the North Carolinian's statements on human rights, free speech, and Watergate. Whereas Fulbright was scholarly but caustic, Ervin was legalistic but affable.

Harold Mixon's "The Rhetoric of States' Rights and White Supremacy" emphasizes the opposition of white Citizens' Councils to the *Brown* decision and their campaign against all subsequent actions to desegregate southern public schools, churches, and public facilities. Mixon argues that Council speakers attempted to legitimize the tradition of racial segregation by developing arguments of scientific racism and by defending the authority of states to control their own schools. The essay also contrasts the appeals communicated by Council representatives to southern audiences with the statements they made outside the region. Mixon reveals the strategies this movement employed as it attempted to halt and reverse the effects of *Brown* v. *Board of Education*.

Waldo W. Braden became curious about Saxon's depiction of southern rhetoric of the early 1970s as a "rhetoric of optimism." As a consequence, he analyzes the speeches of Deep South governors of that decade and determines that many of those public officials abandoned racist appeals of the past for more "conservative and businesslike approaches." Braden assesses the treatment of the race issue by southern gubernatorial candidates and also examines the moderate character of their inaugural addresses. He contrasts the political environment of the period from 1950 to 1969 with the demands of the new audiences in the 1970s.

John H. Patton examines "moral directions" provided in Jimmy Carter's political discourse, tracing the evolution of the Georgian's sense of justice through gubernatorial and presidential rhetoric. Patton judges Carter's southern heritage to be the source of both the president's moral concern and his difficulty in articulating worthwhile values convincingly.

Martha Solomon contrasts the "intensive," well-organized, and "colorful" southern opposition to the Equal Rights Amendment with the region's support for the measure. She attributes the failure of ERA in the South to the region's "traditional views of women's roles" and to southern fears of further social change.

Public Discourse

With this volume the editors abandon the term *oratory*, displayed so prominently in titles of the earlier works in this series on southern public address. In doing so, they express their feeling that this word no longer adequately represents the various forms of public discourse in the South after 1954. Indeed, it may well be that *oratory*, when applied to southern public discourse, promotes the stereotypic images against which Waldo W. Braden has argued so effectively. To many, the term may suggest the style of florid ceremonial speaking of the mid-nineteenth century.[16] In ad-

16. Waldo W. Braden, "The Emergence of the Concept of Southern Oratory," *Southern Speech Communication Journal*, XXVI (1961), 173–83, and "Southern Oratory Reconsidered: A Search for an Image," *Southern Speech Communication Journal*,

dition, *oratory* may connote formal speeches by prominent leaders in moments of monumental crisis. Therefore, the editors fear that the term will not signify the diversity of public persuasion heard in the South after 1954.

Summary

Perhaps *diversity* is the word that should be emphasized in this brief summary. Waldo W. Braden has expressed concern about past tendencies to stereotype southern speakers. Borrowing a phrase from Bernard Mayo, Braden argued that images of the southern orator have become "heavily myth-encrusted."[17] He applied this argument primarily to images of style and images of the character of the orator himself. However, the editors of the present volume suggest that the thesis can be extended to the question of who has done the speaking.

The mythical southern orator (a difficult stereotype to avoid) has been a white male, not a female and—with the possible exception of Booker T. Washington—not a black. Furthermore, this mythical speaker has been a particular type of male, in the sense that in one way or another he was thought to be larger than life. He was represented as being braver, wiser, more trustworthy, and more eloquent than others; or he was, in the tradition of southern demagogues, depicted as being a marvelous bombast-producing "orator." Indeed, his image tended to gravitate toward one extreme or the other, toward the statesmanship of a John C. Calhoun or toward the political sideshow buffoonery of a Cotton Ed Smith.

However, a significant feature of the contemporary South has been that a more diverse group of rhetors participated in the public forum. This factor alone challenges the established myth of "southern oratory." The essays in this volume clearly demonstrate that a variety of voices were heard as the region responded to radical social change. Furthermore, these speakers often did not belong to an elitist segment of southern society. The essays give clear evidence that men and women, blacks and whites, from di-

---

XXIX (1964), 303–15; Howard H. Martin, "'Style' in the Golden Age," *Quarterly Journal of Speech*, XLIII (1957), 374–82.

17. Braden, "The Emergence of the Concept of Southern Oratory," 173.

verse backgrounds, battled rhetorically to preserve or advance favorite causes.

After 1954, the South became a substantially open forum, which
sharply distinguishes this contemporary period from earlier ones.
Southern society at large was involved: males, females; blacks,
whites; influential public figures, ordinary people. This regional
debate involved all citizens either as speakers or respondents,
and, in a very real sense, the contemporary South became more
democratic than it had been at any other time in the region's
history.

Response of the Main-line Southern White Protestant Pulpit to *Brown* v. *Board of Education,* 1954–1965

Howard Dorgan

On January 18, 1956, Federal District Judge John E. Miller ordered the public school system of Van Buren, Arkansas, to present "concrete plans" for racial integration. Subsequently, Methodist pastor Robert Paul Sessions delivered to his Van Buren congregation a sermon entitled "Days of Decision." Sessions speculated that for the first time his town and the state of Arkansas were experiencing the "full impact" of *Brown* v. *Board of Education.* "The controversy in our courts," he said, "is but a public reflection of a personal dilemma which every Southerner faces today. In the words of a colloquialism from my boyhood," he continued, "we are 'caught between a rock and a hard place.' On one hand we have been taught from the cradle that segregation belongs to the South like fried chicken and corn bread. . . . On the other hand, each of us has become aware, increasingly in the last few years, . . . that segregation because of race . . . is illegal, unconstitutional, . . . un-American, [and] . . . un-Christian."[1]

The "rock and a hard place" image Sessions employed to describe the troubled mind of his congregation could easily have been extended to cover the spiritual dilemma faced by many southern clergymen during the ten years following the *Brown* de-

---

1. Robert Paul Sessions, "Days of Decision," *Pulpit,* XXVII (1965), 13.

15

cision. It was the conflict of soul that Ralph McGill characterized as the "agony of the southern minister" and that Reinhold Niebuhr called the "crisis in American Protestantism."[2] Succinctly stated, this dilemma placed the typical southern white Protestant minister in the position of having only three options for responding to the South's racial crisis: (1) He could take a stance in support of integration—or at least in support of peaceful acquiescence to the "law of the land"—and hazard losing his pulpit; (2) he could affirm the racial attitudes and behaviors then exhibited by typical southern Protestant congregations, thus going against what appeared to be obvious Christian morality; or (3) he could remain silent on the most vital social issue of the time, retreating to the safety of those more innocuous tenets of traditional Christian doctrine. This essay examines the rhetoric of representative main-line Protestant clergymen in each of these categories. The essay also draws conclusions about why southern white clerics were not more dynamically involved on the liberal side of this controversy.

Background of the Crisis

Southern Protestant churchmen entered the decade of the 1950s believing their institutions were making slow but steady progress in race relations. Annual church conferences and special councils had produced numerous documents affirming the universal brotherhood of man, and increased contact between black and white fellowships had resulted in a cautious optimism regarding the future of interracial programs in the region.[3] In fact, after the Supreme Court released its 1954 decision, various annual conferences produced a flood of resolutions affirming the spirit of *Brown*. The 1954 Southern Presbyterian General Assembly urged

2. Ralph McGill, "The Agony of the Southern Minister," *New York Times Magazine*, September 29, 1959, p. 16; Reinhold Niebuhr, "The Crisis in American Protestantism," *Christian Century*, LXXX (1963), 1498.

3. See David M. Reimers, *White Protestantism and the Negro* (New York, 1965), 184–85; Kenneth K. Bailey, *Southern White Protestantism in the Twentieth Century* (New York, 1964), 141–45; William Morris Tillman, Jr., "Representative Actions and Statements Among Southern Baptists Concerning Black-White Relations, 1964–1976" (Th.D. dissertation, Southwestern Baptist Theological Seminary, 1978), 32, 38–39, 52–53.

all Presbyterians "to lend their assistance to those charged with the duty of implementing the decision" and characterized compulsory segregation as "out of harmony with Christian theology and ethics." That same year the Southern Baptist Convention declared *Brown* to be "in harmony with the constitutional guarantee of equal justice and love for all men." The 1954 annual conference of North Carolina Methodists depicted the ruling as a "true interpretation of . . . Christian faith and . . . American democracy" while the Baptist General Association of Virginia formally advised: "The decision of the United States Supreme Court . . . is the supreme law of the land . . . [and] does not violate any cardinal principle of our religion. . . . As Christian citizens we should abide by the law."[4]

After the initial growth of the local white Citizens' Councils, a phenomenon that will be discussed later, a few church conferences took stands that were even more explicit and forceful, and several *ad hoc* groups of ministers produced formal statements supporting integration of schools and churches. For example, the 1956 General Conference of the Methodist church urged local congregations to work "in all good faith" and with "brotherliness and patience" to accomplish a peaceful transition to the new order of things, further recommending that "discrimination or segregation by any method or practice, whether by conference structure or otherwise . . . , be abolished with reasonable speed." That same year Texas Baptists passed a resolution calling upon "Christians of all faiths" to join them in a five-point pledge against racial violence: "To behave with charity and good will toward all persons in a time of racial crisis; not to engage in, or to encourage, any action involving or implying violence; not to join with any group in actions which a person would not carry out openly as an individual; to encourage moderation and patience at all times by word and actions; and to show friendship and consideration for persons of all races with whom a person is associated."[5]

4. Presbyterian Church in the United States, *Minutes* (1954), 193, 197; Southern Baptist Convention, *Annual* (1954), 87; *Southern School News* (Nashville), December, 1954; Baptist General Association of Virginia, *Journal* (Richmond, 1954), 88.

5. Methodist Church, General Conference, *Journal* (Nashville, 1956), 1693; pledge quoted in "Texas Baptists for Racial Justice," *Christian Century*, LXXIII (1956), 1091.

In 1957, there were 80 Protestant ministers who initially signed a document that became known as the Atlanta Manifesto. Later this statement was expanded and reissued as "Out of Conviction: A Second Statement on the South's Racial Crisis," this time signed by 312 ministers of the Greater Atlanta area. Among other points, the Atlanta Manifesto asserted that "freedom of speech must be preserved at all costs," that "Americans and . . . Christians . . . have an obligation to obey the law," that the "public schools must not be destroyed," that "hatred and scorn for those of another race, or for those who hold a position different from our own, can never be justified," and that "communication between responsible leaders of the races must be maintained."[6]

A similar document, released in Dallas, Texas, a few months later, was signed by 300 Protestant ministers of the Greater Dallas area. This statement asked that "law and order be maintained" while the city faced "desegregation of its public schools"; asserted that "churches, service clubs and community organizations, newspapers, [and] radio and television" had a "responsibility to assist the School Boards" as they sought "to lead the community"; charged that "Christian parents" could be "of great help in creating proper attitudes towards race"; and argued that "the exchange of views among people of different races [was] necessary for a reasonable solution to the problem."[7]

The controversial booklet *South Carolinians Speak: A Moderate Approach to Race Relations* also was issued in 1957. Edited and published by five Protestant ministers, this work contained essays by several South Carolinians who urged temperance in the state's struggle to adjust to the Supreme Court's mandate. Judged by 1984 thinking, the essays would not sound even moderate, for they built on many of the basic myths and stereotypes about blacks that had been a part of southern rhetoric since the days of slavery. Nevertheless, the mere fact that these five ministers (three Episcopalians, one Presbyterian, and one Methodist) dared pro-

6. "Out of Conviction: A Second Statement on the South's Racial Crisis," *Christian Century*, LXXIV (1957), 1387. A copy of this statement has been included by Raymond R. McCain in "A Description and Analysis of Speaking by Atlanta Ministers on Public School Desegregation from February, 1961, to August 30, 1961" (M.A. thesis, Louisiana State University, 1961), 135–38.
7. *Christian Century*, LXXV (1958), 619.

mote a moderate position was enough to arouse the ire of many South Carolinians as well as the state's governor.[8]

Finally, in response to the turmoil that developed around the integration of Little Rock's Central High School, thirty-five Arkansas ministers released a statement expressing "deep concern" over the crisis. "As Christian ministers," the statement said, "we confess our own share in the corporate sin and guilt of our state."[9]

The Citizens' Councils

This 1957 declaration provides a bridge to another background factor, the influence of the white Citizens' Councils. In their study of the Little Rock ministry's response to the Central High School crisis, Ernest Q. Campbell and Thomas F. Pettigrew took note of the disparity in mood between the lofty statements of southern white Protestant ministers meeting in annual conventions or *ad hoc* committees and the actual mood, rhetoric, or involvement of pastors back home in their local churches. "Much of the minister's ardor [for desegregation] is dampened," they observed, "when he returns to his flock." In fact, Campbell and Pettigrew were critical of the relative inaction of Little Rock ministers during the Central High racial episodes, charging that "*no* systematic attempts were made by the clergy to appeal to the conscience of the community. Such statements as individual ministers did express," they added, "were usually . . . appeals for 'law and order' rather than a Christian defense of the principles of desegregation."[10] Furthermore, this clerical restraint was often the result of pressures placed upon all actors in the South's racial crisis by local white Citizens' Councils.

The Citizens' Council movement was born on July 11, 1954, when fourteen residents of Indianola, Mississippi, met to form an organization dedicated to opposing the *Brown* mandate. Subse-

8. Ralph E. Cousins *et al.* (eds.), *South Carolinians Speak: A Moderate Approach to Race Relations* (Dillon, S.C., 1957); *State* (Columbia, S.C.), July 4, 1957.

9. *Arkansas Gazette* (Little Rock), September 13, 1957.

10. Ernest Q. Campbell and Thomas F. Pettigrew, *Christians in Racial Crisis: A Study of Little Rock's Ministry* (Washington, D.C., 1959), 2–3, and "Racial and Moral Crisis: The Role of Little Rock Ministers," *American Journal of Sociology,* LXIV (1959), 510.

quent growth of local Citizens' Councils was so rapid that by the end of the first eighteen months, the movement claimed that membership totaled 208,000—with 40,000 in South Carolina, 75,000 in Mississippi, 60,000 in Georgia, 20,000 in Louisiana, and the remainder in Alabama, Texas, Oklahoma, Missouri, and Arkansas. "With the rise of the Citizens' Councils," Hodding Carter III stated, "came the decline of the Southern liberal." This liberal, he continued, "became first an isolated figure, then more and more the subject of comprehensive efforts to silence him. . . . The white South's majority had no need or respect or tolerance for neighbors who did not believe wholeheartedly in its efforts." [11]

This intolerance of liberals—or of moderates—could be directed at a Protestant minister as effectively as at an educator, newspaper editor, politician, or other community leader. In fact, Protestant clerics were particularly vulnerable to local Councils' intimidation. Let them side with proponents of integration and chances were they would find that their churches' enrollments, contributions, and programs began to suffer. If they were of denominations that "call" their ministers, they probably would be forced to leave their posts; if they were appointed by bishops or synods, they would usually remain only until head administrators noted the sharp declines in church membership, offerings, and/or building funds.

Indeed, the Citizens' Councils were well aware of their power in such matters. *Black Monday*, a book by Judge Tom P. Brady that has been credited with inspiring the formation of these organizations, suggested a rough outline of the strategy to be followed. "If the Bishops, the Board of Elders, the Deacons, etc., and the powers that be will not clean up their own back yards," wrote Brady, "then they must be cleaned up for them. Where the church organizations permit it, it can be done from the floor. Committees from the congregation can be formed which, in turn, can advise the governing authorities what is not to be preached and what is not to be done." [12]

Hodding Carter III has argued that as the Councils emerged, there developed a direct correlation between this growth, the si-

11. John B. Martin, *The Deep South Says "Never"* (New York, 1957), 37; Hodding Carter III, *The South Strikes Back* (Garden City, N.Y., 1959), 18.
12. Tom P. Brady, *Black Monday* (Winona, Miss., 1954), 70.

lencing of Protestant pulpits, and the rejection of those moderate and liberal sentiments expressed in many of the 1954 denominational conferences. In fact, the trouble first began in Mississippi, where the Councils originated. After the 1954 Southern Baptist Convention passed its resolution acknowledging the "Christian principles . . . of equal justice and love for all men" embodied in the *Brown* decision, the First Baptist Church of Grenada, Mississippi, threatened to secede from the convention, noting that their membership was "not in accord with the Convention's endorsement" of the spirit of the decision. Next, the Presbyterian Synod of Mississippi informed the General Assembly that Mississippi Presbyterians could not "in good conscience comply" with the assembly's recommendation to "admit persons to membership and fellowship without reference to race." In Birmingham, Alabama, the Association of Methodist Ministers and Laymen was formed December 14, 1954, to counter liberal positions being taken by Southern Methodist administrative bodies. Among other complaints, this Birmingham group opposed the use of Methodist Sunday school literature "as channels of propaganda looking toward integration" and the efforts of Methodist bishops and conference administrative units "to break down long established racial customs." By 1956 even Lutherans were bowing to pressure from conservative laymen and pastors. On a motion from Wynne C. Bolick of Greenville, South Carolina, the 1956 convention of the United Lutheran Church in America declined "to support the U.S. Supreme Court's decision outlawing racial segregation in public schools." Three months later the 1957 Georgia state Baptist convention rejected by a three-to-one vote its own social service commission's statement that Georgia Baptists should "seek to create an atmosphere that would make it possible for those who administer . . . public schools to comply with the instructions of the court." Then in 1958 the Southern Baptist Convention succumbed to state and local pressures when the convention's Home Mission Board "withdrew from circulation *The Long Bridge*, a study guide . . . which contained a discussion of racial problems." [13] Thus it seemed that southern Protestant denominations were moving backward with respect to race relations.

13. Carter, *The South Strikes Back*, 164–65; *Baptist Record* (Jackson, Miss.), June 10, 1954; *Southern School News* (Nashville), December, 1954; *Christian Century*, LXXII

With the increase in organized opposition to the *Brown* mandate, every subject discussed relative to race relations in the South grew in degree of sensitivity. Southern ministers in particular found racial themes to be dangerous material for their pulpit rhetoric. Conservative parishioners tended to regard as suspect even the most general of remarks concerning "Christian brotherhood," and clergymen frequently found themselves with less freedom of speech—at least concerning racial issues—than they had possessed prior to 1954. Thus the dilemma to which Robert Paul Sessions referred when addressing his Van Buren, Arkansas, congregation was a very real challenge for most southern white Protestant ministers during this period. Should they speak out in support of *Brown* and risk losing their pulpits? Should they align themselves with the majority southern view and all its paradoxical implications for Christian morality? Should they avoid the issue of race altogether, devoting themselves exclusively to a traditional Christian theology of sin and salvation, with sin having absolutely nothing to do with institutionalized and mandatory segregation?

For many ministers, the choice of one of these options was neither easy nor safe. Indeed, it may have been that of all southern professionals, no individual was placed in greater jeopardy by this crisis than was the typical Protestant clergyman. Like the region's politicians, this southern man of the cloth experienced a public scrutiny that measured his every word and deed against a fixed standard of orthodoxy. Careers, personal dignity, and well-being of families hung in the balance. Thus, during the first ten years after *Brown*, the positions these ministers took on southern race relations could have significant personal and professional ramifications.

Southern Ministers Speaking in Support of *Brown*

Like most southern white Protestant ministers who elected to sermonize in support of *Brown*, Sessions did encounter some criticism from the community he served. There were midnight tele-

---

(1955), 644–45, 971–72, LXXIII (1956), 1302, LXXIV (1957), 54; Samuel Southard, "Are Southern Churches Silent?" *Christian Century*, LXXX (1963), 1430.

phone calls and vitriolic letters, and he even received from a concerned friend a warning of possible violence: "Bob, one morning we're going to pull you out of the Arkansas River all wrapped in chains, and someone is going to say, 'Why did Bob go swimming carrying all those chains?'" [14]

In a larger sense, however, Sessions' situation was not typical. He did not lose his church. He was not run out of town or moved by his bishop. Instead, he stayed at his charge for six years before being transferred to a larger Methodist church in Booneville, Arkansas. There he remained for another six years, a slightly longer than average stay at one church for a young Methodist minister.

Throughout this twelve-year period, Sessions continued to address issues that had to do with black-white relations. In Booneville he "integrated" his church by accepting a black into membership, and during this pastorate he wrote an essay for the *Saturday Evening Post*, "Are Southern Ministers Failing the South?" In this article he argued that "the average pastor in the South" should experience "little uncertainty" about "the ultimate Christian ideal" with respect to integration. "Every major Christian denomination and Jewish body," he noted, had "voted its approval of the principle behind the 1954 Supreme Court decision." [15]

Thus Sessions met opposition because of his racial stance, but he was allowed to address this sensitive issue without apparent harm to his immediate ministry or to his career. His situation, however, should be compared with the circumstances of a Presbyterian minister in Columbus, Georgia. This second story was probably more typical.

In 1957, Robert B. McNeill was pastor of First Presbyterian Church in Columbus. That year he, too, published an article, "A Georgia Minister Offers a Solution for the South," in *Look*. Adopting a moderate stance, McNeill recommended "creative contact" between the races and argued that the freedoms that should be granted southern blacks would ultimately also liberate southern

14. Telephone interview with Robert Paul Sessions, December 21, 1981. When this essay was written, Sessions was president of Southwestern College, Winfield, Kan.

15. Robert Paul Sessions, "Are Southern Ministers Failing the South?" *Saturday Evening Post*, May 13, 1961, p. 82.

whites. These whites, he charged, were not "spiritually and intellectually free." They could not "make judgments about fundamentals like freedom, democracy, and justice on an absolute standard of right and wrong, because of the presence of a people" for whom exceptions would always be made. The "southern mind," he asserted, would "never be free until it grants freedom." [16]

After the *Look* article was published, McNeill experienced serious conflict with his twelve-hundred-member congregation. In general, the parishioners rushed into two opposing camps, his loyal supporters and those who pushed for his dismissal or resignation. His sermons occasionally repeated some of the sentiments in that article, and apparently he stressed most frequently the benefit of "creative contact" between blacks and whites. "This means," McNeill had written, "representatives of both groups on city councils, grand juries, school boards, medical societies, ministerial associations and other public agencies."

These sermons, and McNeill's excursion into national journalism, "triggered parish extremists into action. They fought every measure he suggested, from televised services to air-conditioning in the church." "His crime," Ralph McGill observed, "was that he had spoken out for human contacts and communication between whites and Negroes. . . . He had denounced segregation on the basis of color alone. . . . In short," McGill continued, "Mr. McNeill believes in the brotherhood of man." [17]

By June, 1957—the *Look* article had appeared in May—there were complaints to the Southeast Georgia Synod about McNeill's ministry. He had been at the Columbus church since 1952, but he now found that seven of the church's twenty-eight elders were demanding his resignation. When he refused to resign, his opponents appealed to the synod. A special judicial commission was appointed to investigate the situation and to recommend whether McNeill should go or stay. Chaired by Frank C. King, then of Valdosta, Georgia, the commission first ruled in McNeill's favor. In fact, in announcing the commission's decision, King issued a strong statement of support for the type of pastoral behavior

16. Robert B. McNeill, "A Georgia Minister Offers a Solution for the South," *Look*, May 28, 1957, pp. 55–58, 63–64.

17. *Look*, July 21, 1959, pp. 34, 59; McGill, "The Agony of the Southern Minister," 16.

McNeill had exhibited: "The pulpit must never be muffled or silenced by threats of any description. . . . A minister who voices only the comfort of the Christian Gospel without its accompanying challenge and call to repentance has ignored his obligation." Amid reports, however, that *Look* was preparing a follow-up article on the case, McNeill's opponents intensified their efforts for his removal. As a result, the synod's special judicial commission reversed its position, and King was soon standing in McNeill's pulpit to announce the dismissal of the forty-four-year-old pastor, who two years earlier had written somewhat prophetically: "The true prophet stays behind with his people, pleading, cajoling, lashing, soothing their wounded spirits, praying out their prejudices, taking their blows of resentment upon his own back, loving and forgiving them. Having spoken he must remain to bear the brunt of his own words." [18]

Three days after his dismissal, McNeill was bowling with his son when he suffered a heart attack. The attack did not kill him, but neither did it soften the hostile attitude of many who had opposed his ministry. In fact, McGill reported that some of McNeill's former parishioners interpreted the incident as a "fake attack" designed to win sympathy, or—if real—as a punitive act of Providence. [19] During his convalescence, McNeill accepted a call from a church in Charleston, West Virginia.

There were abundant parallels in the South to McNeill's experience. Most white ministers who made any statement, or took any action, in support of integration quickly found that the clerical cloth did not protect them from the abuse typically given violators of segregationist principles. The following serve as examples of what usually happened to these ministers.

In September, 1965, Donald Clark of Timothy Episcopal Church in Fort Worth, Texas, went to the aid of three black teenagers who were enrolling in what had been the white-only high school in Mansfield, Texas. Clark denounced—on the spot—the activities of some two hundred segregationists gathered to prevent the enrollment. The result was that he had to be led away from the scene by a squadron of Texas state troopers, "with the crowd yelling

18. *Look*, July 21, 1959, p. 34; McNeill, "A Georgia Minister Offers a Solution for the South," 64.
19. McGill, "The Agony of the Southern Minister," 18.

close behind." That same year, after an unsuccessful attempt by ten black students to attend the all-white high school in Clinton, Tennessee, Paul Turner, pastor of First Baptist Church there, tried to help. He met six of the black students at the edge of the Clinton "Negro quarter" and escorted them to school. But when Turner left the campus and walked back through town, he was attacked by several members of the local Citizens' Council. He suffered a bloody nose and facial scratches. In Durant, Mississippi, all that Marsh Callaway did was defend a doctor who had spoken of "the inevitability of integration." For that offense he got "crossed up" with the Citizens' Council and lost the Presbyterian church he pastored. Lloyd Foreman, a Methodist minister in New Orleans, defied a white boycott of William Frantz Elementary School by escorting to the school his own five-year-old daughter, Pamela Lynn. The school had been "integrated" by the enrollment of one black child. An angry crowd subsequently gathered outside Foreman's parsonage, throwing stones and chanting, "Nigger lover, nigger lover, nigger lover, boo! We hate niggers and we hate you." Frightened by these events, Foreman moved his family to temporary quarters. While they were away, "vandals tossed a brick through a window . . . , dumped red paint inside and on the porch, and damaged an air conditioner."[20]

Events such as these became so intimidating that when southern white ministers preached liberal or moderate sermons on racial matters, they frequently did so only after months of soul-searching hesitancy. Indeed, the decision finally to "speak out" occasionally was triggered by some dramatic event. Such was the case with Lucious B. DuBose and Charles L. Stanford, Jr., both Presbyterian ministers.

In 1963, DuBose pastored First Presbyterian Church in Mullins, South Carolina. Two years earlier, shortly after DuBose had become minister of this charge, a joint meeting of the church's elders and deacons had "reaffirmed a previous policy not to seat Negro visitors at worship services." At that time DuBose declared his opposition to the policy, but he made no immediate effort to change it, preaching no sermon against its principles. However, on Sep-

20. *Christian Century*, LXXIII (1956), 1155; *State* (Columbia, S.C.), July 8, 1957; Stan Opotowsky, "Silence in the South," *Progressive*, XXI (August, 1957), 12; Sessions, "Are Southern Ministers Failing the South?," 37.

tember 22, 1963—one week after the bombing that killed four black girls at Sixteenth Street Baptist Church in Birmingham—DuBose felt compelled to deliver his sermon "My Home Town." "It makes one wonder," declared DuBose, "what the churches of Birmingham, and the churches of the whole South, have been talking about all these years. It makes one wonder if it's too late for them to recover their lost opportunity to do something meaningful and constructive about human relations. . . . Will the churches of Birmingham, the churches of the South, *this* church, ever begin to take seriously the implications of Jesus' teaching about love for neighbor?" Birmingham was DuBose's "home town," and at the beginning of his sermon he begged his congregation's indulgence while he reminisced. "If what I have to say seems too personal," he said, "it is because I know no other way to express what has come home to me so deeply this last week." The personal quality of his message, however, did not move one influential element of his congregation, and before long, DuBose lost his church. The following is his account of the events that transpired soon after his sermon:

> Long before September 15, I had planned to be away from town for two weeks beginning September 22. This was unfortunate. While I was gone meetings were held, and when I returned a member of the session called on me to inform me that a joint meeting of the officers had decided that I should seek a call elsewhere as soon as practicable. No resolutions were recorded; no reason was given in writing. In the remaining two months of my time in Mullins I was to discover that the officers had succumbed to the pressure of a vocal minority. The majority, I discovered too late, remained loyal and heartbroken.[21]

The 1962 riot at the University of Mississippi—precipitated by a move to integrate the Ole Miss campus—motivated Charles L. Stanford, Jr., to address the southern racial crisis. Stanford had been pastor of Jones Memorial Presbyterian Church in Meridian, Mississippi, for three years when the Ole Miss disturbances induced him to deliver "his only sermon devoted completely to the subject [of integration]": "My dear friends and fellow Mississippians," he began, "this is a sermon that I really do not desire to

---

21. Donald W. Shriver, Jr. (ed.), *The Unsilent South: Prophetic Preaching in Racial Crisis* (Richmond, 1965), 84–90.

preach and which I kept hoping would never have to be preached. But now I find that my hope was only wishful thinking, and my silence was cowardice." The "horror of Old Miss," he claimed, was at least in part a consequence of pulpits that had been passive: "Those of us who have remained silent on a great and grave moral issue have lent support to those who have spoken out on the side of error and evil. We are reaping what we have sown—the violence that comes from hatred, a hatred that we have allowed to develop because we never said it was wrong." Stanford procéeded to say pointedly that racial hatred and violence were wrong. He also called attention to the designation of that Sunday as "World-Wide Communion Sunday" and challenged his congregation to participate in the eucharist with true repentance for the "sin" that was in their collective soul. After the sermon, however, Stanford noticed that one of the elders "refused the sacrament." "Following evening worship that day," Stanford reported, "I happened to ride by the home of one of the elders, and seeing the familiar automobiles, realized that the session had gathered secretly." The following Sunday, Stanford was presented with a resolution calling his sermon "untimely" and asserting that "references made to alleged sins of the congregation" were unwarranted. The resolution further demanded that he "refrain from participating in any matter that might tend to involve the congregation in political, social, or racial controversy." Stanford remained at this church for sixteen months, experiencing a sharp decline in attendance for his sermons. Finally he accepted a call to a church in Louisville, Kentucky.[22]

The circumstances experienced by ministers such as Stanford, DuBose, and McNeill were typical but not universal. As was the case with Sessions and his Van Buren, Arkansas, sermon, there were, within this genre of responses to *Brown*, examples of moderately successful pulpit persuasion. One such example was the sermon delivered by Marion Boggs to Second Presbyterian Church in Little Rock, Arkansas, on July 7, 1957. This message, entitled "The Crucial Test of Christian Citizenship," represented Boggs's attempt to prepare his congregation for the forthcoming integra-

22. *Ibid.*, 72–76, 85. Stanford's sermon was also published as "Love Disqualified," in *Pulpit*, XXXIV (February, 1963), 15–16.

tion of Central High School. He apparently was one of the few pastors in Little Rock who used their pulpits for this purpose.[23]

At the beginning of his sermon Boggs told his congregation that he wanted to have a "heart-to-heart talk" with them. Then he proceeded to deal very explicitly with the situation, calling the plan for integration "wise and sound" and characterizing "segregation by force of law" as a "vestige . . . from slavery days." There were, he added, three reasons why segregation should be eliminated from the "American way of life": It was a "direct contradiction to the Christian Doctrine of the Dignity of Man"; it was "in direct contradiction to the spirit and purpose of American freedom"; and there was a "rising tide of resentment against it throughout the world," thus detrimentally affecting Christian missionary efforts.[24]

According to Campbell and Pettigrew, response to Boggs's sermon was "gratifying": "Many members told their pastor they were proud of what he said and because he had made his position known so early." A condensation of the address was published in the *Arkansas Gazette*, and "members of other churches who heard of the sermon expressed the wish that their ministers would take an equally forthright stand."[25]

All this should not suggest, however, that Boggs's message significantly altered Little Rock's response to the Central High School episode. Boggs did end up being one of the thirty-five-member ministerial group that wrote a statement calling for a peaceful integration of Central High and that organized an hour of prayer for "goodwill and understanding" when that integration was not so peaceful; but his sentiments did not mirror those of a significant portion of the Little Rock population.[26] What seems important, however, is that he preached the sermon and still held the leadership of his congregation.

23. Campbell and Pettigrew, "Racial and Moral Crisis," 510.

24. Marion Boggs, "The Crucial Test of Christian Citizenship," *New South*, XII (July–August, 1957), 4–8.

25. Campbell and Pettigrew, *Christians in Racial Crisis*, 18; *Arkansas Gazette* (Little Rock), September 1, 1957.

26. *Arkansas Gazette* (Little Rock), September 13, 23, October 12, 13, 1957.

Southern Religious Rhetoric in Favor of Segregation

Sermons of white southern Protestant ministers who spoke in support of segregation did not find their way into print in national publications quite as frequently as did sermons of churchmen who advocated integration. Major religious journals such as *Christian Century, Pulpit, Christian Advocate,* and *Religion in Life* have tended to represent the interests and ideologies of the more established, main-line denominations and have not become repositories of that more conservative or fundamentalist rhetoric. In addition, these publications seemed particularly disinclined to print racist rhetoric, except as they performed a strictly journalistic, reportorial role, and popular magazines like the *Saturday Evening Post* and *Look* tended to publish this rhetoric only in articles that were critical exposés.

As a group, these overtly racist ministers were more likely to be the conservative or fundamentalist churchmen who had received little or no formal seminary training and who did not even write their sermons in manuscript form, much less try to publish them. The established homiletic publications, therefore, seldom became forums for the segregationist point of view.

Nevertheless, there was a great deal of prosegregation religious rhetoric published in various print media. In fact, some racist pulpit rhetoric did make its way into religious journals. For example, throughout the 1950s the *Southern Presbyterian Journal*, a conservative publication that editorially promoted "voluntary segregation," supplied a steady stream of anti-integration rhetoric. One of the most prolific segregationist ministers, Dr. G. T. Gillespie, found this journal receptive to his views. Gillespie consistently argued that integration would mean amalgamation, that compulsory integration was clearly unconstitutional, and that the integration movement in America was communistic in inspiration and organization. He also charged that the Bible sanctioned segregation, that since separation of the races was a mandate of natural law, discrimination was "a spontaneous human reaction," and that in the United States, racial segregation had been a "time-tested national policy" resting on "moral and ethical principles and not upon blind and unreasoning prejudice."[27]

27. *Southern Presbyterian Journal*, XIV (August 17, 1955), 4; G. T. Gillespie, "A Southern Christian Looks at the Race Issue," *Southern Presbyterian Journal*, XVI

Of course the largest print source for this racist religious rhetoric was the South's newspapers. Newsworthy events such as large Citizens' Council rallies and heated school integration conflicts gave opportunity for conservative pastors to be heard and for their words to appear in print. For example, on September 17, 1957, the Citizens' Council of Greater New Orleans sponsored a massive rally at the municipal auditorium. Those who gathered for this event heard two prominent segregationist ministers, Carey Daniel, pastor of First Baptist Church in west Dallas, Texas, and L. D. Foreman, pastor of Antioch Missionary Baptist Church in Little Rock. Daniel was one of the most widely recognized anti-integration southern ministers, having begun his own personal campaign against *Brown* soon after the decision was handed down. One of his main arguments was that God was the "original segregationist." "When first He separated the black race from the white and lighter skinned races," Daniel told his congregation in May of 1954, "He did not simply put them in different parts of town. He did not even put them in different towns or states. . . . He did not even put them in adjoining countries. *He put the black race on a huge continent to themselves, segregated from the other races by oceans of water to the west, south, and east, and by the vast stretches of the almost impassable Sahara Desert to the North.*"[28]

At the New Orleans rally, Daniel blamed America's racial crisis on the United Nations and communism, both of which, he charged, "symbolized the modern anti-Christ forces." He also promoted a five-point program for dealing with the integration issue: (1) pressure for passage of the Langer bill, which would have provided "federal aid for Negroes" who wished "to move to Africa"; (2) "withdrawal of the United States from the U.N."; (3) "refusal to send children to integrated schools"; (4) pressure on ministers "to tell the truth about the subject"; and (5) "boycott of firms encouraging integration." Foreman, the other minister at

---

(June 5, 1957), 7–8, and "A Christian View on Segregation," a sermon preached before the Presbyterian Synod of Mississippi in Jackson, November 4, 1956, quoted in Jerry Butler, "God, Preachers, and Segregation, 1955–1964" (Paper presented to the Fifty-first Annual Convention of the Southern Speech Communication Association, Austin, April 9, 1981).

28. Carey Daniel, "God the Original Segregationist," in Dewitte Holland (ed.), *Sermons in American History: Selected Issues in the American Pulpit, 1630–1967* (Nashville, 1971), 502–22.

the rally, praised the Citizens' Councils for awakening a "sleeping giant," the South, to the evils of integration.[29]

On one prominent occasion a well-known segregationist minister was called upon to address a southern state legislative body, and of course the resulting rhetoric found its way into the newspapers of the region. The minister in question was W. A. Criswell, pastor of "the largest Baptist church in the world," First Baptist Church in Dallas. He was in Columbia to address a Baptist conference on evangelism and spoke, by invitation, to a joint session of the South Carolina legislature on February 22, 1956. Both audiences were told that integration would be detrimental to southern families and that desegregation in general was a policy of "foolishness" and "idiocy." "Who's stirring up all this stuff?" Criswell asked. "Is it God's people or someone else? I happen to know it is somebody else. If they will leave us alone and stay up there with their dirty shirts, we'll save some souls and do more good than they." The minister also attacked the National Council of Churches, charging that "they teach that spurious doctrine of the universal fatherhood of God and brotherhood of man," which he called "a denial of everything in the Bible."[30]

Criswell's rhetorical style for the occasion was characterized by the *State* (Columbia) as "homespun," but in truth it was so intemperate that it embarrassed many of his fellow Texas clergymen. He described all advocates of integration as "a bunch of infidels, dying from the neck up," and he attacked the black leadership in Texas with a crude but popular anecdote of the period: "Why the NAACP has got those East Texans on the run so much that they dare not pronounce the word chigger any longer. It has to be cheegro." The Dallas *Morning News* reported that this rhetoric was received by Texas Baptist officials "with a mixture of surprise and silence" while *Christian Century* described the response of the Texas Baptist establishment as one of "shock." Evangelist Billy Graham, who at that time was a member of Criswell's church, told the Associated Press in Tokyo, where he was conducting a revival, "My pastor and I have never seen eye to eye on the race question. My views have been expressed many times and are well known."[31]

29. New Orleans *Times-Picayune*, September 18, 1975.
30. *Christian Century*, LXXIII (1956), 338; Dallas *Morning News*, February 23, 1956; *State* (Columbia, S.C.), February 22, 1956.
31. *State* (Columbia, S.C.), February 22, 1956; *Christian Century*, LXXIII (1956),

Graham did not elaborate on his "views," but they may not have been particularly progressive or have indicated that the racial question prompted any sense of urgency among ecclesiastics. The next year (1957), when racial conflicts were heating up in Little Rock and Van Buren, Arkansas; Clinton, Tennessee; and Columbus, Georgia, Graham conducted a crusade in New York City. There he told an audience that America was facing its "third crisis" since the founding fathers came to this continent. Nevertheless, he did not identify the conflict over race relations as that third crisis. Instead, he named the Revolution, the Civil War, and the threat of communism.[32]

Criswell was the pastor of a very large southern church, but there were thousands of small churches throughout the region whose pastors occasionally went public with their own conservative positions on this issue. One way in which this occurred was that when a group of liberal, uptown, main-line clergymen published a call for compliance with *Brown,* almost invariably a countergroup of prosegregation ministers—usually from much smaller churches, denominations, or sects—went to the newspapers with their own statement. Take, for example, the events that transpired in Little Rock during the Central High School integration disputes in 1957.

As students of this civil rights crisis will recall, Governor Orval Faubus had mobilized the Arkansas National Guard in an attempt to thwart integration of Central High, justifying his action as an effort to "preserve the peace." President Dwight D. Eisenhower, however, finally stepped in with federal troops to see that the Court-ordered integration plan was carried out. As previously noted, these circumstances generated some pro-*Brown* rhetoric and activities among the more liberal, high-church, uptown elements of the Arkansas ministry. On September 12, thirty-five moderate pastors, representing churches of nine denominations and from fourteen Arkansas cities and towns, released their public expression of "deep concern." Aimed at cooling mounting racial tensions in the state, this statement read in part: "Because we have not walked in the way of the Lord we now find ourselves

---

325; Dallas *Morning News,* February 24, 1956; *Christian Century,* LXXIII (1956), 338; Dallas *Morning News,* February 23, 1956.

32. *State* (Columbia, S.C.), July 12, 1957.

confused, disturbed, and distressed. As Christian ministers we confess our own share in the corporate sin and guilt of our state and our own subjection to the holy judgment of God. Our one hope in this hour of crisis lies not in our own ability to change ourselves, our people, or the social structure of which we are a part, but in the power and grace of God to bring order out of confusion, good out of evil, and redemption beyond judgment."[33]

Many of the Little Rock ministers who signed this document were also among those pastors who organized a citywide "prayers for peace" service held at 11:00 A.M. on October 12. All businesses in the area were asked to halt their activities for a few minutes while the city prayed for racial peace. But as soon as the call went out for participation segregationist clergymen let it be known that they would have nothing to do with the event. The president of the local Missionary Baptist seminary announced on October 6 that his followers would not cooperate with the effort because it was "merely an attempt to promote integration under a veneer of prayer." Then thirty-eight anti-integration ministers called their own prayer meeting for the evening of October 12, arguing in their statement to the press that "the only way to have real and lasting peace" in the city was "for the nine Negro children to return to Horace Mann High School," where they "legally and morally" belonged.

More than six hundred segregationists crowded into Central Baptist Church—an independent fellowship and not a member of the Southern Baptist Convention—for this anti-integration prayer meeting, where they heard M. L. Moser, Jr., call down divine blessings upon the activities of Governor Faubus. "We feel that he has been raised up for such an hour as this," Moser prayed, "and we thank Thee for this commendable stand in using the Arkansas National Guard for the preservation of peace in our community, which was preserved until federal troops moved in to disrupt the peace and order of the city." Moser's prayer merely echoed sentiments that had been expressed in a public statement signed by fifteen segregationist Little Rock ministers. Like Moser, these individuals also praised Faubus' use of the state's National Guard:

33. *Arkansas Gazette* (Little Rock), September 13, 1957.

Believing that Arkansas faces a critical situation that could lead to violence, we . . . wish to publicly commend Governor Faubus for his courageous action in calling the Arkansas National Guard into service for
the protection of all citizens in the opening days of our public school
system.

We believe that among the first duties of our governor is the one of
the preservation of law and order. The Constitution of the United
States of America leaves the education of the citizens of the various
states in the hands of the various states. It is the duty of the governor
of the state to do his utmost to see that the laws of the state are
enforced.

There were individual anti-*Brown* Little Rock ministers who
charged into the fray early in the Central High School dispute and
who thus received some notoriety in the press. Wesley Pruden,
pastor of Broadmore Baptist Church, was one such individual. He
became a spokesman for anti-integration forces when in June,
1957, he appeared before the Little Rock School Board to ask some
questions about the ramifications of the planned integration. The
board asked Pruden to put his questions in writing, and at the
July meeting the minister submitted a letter containing the following seven queries: (1) Would desegregation at Central High "automatically integrate the white and colored mothers of the . . . PTA";
(2) would "Negro women be permitted to hold office and serve as
committee chairmen"; (3) would "white girls be forced to take
showers with the Negro girls, using the same facilities"; (4) would
"Negro boys and girls be allowed to join the school sponsored
clubs," and when out-of-town trips were taken, would "Negro
boys and girls be permitted to go along" and "stay in the same
motels, hotels, or private homes with the white children"; (5)
would "white children . . . be forced to use the same rest rooms
and toilet facilities with Negroes"; (6) would integration "throw
white and Negro children together in the dramatic classes," and
when scripts called for the "enactment of tender love scenes,"
would "these parts be assigned to Negro boys and girls without
respect for race"; and (7) would "Negro boys and girls be permitted to attend school sponsored dances," and would "Negro boys
be permitted to solicit . . . white girls for dances?" With these
questions, Pruden gave voice to what were perhaps the deepest

fears and passions experienced by anti-integration whites. There was an obvious sexual dimension to the queries, and they also probed the delicate issue of social status in black/white relations. These questions moved Pruden, and any other minister who asked them, away from strictly theological arguments against integration. They did not mention the "curse of Ham"; instead, they hinted at the "horrors" of interracial sexual union and the "indignity" of whites being subservient to blacks.

There is one last example from the Little Rock situation that should be examined, if for no other reason than the style of the rhetoric involved. After Eisenhower called in the federal troops, E. T. Burgess and his congregation at Barean (Missionary) Baptist Church sent Eisenhower a telegram, which they released to the press. Among other things, the wire suggested that if the president "had been spending as much time" on his "knees in prayer" as he had "spent on the golf course," he "would never have sent troops into Arkansas." The telegram continued:

> If we have the privilege of freedom of speech left, we wish to lift our voice in strong protest against the unholy invasion of the customs, rights, and privileges of the citizens of Arkansas. . . . By your action, especially in sending armed troops (including Negroes), you have taken away every vestige of dignity and pride ever possessed by people of the South. You have created a situation that is causing mounting tension and will have repercussions for many years to come. You have brought more shame on the high office of President than you have brought on the once sovereign state of Arkansas. May God have mercy on you for it.

There was a PS: "We are not extremists, and none of us have been imported from out of Arkansas. And those of us here on the scene probably know a little bit more about the situation than those a thousand miles away, who are feeling called to go on the networks and speak their mind about it."[34]

One final newspaper source of prosegregation rhetoric needs to be mentioned, the small, limited-circulation, religious papers published for fundamentalist denominations and sects. There are many of these periodicals printed in the South, with titles such as *Gospel Guardian, Wings of Truth, Mission, Gospel Herald,* and *Sword*

34. *Ibid.,* July 8, September 5, 27, October 10, 12, 1957.

of the Lord.[35] The *Sword* will be used to represent this genre of publications, not only because its pages contain prosegregationist articles, but also because its editorial position provides a logical bridge to the final section of this essay, an analysis of the rationales of the "silent" southern pulpit.

On its front page the *Sword* describes itself as "An Independent Christian Weekly, Standing for the Verbal Inspiration of the Bible, the Deity of Christ, His Blood Atonement, Salvation by Faith, New Testament Soul Winning and the Premillennial Return of Christ." Founded and originally edited by the well-known southern evangelist, John R. Rice, the paper has, throughout its existence, waged a constant battle against "modernism," Catholicism, non-evangelical Christianity, communism and socialism, the Revised Standard Version of the Bible, nonliteral interpretations of Scripture, progressive theological seminaries, and even the "liberal" activities and pronouncements of the Southern Baptist Convention. With these strictly conservative editorial positions, the paper also might have been expected to carry on an extended war against the *Brown* decision and subsequent practices of desegregation. Nevertheless, between 1955 and 1965, there were only two major articles published in the *Sword* about racial issues, though there were six front-page sermons or essays run between March and October, 1960, warning against the dangers of a Catholic American president.[36]

These two articles, however, are significant—they were written by John R. Rice and apparently expressed the editorial position of the paper. Furthermore, they represent a response to *Brown* that lies midway between the more overt prosegregation rhetoric and the silence that emanated from some pulpits.

At the outset of the *Brown*-initiated integration disputes, the editorial position of the *Sword* appeared to be one of quiet acquiescence to the new mandate. Rice let all of 1955 and half of 1956 go by without any direct mention in his paper of *Brown* and the resulting debates. In fact, he seemed to go out of his way to avoid specific reference to the issue. For example, in Febru-

35. For additional information about these periodicals, see David Edwin Harrell, Jr., *White Sects and Black Men* (Nashville, 1971), 135–52.
36. *Sword of the Lord* (Murfreesboro, Tenn.), March 18, May 20, August 12, September 16, 23, October 21, 1960.

ary, 1956, when W. A. Criswell delivered his two heavily segregationist speeches in Columbia, South Carolina, the *Sword's* coverage mentioned only Criswell's attack against the National Council of Churches and nothing about his anti-integration rhetoric. Nevertheless, the article did become a veiled defense of segregation when it favorably reported Criswell's specific remarks about the National Council of Churches: "They teach that spurious doctrine of the universal fatherhood of God and brotherhood of man, which is a denial of everything in the Bible." Still, for about seventy-five weekly issues, this type of article represented the most direct opposition to *Brown* mounted by *Sword of the Lord.*

By July, 1956, however, Rosa Parks, Martin Luther King, Jr., and the Montgomery bus boycott—among other persons and events— had brought additional pressure to bear on southern racial policies, and Rice seemed compelled to address the issues in a more direct way. The result was his July 6, 1956, lengthy article, "Race Desegregation—Principles and Problems." Six years later, following the violent integration-related confrontations at the University of Mississippi, Rice wrote the second of his essays on race relations, "Mississippi Tragedy." These two writings apparently summed up what this fundamentalist minister felt about the new racial codes instituted by *Brown.* In addition, they undoubtedly mirrored views he expressed in numerous evangelical sermons.

Oddly enough, Rice did not declare that the basic principle behind *Brown* was completely wrong. "I personally feel that the Jim Crow laws are not wise," he wrote, "and that slowly, as fast as sentiment can be properly created so that the thing will be done righteously and calmly with the best results for both white and colored peoples, the Jim Crow laws ought to be abolished." Nevertheless, he quickly added that the time was not right for this social change and that there were conditions far worse than racial segregation. "Most intelligent people would prefer to have Jim Crow laws," he argued, "than to have unrestrained intermarriage between the races."

The most telling aspect of Rice's ideology, however, was that he found non-Christian, anti-Christian, or un-American motives behind every agitation for racial equality. For example, consider how Rice characterized King's involvement in the Montgomery bus boycott. "The Negro minister," Rice charged, "led that fight

. . . not as a Christian leader trying to make good Christians and to lead in Christian understanding between the races . . . , [but] as a modernist and socialist who was more concerned about racism than he was about Christianity." Consider also the aspersions this editor-evangelist cast on James Meredith when the latter became the first black to enroll at the University of Mississippi. "A twenty-nine year-old Negro," reported Rice, "selected and financed by the National Association for the Advancement of Colored People, . . . was hand picked by NAACP as a political instrument to further the left-wing goals of the radical organization led by the modernist and procommunist, Martin Luther King."

"Communists," Rice wrote, "have always been set to . . . take advantage of every labor fight, every racial issue, and to stir up trouble in America and other free countries in every way possible. They have pictured America as a land of oppression . . . where colored people are abused and exploited and almost enslaved. That false and deliberately misleading picture . . . helps in the fight of communists to raise sentiment in other countries against America." Rice also saw Communist interests at work in the operations of the National Council of Churches and the World Council of Churches. Leaders of these organizations, he argued, had "openly opposed the Congressional Committee on Un-American Activities," had "worked for the freeing of convicted communists and for seating Red China [in the U.N.]," had "admitted [as members] Russian church leaders" who were "for communism," and had been "strong for racial integration by armed force."

From the point of view of the editor of *Sword of the Lord*, any social-issue orientation that resulted in a church's sublimating its evangelical goals was highly objectionable. "No well-known church in the world," he declared, "which is much occupied in campaigning for uniting races is a strong soul-saving church. God does not want me to spend my time crusading for racial equality. He just wants me to preach the Gospel and help people do right. The churches are not meant to be political arenas." Besides, he added, "colored people are happier and make much better Christians and do better Christian service when they go where people sing the kind of songs they like to sing, where they hear the kind of preaching they like to hear, where their young people can meet together on the happy basis that young people like, and where the young people, of course, will find their mates for life, and their friends for a lifetime."

Thus a close examination of these two articles reveals the principles that undergirded the evangelist's position on the racial issue: American blacks had not been abused by the segregated social and political systems; any agitation for social and political equality for blacks was at best an activity that played into Communists' hands and at worst a direct Communist ploy; Christian ministers should "help people do right," but the achievement of racial equality was not one of those "rights"; the manifestation of Christian character is something apart from and definitely not tied to the practice of any system of racial equality; and for Christian churches to campaign for racial equality was to be political and thus to be disallowed. The last of these principles is particularly interesting in light of Rice's efforts to organize fundamentalist churches against the election of John Kennedy. During September and October, 1960, Rice used the *Sword* and its subscription procedures to distribute an anti-Kennedy booklet. The *Sword* also urged fundamentalist pastors to campaign actively against the election of a Catholic president.[37]

Rice began by trying to be silent on the racial issues generated by *Brown*. When he did participate in the rhetorical fray, however, he did so by dismissing the racial equality movement as a legitimate Christian enterprise, by denying the harms of segregation, by proclaiming the harm integration would allegedly cause, and by questioning the motives of all who came to the defense of the desegregation cause. Thus he has to be counted among those ministers defending racial segregation.

The Silent Southern Pulpit

Southern white Protestant ministers who chose to remain silent on the integration issue appear to have done so for one or more of three reasons: They believed that their speaking out on racial issues would have absolutely no constructive effect on the behavior of their congregations; they privately supported the principles behind *Brown* but saw their ministries as having larger goals than

37. *Ibid.*, March 30, July 6, 1956, November 16, 1962.

"social causes" and envisioned these goals being threatened if they advocated integration; or they actually believed—using a kind of "render unto Caesar what is Caesar's" rationale—that such sociopolitical causes as civil rights fell outside the purview of the Christian gospel. As a result, southern Protestant clergymen often justified their silence on the issue with statements such as the following:

> There's not one thing I can do about the race problem. . . . Look at it this way: there are five leading churches in my town. Let's say that all five of us clergymen got up and said we were for integration. Why we'd be crucified!
> And why should we allow ourselves to be? Where would we go? Our training has been in religion and our lives have been spent as southerners. Why should we have to go off to the North?

> Suppose I do tell my people our schools should be integrated? I would get fired immediately. That wouldn't worry me; I could go to a better church in the North right now. But what would I have accomplished? My people would still be just as they are. They would have made a fuss. Their next minister would be someone they could depend on not to disturb them.

> This thing [integration] is not a Christian issue. It is political and certainly the church has no business supporting it.

> As I see it, this whole question is a political one. . . . The politicians started it; let them end it.[38]

As a consequence of such rhetorical stances, many southern ministers passed through this period of controversy without addressing in any significant fashion the issues of social ethics and morality that *Brown* brought into focus. It became easy for these particular clergymen to say, "I have a greater cause to pursue, that of saving souls." This sidestepping maneuver allowed "silent" southern churches to slide comfortably into what Reinhold Niebuhr characterized as "the abject capitulation of American Protestant Christianity to perpetuation of this social injustice."[39]

38. George McMillan, "Silent White Ministers of the South," *New York Times Magazine*, April 5, 1962, p. 114; Colbert S. Cartwright, "What Can Southern Ministers Do?" *Christian Century*, LXXIII (1956), 1505; McMillan, "Silent White Ministers of the South," 114; *Pulpit Digest*, XXXIX (December, 1958), 17.
39. Samuel S. Hill, Jr., "Southern Protestantism and Racial Integration," *Re-*

Some clergymen, however, grew irritated by the frequent depiction of southern churchmen as those silent white ministers of the South. They felt they were being harshly judged by critics who simply did not understand the situation. "Sometimes, when things are really sticky, and one of my friends is right in the middle," complained Methodist minister Robert Collie, "and I read a big, brave statement on the situation down here, coupled with a charge about the ministers' failure to do their duty, I feel like chucking the whole thing. What does such a person know, a thousand miles from where he can get hurt?"

Because Collie felt he and his fellow Protestant clergymen *could get hurt*, and because he believed he and these other ministers were caught between two uncompromising forces, neither of which they could materially control, he was offended by George McMillan's 1962 article in the *New York Times Magazine*, "Silent White Ministers of the South." "The truth is evident," McMillan had declared. "On the issue of race, the white Southern minister refuses to lead. He follows and parrots the feelings of his congregation. His publicly expressed racial attitudes are very likely to be a good clue to the . . . social and economic make-up of his flock: the more deeply segregationist the minister, the less education he has." Angered by these generalizations, Collie, pastor of the Methodist church in Kentwood, Louisiana, wrote his own article for the *New York Times Magazine*. The essay was reprinted in *U.S. News & World Report*.

Collie charged that critics were overrating the influence of a Protestant minister. "Does anyone really believe," he wrote, "that the community in general and the power structure in particular will reverently bow their heads in obedience if a pastor tells them what their attitudes and actions on a given course of action would be? Our society just doesn't accord that kind of power to ministers; it hasn't since the time of the Puritans." This may have been Collie's answer to President Lyndon Johnson, who three months earlier had addressed a gathering of Southern Baptist ministers, urging them to be more influential in defusing the racial crisis. "You people are part of the power structure in many communities in our land," Johnson had said. "The leaders of the cities, states,

---

ligion in Life, XXIII (1964), 425; Niebuhr, "The Crisis in American Protestantism," 1500.

and towns are in your congregations. . . . Their attitudes are confirmed and changed by the sermons you preach . . . and by the examples you set."

Collie obviously felt that this statement simply exaggerated the power of the southern pulpit. "I can preach in the field of social concerns," he said, "but . . . I have every assurance that the next Sunday I would have a congregation . . . of one lay person. . . . I believe that we must destroy the evils represented in segregation," he declared, "but I am committed to the much larger social ideals of the Methodist social creed, and I am inclined to view my own success or failure . . . more in terms of this larger social concern than just civil rights." He was willing, he added, "to bear the stigma of being a *silent* minister" if he could practice his "ministry of reconciliation." This meant, Collie said, "having two faces": "When I am dealing with the segregationist, I try to show him where he is wrong; but when I am dealing with a person from another section of the country, I try to show him where the segregationist is right." This duplicity, he argued, was necessary for him to be able to work within a social climate that had become increasingly tense. "We simply have lost ground in the South in respect to good will," he charged, with the result that the region had regressed in race relations:

> Ten years ago . . . it was part of our way of life for a man to feel a responsibility toward a Negro. If a family was hungry, you gave them food; you put $10 in the collection being taken up for the Negro church or a hospital bill or burial; you signed his note at the bank if you knew him well; if he was out of work, you gave him a job if you possibly could. Today, the same man couldn't care less.
>
> A pastor is conscious of these things, and when he wants to move ahead, to put the evils of segregation behind him, he knows that real progress is more than forcing a Negro child into a white classroom. . . . I want real progress in terms of human relationships, and the stance I take is often different from that of those who are concerned with civil rights.[40]

Collie's reasoning obviously would not have pleased black activists of the 1960s who placed more value on freedom and human dignity than upon paternalistic good will and handouts. To the

40. *U.S. News & World Report*, June 15, 1964, pp. 76–79; Johnson quoted in Atlanta *Constitution*, March 26, 1964.

degree that Collie could not perceive this difference, he also could not envision the real "evils of segregation." Thus he remained silent on those evils, placing more emphasis upon a return of social harmony—a harmony that would facilitate the slow progress in race relations that had been a feature of the period immediately preceding *Brown*. Collie's situation illustrates the conflict in values faced by many southern Protestant ministers, but his rationales exemplify how the "silent" pastor justified failure to act decisively in the face of monumental social wrongs.

Conclusions

In 1955 when several Roman Catholic parishioners of Erath, Louisiana, assaulted a lay catechism teacher who had instructed white and black children in the same classroom, Bishop Jules B. Jeanmard of Lafayette took swift action and excommunicated the perpetrators of the violence. The punishment apparently worked, for Bishop Jeanmard later announced that the excommunicated individuals had "indicated . . . repentance for their actions." He subsequently lifted the excommunication.[41]

This account illustrates a position the Roman Catholic church occasionally took in dealing with integration disputes. It is certainly possible that these parishioners in Erath, Louisiana, did not experience a true change of heart about the rights of blacks, but they did formally express contrition for their acts and probably were reluctant to repeat them if and when similar circumstances arose. Thus Bishop Jeanmard played a small but significant role in preparing the way for the social changes *Brown* demanded. Indeed, the part Jeanmard performed was similar if not identical to that assumed by courts and federal law enforcement agencies. Although the bishop may not have made these Catholics like the new rules of race relations, he did force them to behave while time took over to forge those more meaningful changes in human attitudes. Why were white Protestant clergymen of the South unable to do the same thing?

There are some obvious answers to this question: (1) Protestant churches of the South do not belong to a unified hierarchy of ec-

41. *Christian Century*, LXXII (1955), 1453.

clesiastical power; (2) the democratic structure of most Protestant denominations gives their laymen more influence over clerical pronouncements and behaviors than exists under Catholicism; (3) between Catholic and Protestant churchmen, there has tended to be a somewhat different attitude toward who serves whom, cleric or layman; and (4) the practice of racially segregating worshipers into independently administered subdenominations has been, for the most part, a Protestant phenomenon and not a Catholic one. Robert Collie alluded to some of these factors when he wrote his 1962 article for the *New York Times Magazine:* "I appreciate what the Roman Catholic Church has done in the area of integration," but "there are some things that a priest can do that I can't. He has an authority system that can make his judgment felt whether on integration or birth control. I have none." [42]

Nevertheless, Collie's statements did not fully explain why southern Protestant ministers were not more influentially involved on the pro-*Brown* side of this controversy. There appear to be at least two other explanations that could be advanced. First, it would be a mistake to conclude automatically that most of these ministers really wanted to become active in support of *Brown* but were prevented from doing so by congregational pressures. Indeed, it seems more probable that many of these pastors—and perhaps a majority in certain areas of the Deep South—were squarely in favor of segregation. Second, although most of the region's major denominations' administrative bodies verbally supported *Brown*, their personnel policies tended to favor the parishioners' desire to suppress pro-integration ministers.

The question that must be asked is, Did a majority of southern white Protestant ministers really favor *Brown?* In 1958, *Pulpit Digest* sought to answer this question. Their survey of Protestant ministers in "*seventeen Southern* states" indicated that an amazing "four out of five" of these individuals were in favor of "compliance with the Supreme Court's order." [43] However, a close examination of the survey's methods and results suggests that this conclusion ought to have been heavily qualified.

Three observations should be made immediately. First, the poll

42. *U.S. News & World Report,* June 15, 1964, p. 79.
43. "Southern Ministers Speak Their Minds," *Pulpit Digest,* XXXIX (December, 1958), 13 (emphasis added).

was voluntary, and it might be surmised that a higher number of replies were received from ministers of uptown, main-line churches than from pastors of rural or poor urban denominations or sects, simply because these latter groups were less likely to have been subscribers to *Pulpit Digest*. If this reasoning is valid, then we might also suspect that the results were skewed toward a liberal bias. In *White Sects and Black Men*, David Edwin Harrell, Jr., argues that upper-class southern Protestants have been more likely to exhibit liberal or moderate racial postures than were their lower-class or rural counterparts.[44]

Second, it should be noted that the survey also went to black clergymen (6 percent of the total respondents), and it would be expected that this population almost unanimously favored the *Brown* decision. Third, the seventeen states included Delaware, Maryland, West Virginia, Kentucky, and Oklahoma, where integration plans typically were instituted with greater ease than in the Deep South.

When responses were tallied by state, 60 percent of those from Georgia were procompliance; Mississippi and Arkansas registered 54 percent procompliance; and Alabama and South Carolina, only 53 percent and 50 percent procompliance, respectively. If the assumption that results were skewed toward a liberal bias is correct, then these percentages should also be viewed in that light. Further, replies from black ministers should be subtracted. So it seems reasonable to conclude that a majority of 1958 white Protestant clergymen in at least South Carolina, Alabama, Arkansas, and Mississippi were not in favor of compliance.[45]

But this is not the only argument suggesting that a majority of these southern ministers may have been anti-*Brown*. "Fundamental to an understanding of the race problem in Protestantism," David M. Reimers has charged, "is the fact that churches are social institutions that are shaped by the culture in which they exist. A correlate to this thesis would be that the values and ideologies of Protestant ministers seldom are separated widely from the values and ideologies of their congregations. If this is so, then a 1956

44. Harrell, *White Sects and Black Men*, 116–18.
45. *Pulpit Digest* did not report the individual results from Louisiana and Florida.

National Opinion Center poll indicating that only one in seven white southerners approved of school integration is revealing."[46] Seen in this light, the *Pulpit Digest* survey results look less than conclusive. If only one in seven southerners approved of *Brown*, could the region's Protestant ministers have been considerably ahead of this figure?

But even if a minister did support the *Brown* decision, there was still one final reason why he might have remained silent: throughout this period, pastors were carefully watched by administrative hierarchies—conferences, synods, etc.—that, according to Samuel S. Hill, Jr., were primarily interested in the "preservation and enhancement of the institutional church" and "the avoidance of any policy" that threatened "the growth of local churches in size and wealth." As we have seen, if a minister clashed with the established racial attitudes of his congregation, that congregation was apt to abandon him, in both attendance and financial support. Bishops and presbyteries responded pragmatically—as was the case with McNeill—and arranged for the offending cleric to be moved to another church, reasoning that he had lost his effectiveness with the present congregation. Conservative laymen interpreted these actions as victories for their side and were conditioned to use similar tactics in future confrontations. Even Methodist pastor Robert Sessions, who was successful in Van Buren, Arkansas, complained that in these disputes, local Methodist ministers did not receive a great deal of support from their district superintendents and/or bishops.[47]

Operating in a profession where success is often measured by growth in church membership, expansion of the church facility, and general increases in financial contributions, most young Protestant ministers understood fully the price they might have to pay were they to advocate social values far in advance of their congregations. Furthermore, these congregations obviously appreciated the influence they could wield with denominational governing bodies should a young, upstart cleric decide to disrupt the

46. Reimers, *White Protestantism and the Negro*, 180; see H. H. Hyman and P. B. Sheatsley, "Attitudes Toward Desegregation," *Scientific American*, CXCV (December, 1956), 35–39.

47. Hill, "Southern Protestantism and Racial Integration," 423–24; telephone interview with Sessions, December 21, 1981.

peace of a church by pushing liberal racial policies. In his *New York Times Magazine* article, McMillan quoted a "prominent businessman and church leader" speaking about the typical young, liberal minister: "Give him a couple of years to get the highfalutin seminary ideas out of his head, let him get his family started, give him a decent salary and nice parsonage, and a membership in the local country club, and he's got a good living and knows it. And when it comes to dealing with the colored folks, he's as likely to be as conservative as any of us." [48]

Still, there were some ministers—Sessions, McNeill, Boggs, DuBose, Stanford, among others—who did speak out for the new social ethic embodied in *Brown*. Driven by whatever motive it was that sent them against established southern traditions—an above-average sense of social morality, a feeling of personal or regional guilt, or, as some opponents accused, a need for notoriety—these pastors did attack segregation of schools, churches, and public facilities. And for their actions they often paid a heavy price. Were these rhetorical acts of courage effective? Did pro-integration ministers ever materially change the attitudes of southern congregations?

Journalist Ralph McGill felt that there were some cases in which they did. At least McGill reported one such story. A Protestant minister in Georgia had taken his stand and had subsequently been harassed by some influential members of the congregation. His programs lost support, the board of deacons frustrated his every effort, and he eventually found that he was completely ineffective in church affairs and politics. So he accepted a call from a congregation in the Southwest. But before he left town he was told by one of his former parishioners: "We had a meeting to discuss your replacement. And you know, we found that we had just about fifty-three die-hard segregationists in our congregation of more than 2,000. We are going to engage a man with convictions like yours." [49]

McGill's story suggests a more idyllic resolution of the conflict, however, than was the case in most southern Protestant churches. For the most part, the attitudinal and structural changes requisite

48. McMillan, "Silent White Ministers of the South," 114.
49. McGill, "The Agony of the Southern Minister," 60.

to the new order of race relations did not come so quickly or so easily. Indeed, in many instances, these changes did not come at all until the 1970s, when the entire South finally began to make its peace with the realities of the new social order. Even after integration of public schools was a *fait accompli*—or at least well on the way to realization—local churches often voted to maintain a racially pure membership. As late as 1977, President Jimmy Carter found that his own church in Plains, Georgia, could cause him embarrassment by maintaining, in very public fashion, its white-only membership.[50]

If one were to go, as I did, to the Library of Congress and skim the many one-volume histories of local southern churches, it would become obvious that during the 1960s, numerous congregations simply refused to integrate. In fact, the prototypical scene played out in these dramas of conflict between the old and the new is probably the one that occurred at First Baptist Church in Holt, Alabama. One page in *Bow of the Hill Above the Warrior: History of the Holt Baptist Church* pointedly tells the story:

Changing Times . . . Integration
To Live is to Change; To Have Lived
Perfection, is to have Changed Often.

Down through the centuries one of the fundamental principles of the Baptist Denomination has been the complete Separation of Church and State. The Holt Baptist Church has always ascribed to this policy; thus, during the Civil Rights upheaval of the early sixties, which resulted in riots, demonstrations, marches, burnings (churches included), violence of all kinds and killings, the question of integration was a burning issue across America, particularly in the South, hence in the Holt Baptist Church.

Churches everywhere were confronted with the dilemma of old traditions and customs conflicting with modern, moral questions concerning separation of the races.

Congregations and individuals began to search their conscience and the Scriptures to determine what the Christian policy on integration of the Church should be. Many Churches were divided on this question just as they had been divided a century before over the question of slavery.

On February 28, 1962, at a meeting of the Board of Deacons of the

50. "Schism in Plains," *Christianity Today,* XXI (July 8, 1977), 37.

Holt Baptist Church, the question of what the Church should do if the Black People came to the Church service was discussed. Many different opinions were expressed. It was pointed out that the Black People had many nice churches of their own in the area, that they enjoyed having their own Pastor and their own form of worship. The white Pastors had always cooperated with them; so, if they came to this Church they would not be coming for the worship only, but to force Integration of the Church.

After much prayer and discussion, the decision was that if the Black People came, the Church would not receive them, but would furnish transportation to the Black Church of their choice.

NOTE: The above decision was rescinded at a meeting of the Board of Deacons, held April 28, 1974. It was decided that if any of the Black People, or people of any other race, sought admittance to the worship service of the Holt Baptist Church, they would be received.[51]

A telephone call to Nancy Dean Blackman, author of this history of Holt Baptist Church, revealed that the 1974 reversal vote had not been particularly meaningful, since no blacks had ever sought to attend services there. In fact, Blackman repeated that blacks in Holt, Alabama, have "many nice churches of their own" and therefore have no need to worship at a white church.[52] Thus the racial progress that has been made in some southern Protestant churches has been mainly symbolic: No longer is something formally prohibited, but often it still does not happen.

Some Final Thoughts

The *Brown* v. *Board of Education* decision wrought immense changes in the South, but for the most part the South's white Protestant clergy did not join that vanguard of individuals who actively promoted these causes. The argument advanced by McMillan, that these ministers tended to mirror the values of their respective congregations, appears to have been valid. To the degree that individual communities were open to this new relationship, Protestant pastors were able to assume leadership in bringing it about. In comparison, however, Citizens' Councils became more influential, but in support of racial segregation.

51. Nancy Dean Blackman, *Bow of the Hill Above the Warrior: History of the Holt Baptist Church* (Tuscaloosa, Ala., 1976), 182.

52. Telephone interview with Blackman, June 24, 1983.

Changes that occurred in the churches themselves—integration of worship services and memberships—tended to follow, not precede, those advances made in the community at large. Furthermore, these changes may have been largely symbolic, as apparently was the case with Holt Baptist Church. The Supreme Court could not mandate integration of churches, and for Protestant southerners, the Sunday morning worship hour has continued to be perhaps the most racially segregated daytime interval of the week. This fact alone would suggest that Protestant clergymen of the South have not been particularly effective in promoting the spirit of *Brown*.

Nevertheless, there may have been ways in which southern churchmen who were so inclined could have been more successful in supporting *Brown* than they were. Robert Sessions suggests that the secret of success lay more in the minister's attitude toward his congregation and in his mastery of interpersonal skills than in his precise rhetoric. "I never tried to get above them and preach down to them," he said. "I just tried to love them into progress."[53] Therefore, it is possible that southern pastors like Sessions and Boggs were more successful than other ministers such as McNeill and DuBose not because of superior rhetorical talents but because of superior interpersonal skills. Indeed, there may be times when the power of direct and explicit rhetoric is severely limited. Such seems to have been the case in southern Protestant churches in the ten years immediately following *Brown* v. *Board of Education*.

53. Telephone interview with Sessions, December 21, 1981.

A Black Rhetoric of Social Revolution

G. Jack Gravlee

On occasion, Martin Luther King, Jr., quoted for his audiences an old black preacher's ungrammatical expression of gratitude: "Lord, we ain't what we oughta be. We ain't what we wanna be. We ain't what we gonna be. But thank God, we ain't what we was."[1] Unknowingly, that preacher encapsulated the black South's social revolution. Initiated in the 1950s by the Supreme Court and internal combustion, it roared through the 1960s and matured in the 1970s. Black rhetoric during that period was less a communication "movement" and more a series of communication "crises." The leadership, style, values, and tactics of the southern black protest movement of the mid-twentieth century arose and, in large part, continues from the southern blacks' musical and rhetorical religious experience. In its quest for support from both religious and nonreligious followers, the movement incorporated a quality of "soul" that made it at once personal and universal—personal in its appeal to the black audience; universal in its appeal to the international conscience. Any study of black rhetoric in the South must recognize its background of white insult and degradation, its entrenchment in religion, its unity with music, its apparent rejection of violence, and its evolution from clerical to

1. "Humor in Black and White," *Ebony*, XX (August, 1965), 102–103.

secular leadership. Four major divisions here develop these premises: the rhetorical degradation that was a southern black legacy during the period; the black church, from which evolved inseparably the music and the rhetoric; the militant, black reactors who never registered any significant rhetorical impact in the South; and the contemporary southern black rhetoric that, while religiously rooted, appears to be emanating presently from legal, political, and academic arenas.

Rhetorical Degradation

Language probably coerces or enslaves a subordinate group as rigidly as does force. Unlike warfare, it can deceive the victim over an extended period of time by clever metaphorical selection. Hence, the degrading, contemptuous label uttered repetitiously may become tolerated, or even accepted, by the subordinate. Base epithets became all too common in southern white speech. Adult black males often were called "boy," "shine," "Rastus," "slim," "preacher"; adult black females were "girl," "mammy," "Aunt Jemima"; black children were "pickaninnies"; and blacks collectively were "coons," "darkies," and "niggers." Polite and honorific titles—Mr., Mrs., Miss, Ms., Doctor, Professor, Reverend, Pastor, Sir, Madam—rarely were used by whites toward blacks in the South as late as the 1950s. The labels "White" and "Colored" were posted over separate public facilities such as drinking fountains, ticket windows, rest rooms, pay windows, waiting rooms, and seats on mass transit vehicles. For years a Birmingham laundry boldly announced on the sides of its trucks: "We wash for white people only." As Martin Luther King, Jr., repeated on many occasions, blacks were drained of a sense of "somebodiness" after undergoing protracted white rhetorical tyranny.

In story, joke, and cartoon, the southern white chortled over the plight of blacks. Earlier in the century, "the most popular subject for Southern humor was the Negro in all his guises: faithful slave and freedman, upstart Negro, philosopher, picaro, reconciliator, and comic mouthpiece for the white man's political and social ideas." Prominent white figures from the South, such as Senator Tom Heflin of Alabama, developed national reputations as "tellers of darky dialect stories." Prior to the mid-1950s, blacks had no practical defense against such degradation. Braden points out that "the Establishment was formidable because it monopolized the principal means of communication. . . . Anyone who recommended moderation, deplored racism, suggested abiding by federal court decisions, or urged respect for federal authority could be chastised and disciplined. . . . Church burnings, beatings, economic reprisals, shootings, bombings, murders, cross burnings, lynchings, unlawful imprisonment, heavy fines for minor offenses, delays in processing legal documents, and harassment on streets and highways were weapons used against those who dared to oppose the Establishment."[2]

Over the years, as a defense mechanism in communicating with "The Man," blacks used "tomming" and "shucking" in "degradation rituals."[3] These behaviors were likely handed down from the slave period when "seldom were blacks free 'senders' of messages" but "remained strategically in a receptive state: attentive, defensive, discriminate, and adaptive" when speaking to whites. It was a *"language conceived more to conceal and to please than to enlighten."* Gradually, blacks became more assertive in denouncing such conditions. In *Phylon,* the Atlanta University review of race and culture, black reaction was identified in a thematic analysis of editorials on the black protest movement that were published in four large regional black newspapers between 1946 and 1972. Out of the ten most frequently occurring themes, "The South as Enemy" ranked as follows:

2. Wade Henry Hall, "A Study of Southern Humor: 1865–1913," *Dissertation Abstracts,* XXII (1962), 3644–45; New York *Evening Times* quoted in G. Allan Yeomans, "A Rhetorical Study of the Cotton Advocacy of James Thomas Heflin, 1904–1920" (Ph.D. dissertation, Louisiana State University, 1966), 84; Waldo W. Braden, "The Rhetoric of a Closed Society," *Southern Speech Communication Journal,* XLV (1980), 336–38.

3. "Tomming" occurs "when a member of a subordinate group . . . communicates with members of the dominant group exactly as they expect him/her to do." "Shucking" is "a form of communication in which [blacks] behaviorally conform to racial stereotypes while cognitively rejecting the meanings associated with those behaviors and stereotypes. . . . Those who 'tom' do so consistently; those who use shucking do so only when they must." Marsha Houston Stanback and W. Barnett Pearce, "Talking to 'The Man': Some Communication Strategies Used by Members of 'Subordinate' Social Groups," *Quarterly Journal of Speech,* LXVII (1981), 21, 24–26.

1946–1949	#1	22.8%
1950–1954	2	19.7
1955–1959	1	35.9
1960–1964	1	29.5
1965–1969	3	14.4
1970–1972	5	11.3[4]

The "enemy" specter of the South was most intense during the Montgomery and Birmingham crises and the March on Washington. Apparently, it did not abate until after the passage of the 1964 Civil Rights Act. Even then, the "enemy" could have been perceived as diffused nationally rather than concentrated regionally. But the perception of the South by leading black editorialists did not seem to improve until it became unlawful for the region openly to practice rhetorical subjugation.

Commercially, blacks in the South remained "nobody" for the better part of the twentieth century. If they ever were considered a "market" worthy of attention, it was usually for hair straighteners and skin bleaches. Certainly people with no status could expect only bare subsistence with no need for manifestations of leisure—hotels, restaurants, golf courses, tennis courts, country clubs, or even libraries. They could consume finished products only in specified categories. In the movies, blacks were caricatured as Stepin Fetchit; on the radio, they were Jack Benny's Rochester or whites in blackface on "Amos and Andy" torturing the language in a parody of minstrel shows. In the newspapers, they rarely appeared pictorially or narratively except in crime reporting. White media ignored them as potential viewers, auditors, readers, and ultimate purchasers. Both blacks and poor whites became the reflections of *Gone With the Wind* and *Tobacco Road*.

In launching their own counterattack against centuries of rhetorical degradation, blacks introduced a new application of the word *soul*. The term assumed qualities of endearment or contempt, depending on application and the recipient's perspective.

4. Cal M. Logue, "Transcending Coercion: The Communicative Strategies of Black Slaves on Antebellum Plantations," *Quarterly Journal of Speech*, LXVII (1981), 39; Charlotte G. O'Kelly, "Black Newspapers and the Black Protest Movement, 1946–1972," *Phylon*, XLI (1980), 313–24.

Soul brothers and *soul sisters* entered the language along with *soul food* and *soul music*. Record makers, "hot on the scent of a marketable commodity," turned out such numbers as "Soul Junction" and "Sin and Soul" while "collard greens and ham hocks, chitterlings, pig ears and pig feet" suddenly gained gastronomic fame. A new magazine, *Soul*, appeared in the 1960s, and an all-black televised musical program, "Soul Train," surfaced a decade later. Thus, with the word *soul*, blacks appropriated for their own use a piece of the white vocabulary. Soul became "the essence of Negroness"; you had to be black to have soul. It came in elusively measured quantities: "Man, he got a lot of soul." On the contrary, if "'soul' is Negro, the non-Negro is 'non-soul,' and, it appears, somewhat less human." So, using "'soul' rhetoric is a way of convincing others of one's own worth."[5] What originated as an ingroup term of empathy that had religious overtones became a commercial metaphor widely applied to the marketing of products to blacks.

There seemed to be no calculated campaign by blacks to reverse specifically the legacy of rhetorical degradation. Trite, demeaning labels were simply ignored by those blacks who became assertive senders of messages. Previously submissive practitioners of tomming and shucking now joined demonstrations and verbalized demands for equality. Some whites charged "outside agitators" and "uppity niggers" with complicity in disrupting "the system." Apparently, those in the power structure had difficulty believing that rhetorical challenges could evolve from local black populations. Old terms assumed new meanings as blacks began creating their own metaphors. Once the oppressed had their personal terminology broadcast widely over a variety of media, the escape from former semantic shackles probably was accelerated. The process continues in the contemporary South.

The Black Church

It is not surprising that a concept of soul should evolve outside of official ecclesiastical circles. Religion has been a potent force in

5. Lerone Bennett, Jr., "The Soul of Soul," *Ebony*, XVII (December, 1961), 112; Ulf Hannerz, "The Rhetoric of Soul: Identification in Negro Society," *Race* [U.K.], IX (1968), 454–55, 462.

black history even among those who were not active church members and who did not consider themselves religious. The black church, "a center for the total life of the people," guided its membership toward "fuller participation in American life." The black clergy was the source of community leadership; many church members first learned to read in Sunday schools; these same members developed their thought processes by interpreting Scripture; church burial societies launched black insurance companies; the church service offered an arena for the emotional release of suppressed frustrations; and the building became the community center for all types of meetings. The black church has been defined as school, forum, political arena, social club, art gallery, conservatory, lyceum, gymnasium, and sanctum sanctorum. As such, unfortunately, it became a symbolic target for white bombers lashing out against the entire black population.[6]

The Baptist denomination particularly suited black needs because it did not possess a ruling ecclesiastical hierarchy. A "call" to preach was beyond effective challenge, the liturgy was sufficiently unstructured to permit a relatively wide range of emotional expression, and it was not necessary to rely on white tolerance or largess. Consequently, over one-half of all black church members and more than one-fourth of the entire U.S. black population are Baptists.[7] Their "old-time religion" orientation fit comfortably into the southern Bible Belt. Most important, each congregation supported its own clergy, which produced the absolute independence of its leadership from potential interference by a white power structure.

BLACK MUSIC

Bernice Johnson Reagon, one of the avid participants in the demonstrations during the 1960s, observes that the "few successful studies" of the civil rights movement "acknowledge the songs as the language that focused the energy of the people who filled the streets and roads of the South during that period." The music and

6. Hannerz, "The Rhetoric of Soul," 454–55; Richard I. McKinney, "The Black Church," *Harvard Theological Review*, LXIV (1971), 452–81; C. Eric Lincoln, "Forward," in Henry H. Mitchell, *Black Preaching* (Philadelphia, 1970), 6.
7. McKinney, "The Black Church," 459; W. Augustus Low and Virgil A. Clift (eds.), *Encyclopedia of Black America* (New York, 1981), 227, 159.

the lyrics often captured black pathos in a rhythmic, abbreviated, memorable form.

> In 1960, when Black students sat in and were beaten at segregated lunch counters across the South, they sang. They sang as they were dragged into the streets. They sang in the paddy wagons and in the jails. And they sang when they returned to the Black community's churches for strategy rallies.
>
> When the buses carrying the Freedom Riders were stopped and burned, when the riders were pushed to the ground and beaten, they sang. When the Freedom Riders were jailed in Mississippi's Hinds County Jail and Parchman Penitentiary, they sang again. During the summer of 1961 when students in McComb, Mississippi, were suspended from school for participating in SNCC's [Student Non-violent Coordinating Committee's] first voter education project, they sang. In 1962, when mass arrests followed the first testing in Albany, Georgia, of the Interstate Commerce Commission's ruling that interstate travel be integrated, songs thundered from the massive community-based movement that was born. In Selma and Birmingham, in Greenwood and Hattiesburg, in Danville and Pine Bluff and Baton Rouge and Cambridge, in segregated cities across the nation, communities of activists came together. Central to their gatherings—mass meetings, rallies, marches, pray-ins, jail-ins—were their freedom songs.[8]

In their seminal essay, James Irvine and Walter Kirkpatrick suggest that scholars of rhetoric may need on occasion to address themselves to "the place of music in the rhetoric of social movements," including "how movement-oriented music evolves" and "the impact of the music upon the traditional rhetorical engines normally found within movements." Such topics are particularly important in any attempt to understand black rhetoric. "Whereas the traditional discursive form of the message emphasizes intellectual participation on the part of the receiver," reasoned Irvine and Kirkpatrick, "the musical form necessarily involves and stimulates the body and its capacity for sensation. . . . When listening to a message couched in music, one is less prepared to argue in opposition to the projected message. Listeners do not ordinarily

8. Booklet accompanying three phonodiscs, *Voices of the Civil Rights Movement: Black American Freedom Songs 1960–1966* (Washington, D.C., 1980), 4, 11–12. This compilation probably is the single most representative collection of recorded songs that evolved during the period.

anticipate persuasion and, as a result, they are ready recipients of the rhetorical statement without being aware of its complete implications." Furthermore, Stephen Kosokoff and Carl Carmichael found some empirical evidence to support this argument, concluding that "songs can add to the attitude change resulting from a speech of social action" to the point that a "poor speech" can be "saved" when "combined with a song that, by itself, had also failed to produce statistically significant attitude change."[9] This result is instructive inasmuch as southern black rhetoric of protest often was embellished by musical lyrics. Perhaps there is some wisdom in the old cliché "I care not who makes the nation's laws so long as I can make its songs."

Black music in general, and black church music in particular, can be traced to African origins. While bondage destroyed most of their roots, the slaves' music was the one element of their previous existence that was preserved with some authenticity. African music was both pervasive and complicated. In its execution, "virtually everyone is performing and everyone is listening." From this complexity, which often "contained coded information essential to survival," evolved the work song, the shout, the holler, the spiritual, and, ultimately, the street cry. Deluded in believing that blacks were happy and working hard while singing, a myth alive in the twentieth-century South, whites encouraged "cheerful" and "nonsensical" songs, unaware that such singing was neither. As long as "the *sound* of the singing created a mood acceptable to whites or the language was perceived by owners as being meaningless, blacks could communicate thoughts and concerns unmentionable publicly in other forms." Some contemporary spirituals, such as "Down by the Riverside" and "Steal Away to Jesus," supposedly were sung originally as signal songs.[10]

9. James R. Irvine and Walter G. Kirkpatrick, "The Musical Form in Rhetorical Exchange: Theoretical Considerations," *Quarterly Journal of Speech*, LVIII (1972), 284, 273; Stephen Kosokoff and Carl W. Carmichael, "The Rhetoric of Protest: Song, Speech, and Attitude Change," *Southern Speech Journal*, XXXV (1970), 301.

10. Leonard W. Doob, *Communication in Africa* (New Haven, 1961), 79; Richard Alan Waterman, "African Influence on the Music of the Americas," in Sol Tax (ed.), *Acculturation in the Americas* (New York, 1967), 207–18; David N. Baker, "The Rhetorical Dimensions of Black Music: Past and Present," in Jack L. Daniel (ed.), *Black Communication* (New York, 1974), 15; Logue, "Transcending Coercion," 44; McKinney, "The Black Church," 458.

The call-response, a feature of group rather than solo performance, is a characteristic of black music that has a direct relationship to black speech. A lead singer, or "caller," sings a solo verse line and is followed by a choral group, or "responders," singing a word or a short phrase. The leader's call changes as the song progresses, but the choral response usually remains fairly constant. The call-response set an "elemental rhythm" in motion with tapping, clapping, and swaying, followed by audience humming and spontaneous verbal responses. Black churches in twentieth-century America could rarely afford a musical instrument, so "the sisters sat in the 'amen' corner and kept rhythm by clapping their hands." As a result, some people went to church "for the rhythm." This circumstance should not be treated lightly. Rhythm "is capable of producing a change, both physiological and psychological" in audience and performer. But, more important, rhythm functions "as a *carrier of rhetorical impact.* Here rhythm acts to reduce the inhibitions and defense mechanisms of the listener and to render him more susceptible to the rhetorical aspects of the musical message."[11]

Unlike the white community, blacks seemingly were able to sing religious songs outside of church without a sense of guilt or embarrassment. Religious lyrics had no institutional limitations. Most of the music was familiar to all southern audiences inasmuch as whites and blacks shared the traditional Baptist hymns of the region: "This Little Light of Mine," "Leaning on the Everlasting Arms," "Go Tell It on the Mountain," "Will the Circle Be Unbroken," "City Called Heaven," "Walk with Me, Lord," "I Told Jesus." Thus, the musical foundation was sacred to all concerned, which meant that a fundamental communicative element of the civil rights movement was mutually revered by all sides. This significant point of basic understanding often is overlooked by those who ignore black music.

With this common religious foundation, blacks were able to intersperse other lyrics that often were more secular and more polemic. Themes emphasized militancy, freedom, and even de-

11. LeRoy Moore, Jr., "The Spiritual: Soul of Black Religion," *American Quarterly,* XXIII (1971), 671; Bennett, "The Soul of Soul," 120; Irvine and Kirkpatrick, "The Musical Form in Rhetorical Exchange," 277.

fiance. Military metaphors abound in "We Are Soldiers in the Army," "Which Side Are You On?," "We'll Never Turn Back," "We Shall Not Be Moved," "We're Marching On to Freedom Land." Freedom had its thematic roots in the Underground Railroad, and the metaphor was carried into the 1960s: "Get on Board, Children," "Woke Up This Morning With My Mind on Freedom," "Freedom Train," "Oh Freedom," "Don't You Think It's About Time That We All Be Free." The defiant lyrics often made it possible to sing poetically what an individual might be reluctant to state: "If You Miss Me From the Back of the Bus," "Ain' Scared of Nobody," "Oh Pritchett, Oh Kelly," "99 1/2 Won't Do," "Governor Wallace," "Get Your Rights, Jack," "Ain' Gonna Let Nobody Turn Me 'Round."[12]

Some of the defiant lyrics spontaneously targeted local figures: "Tell Jim Clark," the Selma sheriff; "Tell Al Lingo," head of the Alabama Highway Patrol. More pointedly, "If you miss Jim Clark, can't find him nowhere. Come on over to the graveyard, he'll be laying over there." "If you miss Governor Wallace, can't find him nowhere. Come on over to the crazy house, he'll be resting over there." "Ain' Scared of Nobody" was directed at Birmingham's police commissioner, Bull Connor, in 1963. "Oh Pritchett, Oh Kelly" refers to Police Chief Laurie Pritchett and Mayor Asa Kelly of Albany, Georgia. A Georgia court order banning demonstrations stimulated "Ain' gonna let no injunction turn me 'round," which became "Ain' Gonna Let Nobody Turn Me 'Round." According to R. Serge Denisoff, "The songs of the civil rights movement of the South . . . were repetitive and so structured that verses could be improvised to meet any contingency. 'Ain't gonna let ———— turn me round' could be sung for any occasion on the streets of any community. The simplicity and repetitiveness made the song easy to learn within a matter of minutes."[13]

Some of the songs were adapted from other periods, other subjects, other performers, and even other countries. "Oh Freedom" was used by blacks protesting the Atlanta race riots of 1906. Then, with some alterations, it was used by the Southern Tenant Farm-

12. Booklet accompanying *Voices of the Civil Rights Movement*, 12–21.
13. *Ibid.*; R. Serge Denisoff, "Protest Songs: Those on the Top Forty and Those of the Streets," *American Quarterly*, XXII (1970), 820.

ers' Union in the 1930s. Harry Belafonte's "Banana Boat Song" of the 1950s was converted into "Calypso Freedom" by the Nashville Freedom Riders. "Wade in the Water" evolved from tales of Harriet Tubman and the Underground Railroad. "Cum Bah Yah" was imported from Liberia, West Africa, as an alteration of the spiritual "Come By Here." "Hit the Road, Jack" by Ray Charles was converted to "Get Your Rights, Jack." James Farmer, the CORE (Congress of Racial Equality) leader, rewrote the words to "Which Side Are You On?," a union song from the Harlan County, Kentucky, coal miners' strike of the 1930s. "Woke Up This Morning With My Mind Stayed on Jesus" was altered to "Woke Up This Morning With My Mind on Freedom." "We Shall Not Be Moved" was used in attempts to unionize black workers during the 1930s and 1940s. In an old spiritual, "I'm On My Way," Canaan Land became Freedom Land. Mother Bell, a gospel singer of the 1940s, originally made "99 1/2 Won't Do" popular. The hymn "Old Ship of Zion" became "Union Train," a labor organizing song of the 1930s and 1940s, then evolved into "Freedom Train" in the 1960s.[14]

But one song deserves special notice. "We Shall Overcome," a reworked nineteenth-century revival hymn, became the civil rights anthem. It was "particularly effective in marches and other situations of confrontation, since it reaffirms the valor of the marchers and the righteousness of the cause in a highly repetitive manner:

> We are not afraid, we are not afraid
> We are not afraid today.
> Oh, deep in my heart, I do believe,
> We shall overcome someday."

In addition, unlike other freedom calls, it was a gentle, convivial, soft, nonthreatening, hymnlike melody. In a television interview, Martin Luther King, Jr., contended that "freedom songs and the great spirituals" invigorated, unified, and provided renewed courage to those in "the Movement" who faltered and almost gave up in despair during especially trying periods.[15]

14. Booklet accompanying *Voices of the Civil Rights Movement*, 12–21.
15. Jerome L. Rodnitzky, "The New Revivalism: American Protest Songs, 1945–1968," *South Atlantic Quarterly*, LXX (1971), 17; King quoted in R. Serge Denisoff,

In addition to a solid foundation of religious songs, there were well-established singing groups that usually had religious affiliations: Gospel Harmonettes of Birmingham, Montgomery Gospel Trio, American Baptist Theological Seminary Quartet (known as the Nashville Quartet), Alabama Christian Movement Choir of Birmingham, Georgia Sea Island Singers. The names of newer groups became focused more directly on the social revolution as it grew in force: CORE Singers, SNCC Freedom Singers, SNCC Freedom Voices, Selma Youth Freedom Choir, Nashville Freedom Riders, Integration Grooves, Jimmy Collier and the Movement Singers. These groups, and many more, acquired a degree of fame during the period by performing at rallies, demonstrations, church services, and speaking engagements. While those with long-standing religious affiliations supplemented their repertoire with more secular pieces, all groups were equally motivated to perform in church, on the street, or in jail.

There was no shortage of individual musical talent. While most of these people did not become nationally renowned, their contributions were significant during the period, among them the brother-sister combination of Emory and Rutha Mae Harris, Chuck Neblett, Cordell Hull Reagon, and Bernice Johnson (later, Dr. Bernice Johnson Reagon). Betty Mae Fikes developed a unique musical yell as a call, Cleo Kennedy was a piercing soprano, and Hollis Watkins often contributed a lyrical shout. From Mississippi came Willie Peacock, an inspirational song leader, and Fannie Mae Hamer, with her raspy voice, singing and speaking in behalf of the Mississippi Freedom Democratic party. From Americus, Georgia, came Amanda Bowens Perdew, Virginia Davis, and Sammy Mahone. Other individual performers included Bill Harris, Brenda Darden, Avon Rollins, and Diane Smith. In addition, the movement could boast many songwriters who often wrote music in jail or were stimulated to compose on short notice following a single tragic event. Like the performers, most did not attain lasting fame but applied a talent that often seemed to surface spontaneously: James Bevel, Bernard LaFayette, Brenda Gibson,

---

"Protest Movements: Class Consciousness and the Propaganda Song," *Sociological Quarterly*, IX (1968), 243.

Marshall Jones, Carlton Reese, Matthew Jones, Bertha Gober, Janie Lee Culbreth, James Orange, Mabel Hillary. These personalities and characteristics contributed significantly to the ultimate universality of a generous portion of black music and its accompanying speech improvisations. When whites imitated such music, blacks made further modifications in an effort to preserve their own musical forms. Jazz became funky jazz, then, after the Supreme Court decision, soul. This music was "consciously revivalistic in form and overtly anti-white in function." Soul was something with which you were born and had to renew periodically by returning "down home" to your roots. The black church was a "basic training center for soul singers," and some graduates became internationally famous—Ray Charles, Diana Ross, Aretha Franklin, Dionne Warwick, Little Richard, Otis Redding, James Cleveland, Dinah Washington, Mahalia Jackson, the Dixie Hummingbirds, Lou Rawls and the Pilgrim Travelers, David Ruffin and the Temptations, and many more. When these performers were not on the road, they usually were "just another voice in the 'amen' corner." Tindall reminds us that whatever "African traits endure, black Americans like other ethnic groups have an experience and an American identity not shared by their cousins who were left behind. *Négritude* may evoke echoes of Africa, but 'soul' evokes echoes of the South." With its birth after the civil rights movement began, soul sometimes had the persuasive aura of music with a purpose. Albums such as *We Insist: Freedom Now Suite*, with a lunch-counter sit-in scene on the cover, attacked segregation directly. Some of the music highlighted Little Rock or the efforts of Martin Luther King, Jr.[16]

The southern black social revolution was assisted immeasurably by a rich tradition of church music woven into the fabric of oral discourse. This music was based on a Christian ethical system that venerated freedom and individual choice; provided instruction through a repetitive call-response method; offered a sense of unity and acculturation, with widespread participation,

16. Booklet accompanying *Voices of the Civil Rights Movement*, 12–21; John F. Szwed, "Musical Style and Racial Conflict," *Phylon*, XXVII (1966), 358–66; James Alexander, "Religious Influence in Soul Music," audiotape, Indiana University, n.d.; George B. Tindall, "Beyond the Mainstream: The Ethnic Southerners," *Journal of Southern History*, XL (1974), 17; Bennett, "The Soul of Soul," 116.

coded messages, and popular fables; served as release for unrestrained feelings openly expressed; supplied an outlet for black musical and rhetorical creativity; was the one black creation accepted with genuine enthusiasm by nonblacks for the quality of its message and expression; gave professional black musicians exposure, livelihood, and ultimate fame; and provided a subtle, nonthreatening vehicle for transmitting black grievances to the entire world.

BLACK RHETORIC

The black clergy had a leadership role that assumed a variety of forms in the twentieth century: "pastor or spiritual leader, political leader, social leader, and very often the leading proponent and exemplar of education." As loving tyrants, they had to teach their flock survival through compromise. Although older, less educated, black ministers could be caricatured by such slapstick representations as Flip Wilson's Brother Leroy, the younger clerics sometimes completed advanced academic degrees in addition to seminary training. In the past, "the Negro's only sense of prestige and dignity was derived vicariously through the person and status" of the minister. "When Negroes were hungry, they fed the preacher; when ragged, they clothed him with expensive suits; while they walked, they bought the pastor a big car." The "Negro community" looked to the minister "as their spokesman before the mysterious white world, and trusted him to keep their affairs in order." When times changed, the one person in the community who had dignity was expected to lead blacks in search of their own dignity. As a result, the "civil-rights movement at the grass-roots level" in the South was largely in the hands of black ministers.[17]

Apparently this authority was clear to both the leader and the led. Researchers over the decades spanning the civil rights movement questioned members of southern black communities concerning whom they perceived as black leaders. In 1966 it was decided, "No other single occupational group receives anything close to the number of leadership nominations given to preachers." Not only did the preacher enjoy a long history of eminence,

17. Lincoln, "Forward," in Mitchell, *Black Preaching*, 6–7; C. Eric Lincoln, "Key Man of the South—The Negro Minister," *New York Times Magazine*, July 12, 1964, p. 20.

but, unlike other professionals, he was practically invulnerable to white pressures. As long as he remained a staunch black advocate, this status was assured. Again, in 1976, it was concluded that "the black minister" was "in the top echelons of black political leadership," which led some observers to argue that the black church is the "spearhead of social protest in the deep South." Thus, when southern blacks began their dissent, they did not estrange themselves from their preachers. Indeed, it was the younger pastors who assumed the mantle of leadership by demonstrating three compelling characteristics: "individuality, devotion to their congregation, and eloquence."[18]

As titular head of and major speaker for the black community, the minister had to know the nuances of both black and white American English. Like southern black music, southern black speech probably has had a more profound impact on the national idiom than has its white counterpart. Neither the blacks' music nor their speech rigidly separates secular from sacred. Through sheer force of numbers, southern blacks are national leaders of their race. Formal instruction in southern-flavored "Black English" evolved, but no comparable courses in southern "White English" have been offered, though it too is a distinct genre. By implication, southern black language has attained a level of importance, appeal, and political clout not yet achieved by southern white speech.

Because black ministers possibly possessed the most extensive knowledge of potential pitfalls in black-white communication, it is fortunate that they led the adversary forces for change. In addition, apart from humane rationales, such knowledge could have stimulated the clergy to insist on a general policy of nonviolence to defuse any misunderstanding before it boiled irrevocably into open warfare. Black preachers led the southern black social revolution in the twentieth century because they possessed independence and power inasmuch as their personal economic support came exclusively from black parishioners; frequently, along with

18. Donald R. Matthews and James W. Prothro, *Negroes and the New Southern Politics* (New York, 1966), 181; William M. Berenson, Kirk W. Elifson, and Tandy Tollerson III, "Preachers in Politics: A Study of Political Activism Among the Black Ministry," *Journal of Black Studies*, VI (1976), 374–75; Low and Clift (eds.), *Encyclopedia of Black America*, 159.

black teachers, they were the best educated and most cultured of the black community and usually were the most fluent in all strata of the black and the white idioms; they were informed on all facets of community life; they were seasoned public speakers who controlled a ready platform for sending and receiving the latest information; they often commanded more physical resources than did any other community member; they "knew the Bible," and therefore acquired a respect from many white southerners that secular occupations did not provide; they understood Establishment methods and agents—police, lawyers, judges, physicians, nurses, morticians, insurers, bill collectors, etc.; they personally negotiated with such agents in dialectical settings on behalf of harassed communicants; they served all generations within the black community; and they adopted respected trappings of the affluent Establishment—they were well dressed, well groomed, well mannered, and frequently adorned with expensive jewelry and a big automobile.

Martin Luther King, Jr., was the most influential black advocate of the period. In retrospect, he single-handedly dominated several major events that remain turning points in the southern social revolution. The following analysis concentrates on King's most noteworthy rhetorical achievements in presenting the black appeal for change: the Montgomery bus boycott, his letter from the Birmingham jail, and the Washington Freedom March.

Montgomery Bus Boycott

On December 1, 1955, in Montgomery, Alabama, a little more than a year after the Supreme Court decision, a weary Rosa Parks chose to remain in her seat, contrary to the orders of a public bus driver. She was promptly removed from the vehicle and arrested. Thus, the "Great Negro Awakening" began. Jesse Jackson contends that Parks "just changed her mind as to what she was worth." A twenty-six-year-old Baptist preacher, Martin Luther King, Jr., "the right man in the right place, stepped forward reluctantly into history."[19] Unquestionably King became the leader of the black social revolution in the South and remained so until his

19. Donald Hugh Smith, "Civil Rights: A Problem in Communication," *Phylon*, XXVII (1966), 383.

death in 1968. His plan was simply to bring to the black southerner the potential for achieving the American dream.

On December 5, King was elected president of the Montgomery Improvement Association and delivered the first of his many mass-meeting addresses. Even at that early stage in his career, he demonstrated the eloquent style and rhythm of his more famous discourses:

> There comes a time my friends when people get tired of being plunged across the abyss of humiliation, when they experience the bleakness of nagging despair. There comes a time when people get tired of being pushed out of the glimmering sunlight of last July and left standing amid the piercing chill of an Alpine November. . . . We are not wrong in what we are doing. If we are wrong, the Supreme Court of this nation is wrong. If we are wrong, the Constitution of the United States is wrong. If we are wrong, Jesus of Nazareth was merely a Utopian dreamer who never came down to earth.

From the outset, King urged nonviolent, unified, fearless action within the law in order to seek proper redress of grievances. When later faced with denials of such superficial instruments as parade permits, he would advocate the disobedience of "unjust" laws. But, for the present, he led a simple, civilized, passive action that hit Montgomery where it hurt—in the pocketbook. It was not blacks' first protest against southern public transportation, but it was by far the most effective up to that time in emphasizing southern racial discrimination for a national audience.[20]

From its nascence, the southern racial struggle was made to order for television. The issue at each juncture was simple and easy to comprehend; the forces for good and evil were identifiable instantaneously; while the drama was intense, the behavior of key characters, such as white sheriffs, became predictable; although there might be short-term setbacks, the ultimate victory of good over evil could be anticipated. Ironically, when it was revealed that

20. King quoted in Donald H. Smith, "Martin Luther King, Jr.: In the Beginning at Montgomery," *Southern Speech Journal*, XXXIV (1968), 14–15; Roger A. Fischer, "A Pioneer Protest: The New Orleans Street-Car Controversy of 1867," *Journal of Negro History*, LIII (1968), 219–33; August Meier and Elliott Rudwick, "Negro Boycotts of Segregated Streetcars in Florida, 1901–1905," *South Atlantic Quarterly*, LXIX (1970), 525–33; August Meier and Elliott Rudwick, "Negro Boycotts of Jim Crow Streetcars in Tennessee," *American Quarterly*, XXI (1969), 755–63.

the press and television cameras would be present at King's December 5 address, "many of the ministers" became "too frightened to take part in the program." This behavior would change as future rhetorical situations multiplied. By early 1956, the Montgomery bus boycott was gaining international press coverage with some consistency. Southern racial stories would become even more common from 1959 on into the 1970s, with Martin Luther King, Jr., for the remainder of his life, the single most-featured civil rights personality.[21]

Those principals who should have been least experienced with televised speech and action, the black ministers, surfaced consistently as heroes. Doubtless they were on the "right" side of most viewers' emotions, and, equally beyond question, television editing can be biased. However, familiarity with both black and white idiom, a knowledge of the communicative culture of the two races, and constant practice before "live" audiences gave the pastors an intuitive sense in handling exchanges at the barricades as well as in delivering formal speeches. Blacks had been adjusting to audiences of different races all their lives; their white adversaries probably found the experience both novel and threatening. Robert MacNeil contends, "Television was a primary agent in conveying to fair-minded white Americans for the first time the depths of Negro humiliation and frustration." But there was a black audience out there as well. By 1968, the date of MacNeil's observations, the black audience was composed of a higher percentage of viewers within their racial group who watched more television and judged it to be of higher quality than did their white counterparts.[22]

Early in the protest movement, King and associates began exploiting two crucial rhetorical elements. They dictated the *exigencies*—those imperfections "marked by urgency," things "waiting to be done" because they are other than they should be. Likewise, despite visible *constraints*, they usually calculated properly the target *audiences* of a broader population who were the ul-

21. Smith, "Martin Luther King, Jr.," 16; for examples, see London *Times*, February 1956–May, 1974, *passim*.

22. Robert MacNeil, *The People Machine: The Influence of Television on American Politics* (New York, 1968), 71; Robert T. Bower, *Television and the Public* (New York, 1973), 45–50.

timate "mediators of change." Often in dictating the time, place, and issue, they controlled two of the three elements of Lloyd Bitzer's "rhetorical situation." Their strategy underscores the potential accomplishments of minority adversaries outside the mainstream who command no Establishment forces, yet who succeed remarkably in bringing intangible pressures to bear on those forces. The bus issue ended successfully after a year of boycotting. A noteworthy accomplishment, it was ranked ninth, just below the "Supreme Court School Decision," on *Ebony* magazine's list, "Ten Most Dramatic Events in Negro History."[23]

Letter from Birmingham Jail

The next significant rhetorical act—King's April, 1963, "Letter from Birmingham Jail"—surfaced amid some of the most frightening circumstances of the movement. Because King responded to the "Public Statement by Eight Alabama Clergymen" and had to do so in writing while he was incarcerated, this time he was least in control of the rhetorical situation. He started from a posture of defense. "Seldom, if ever, do I pause to answer criticism of my work and ideas. . . . But since I feel that you are men of genuine good will and your criticisms are sincerely set forth, I would like to answer your statement in what I hope will be patient and reasonable terms." His critics in this instance were eight Christian and Jewish clergymen whose letter, published in the Birmingham *News*, accused King either directly or implicitly of being an imported agitator, refusing impatiently to await the proper time for integration, failing to use the courts for redress of grievances, disrupting the newly elected city government by not giving it a chance to correct previous wrongs, and being an extremist who, ignoring "law and order and common sense," incited violence. In addition, they praised "the community," "the news media," and "law enforcement officials."[24]

23. Lloyd F. Bitzer, "The Rhetorical Situation," *Philosophy & Rhetoric,*" I (1968), 1–14; "Ten Most Dramatic Events in Negro History," *Ebony*, XVIII (September, 1963), 28–38.
24. All quotations of King's "Letter from Birmingham Jail," April 16, 1963, and of "Public Statement by Eight Alabama Clergymen" are from Haig A. Bosmajian and Hamida Bosmajian, *The Rhetoric of the Civil-Rights Movement* (New York, 1969), 37–57, 35–36.

King's circumstances were repressive and his resources meager. He began his response "on the margins of the newspaper in which the statement appeared . . . continued on scraps of writing paper supplied by a friendly Negro trusty, and concluded on a pad" that his "attorneys were eventually permitted to leave." From this inauspicious beginning, the letter has become a standard entry in literary anthologies. It is a textbook example of responding to the immediate audience of eight clergymen while simultaneously addressing a universal audience that potentially encompasses all races throughout time. It is a "sermon/letter" that partially rings with traditional "old-time Negro preaching," yet incorporates a "devastating logic" often missing from "the traditional Negro minister's resources." It unfolds as debate refutation with King defining terms and answering "each argument on at least two levels, usually a practical, immediate level, perhaps most appealing to a public audience, and an abstract, philosophical level involving unstated moral premises," perhaps most appealing to those "with some concern for philosophical abstractions." Even so, parts of the essay are "eminently quotable"—the reader can "hear the cadences of the evangelist."[25] While obviously not intended as music, the letter incorporates such devices as metaphor and repetition to give it melodious rhythm. These likely are outward manifestations of a deeper black cadence.

Respect for authority is the single most resounding element. This addressed directly or tangentially all five charges registered by the clergymen. Without benefit of library or ordinary research tools, King buttressed each contention with eminent authority— the apostle Paul, Jesus Christ, Socrates, an unidentified "distinguished jurist," Reinhold Niebuhr, the Supreme Court, Saint Augustine, Saint Thomas Aquinas, Martin Buber, Paul Tillich, Shadrach, Meshach, Abednego, Hungarian freedom fighters, Martin Luther, John Bunyan, Abraham Lincoln, Thomas Jefferson, Ralph McGill, Lillian Smith, Harry Golden, James Dabbs, T. S. Eliot, "the founding fathers." He not only cited these people

25. Martin Luther King, Jr., *Why We Can't Wait* (New York, 1964), 76n; Wesley T. Mott, "The Rhetoric of Martin Luther King, Jr.: *Letter From Birmingham Jail*," *Phylon*, XXXVI (1975), 411–21; Richard P. Fulkerson, "The Public Letter as a Rhetorical Form: Structure, Logic, and Style in King's 'Letter From Birmingham Jail,'" *Quarterly Journal of Speech*, LXV (1979), 121–36.

but quoted from memory selected applicable statements. His refutation of "extremist" is an example:

> Was not Jesus an extremist in Love? "Love your enemies, bless them that curse you, pray for them that despitefully use you." Was not Amos an extremist for justice—"Let justice roll down like waters and righteousness like a mighty stream." Was not Paul an extremist for the gospel of Jesus Christ—"I bear in my body the marks of the Lord Jesus." Was not Martin Luther an extremist—"Here I stand; I can do none other so help me God." Was not John Bunyan an extremist—"I will stay in jail to the end of my days before I make a butchery of my conscience." Was not Abraham Lincoln an extremist—"This nation cannot survive half slave and half free." Was not Thomas Jefferson an extremist—"We hold these truths to be self evident that all men are created equal."

Such sources demonstrated King's impromptu command of sacred and secular history; his opponents' arguments presumably mired on the wrong side of revered authority; his willingness, unlike less responsible agitators, to accept that authority; his endorsement of Judeo-Christian morality; his respect for a deductive logical system dependent upon authoritarian concepts; and, finally, the sharp contrast between his own intellectual values and those of the Establishment responsible for his confinement. The opposite of a left-wing radical, King revered deduction and the authoritarianism on which it must be grounded. He was thus squarely within Richard M. Weaver's definition of a conservative. After all, except possibly on those occasions when he chose to disobey unjust laws, he was attempting to conserve and make operational those standards already presumably in force.

Even with such an impressive array of sources, the letter is free from pedantry, pretension, arrogance, or acrimony. He could have cited some of the writers who had contributed to his own thought processes, such as Plato, Aristotle, Thoreau, Gandhi, Mill, Locke, and many more. But with the exception of Gandhi,[26] perhaps none had the recurring influence or the general audience acceptance those had who were mentioned in the letter.

In addressing his fellow clergymen in a "warm, personal tone," King wrote an essay that was "a real letter with a real personality

26. Donald H. Smith, "An Exegesis of Martin Luther King, Jr.'s Social Philosophy," *Phylon*, XXXI (1970), 89–97.

behind it." However, necessary directness is not diluted. He refers to oral coercion that causes black self-perception to degenerate into a sense of "nobodiness": "Your first name becomes 'nigger' and your middle name becomes 'boy' (however old you are) and your last name becomes 'John' . . . your wife and mother are never given the respected title 'Mrs.' . . . you are . . . constantly at tip-toe stance never quite knowing what to expect next."[27] Likewise, King retains an intellectual vocabulary: "unfettered realm of creative analysis and objective appraisal"; "tranquilizing Thalidomide, relieving the emotional stress for a moment"; "an abyss of injustice"; "the bleakness of corroding despair"; "vitriolic words"; "wheels of inevitability"; "forces of social stagnation"; "ominous expressions"; "anesthetizing security"; "pious irrelevancies and sanctimonious trivialities"; "interposition and nullification"; "infanticide and gladiatorial contest"; "paralyzing chains of conformity." But he also recognized the eloquence that could arise from the black idiom when "a 72-year-old woman of Montgomery, Alabama, . . . decided not to ride the segregated buses, and responded to one who inquired about her tiredness with ungrammatical profundity: 'My feets is tired, but my soul is rested.'"

Washington Freedom March

Just a few months after the "Letter from Birmingham Jail" and the fire hoses, guard dogs, and police riot that followed, King delivered his most famous oration, "I Have a Dream," at the Lincoln Memorial on August 28, 1963. Southern white opposition, combined with the necessary intervention of the president, catapulted King into national prominence. He was now in a position once more to dictate the basic elements of the rhetorical situation. As first president of the Southern Christian Leadership Conference (SCLC) since 1957, he had taken a regional organization and made it a national force. It seemed only natural that A. Philip Randolph, who "conceived and became Director of the March on Washington for Jobs and Freedom in 1963,"[28] should include prominent black leaders such as Roy Wilkins of the NAACP, Whitney Young

27. Fulkerson, "The Public Letter as a Rhetorical Form," 124; King, "Letter from Birmingham Jail," Bosmajian and Bosmajian, *The Rhetoric of the Civil-Rights Movement*, 42–43.
28. Kurt W. Ritter and James R. Andrews, *The American Ideology: Reflections of the Revolution in American Rhetoric* (N.p., 1978), 95.

of the National Urban League, James Farmer of CORE, John Lewis of SNCC, and King. But, in view of King's rapid rise, it seems equally natural that he was selected to deliver the final presentation, which became the keynote address for an event of international significance. People descended on Washington from all over the country to assemble peacefully and petition their government for social and economic equality. The attending audience was in the hundreds of thousands, with the electronic media swelling an immediate and expanded audience to uncounted millions all over the world.

It was a hot day; the program was lengthy; the audience was calm but weary; and Lewis' proposed speech preceding King's had been disapproved by the organizers and was subjected to frantic, last-minute revisions. The SNCC speaker adjusted his remarks but not his temperament. His militant stance was a precursor of future events. On that day, if the speaking flagged on occasion, the intervening music performed by top recording talent revived interest. Joan Baez with "We Shall Overcome," Marian Anderson singing "He's Got the Whole World in His Hands," and Odetta's "Oh Freedom" provided excellent supplements to King's message. The program took on the aura of church, leading one writer to declare justifiably that "I Have a Dream" was a "sermon." [29]

Not only did the music evolve straight from the choir loft, but the traditional call-response was used almost from the outset. It was a characteristic that was present in all King's addresses. As the son, the grandson, and the great-grandson of preachers, he had been nurtured on those familiar rhythms that now seemed to sustain him. His ministerial cadence offered measured pauses that encouraged spontaneous audience interjections even in the expanded, multiracial, open-air gathering—"Yeah," "That's right," "Ah yes," "Go 'head," "O Lawd," "Yes it is," "I know it." Eight statements beginning "I have a dream" built up a crescendo of response that signaled the approaching climax with its nine statements beginning "Let freedom ring." These clarion calls for "freedom," recorded in poetic form in the text, precede the final

29. *Ibid.*, 97–105; Hortense J. Spillers, "Martin Luther King and the Style of the Black Sermon," *Black Scholar*, III (1971), 21.

emotionally loaded paragraph delivered in a shout over the thunderous response of the audience. This was "soul force." It was an audience experiencing the "joy" in "knowing that the preacher can play with words and make beautiful, pleasing combinations of sound out of them."[30]

King delivered countless speeches and sermons, thus repetition was unavoidable. Like most great speeches, the Washington presentation was not created suddenly from a vacuum. Many expressions went through a trial-and-error evolutionary process from earlier discourses. As demonstrated below, a surprising number of ideas and symbols seemingly grew directly from the Birmingham letter:

Birmingham letter	Washington sermon
We were the victims of a broken promise.	America has defaulted on this promissory note.
tranquilizing Thalidomide	tranquilizing drug of gradualism
Now is the time to make real the promise of democracy, and transform our pending national elegy into a creative psalm of brotherhood. Now is the time to lift our national policy from the quicksand of racial injustice to the solid rock of human dignity.	Now is the time to rise from the dark and desolate valley of segregation to the sunlit path of racial justice. Now is the time to lift our nation from the quicksands of racial injustice to the solid rock of brotherhood. Now is the time to make justice a reality for all of God's children.
Was not Amos an extremist for justice—"Let justice roll down like waters and righteousness like a mighty stream."	No, no, we are not satisfied, and we will not be satisfied until justice rolls down like waters and righteousness like a mighty stream.
The lips of Governor Barnett [of Mississippi] dripped with words	Alabama . . . with its governor having his lips dripping with the

30. "We Shall Overcome," phonodisc, Broadside Records, 1964. The most authentic printed text is in John Graham (ed.), *Great American Speeches 1898–1963* (New York, 1970), 117–21; Ritter and Andrews, *The American Ideology*, 108; Spillers, "Martin Luther King and the Style of the Black Sermon," 20.

of interposition and nullification.	words of interposition and nullification.
Our destiny is tied up with the destiny of America.	[The whites'] destiny is tied up with our destiny.
police force . . . angry violent dogs . . . ugly and inhuman treatment . . . push and curse . . . slap and kick . . . refuse to give us food	the winds of police brutality

Both conclusions are optimistic. In the letter, King referred midway to "a creative psalm of brotherhood"; in the sermon, he recited words from "America" and soon thereafter ended with his epitaph: "In the words of the old Negro spiritual, 'Free at last! Free at last! Thank God Almighty, we are free at last!'" Thus, he blended musical lyrics intricately into the sermon text, which now is a standard entry in speech anthologies.

The letter was debate refutation that entailed accusation and defense; hence, it was specific, detailed, factual, replete with documentation. It possessed characteristics both of the courtroom and the legislature in treating matters past and future. The sermon was epideictic. It dealt with elements of praise and blame evolving from the present. While the March was for the purpose of urging new legislation, King's sermon did not address that dimension. He recognized that the occasion was not conducive to brazen lobbying. The physical presence of thousands of people at the Lincoln Memorial was lobbying enough. His purpose was to unify the assembly as the agenda drew to a close. His most subtle theme, shared in both messages, involved economics. He wanted the government to guarantee that people would be fed, housed, clothed, educated, trained, and employed. While he categorically rejected communism, he certainly "embraced democratic socialism." This philosophy was consistent with his acceptance of Walter Rauschenbusch's social gospel.[31] In King's view, the church has power only to the extent that it has a conscience in all life's problems.

31. Mergione Pitre, "The Economic Philosophy of Martin Luther King, Jr.," *Review of Black Political Economy*, IX (1979), 191–98; Smith, "An Exegesis of Martin Luther King, Jr.'s Social Philosophy," 90.

The Washington March was the crest of King's career. More than a year prior to the letter and the sermon, he was selected in a poll of five hundred Washington correspondents as the second "most impressive, dependable, and efficient Negro leader" after the aging Ralph Bunche and ahead of Thurgood Marshall, the attorney in the *Brown* case and future Supreme Court justice: "Of those active in civil rights, Dr. King and Judge Marshall dominated the voting." Following the March on Washington, King was named, in September, 1963, one of America's one hundred most influential Negroes by *Ebony; Time* magazine's Man of the Year for 1963, the first black so honored; and Nobel Peace Prize recipient in 1964, the youngest honoree in the history of that award. In less than eight years, he went from an obscure pulpit in Montgomery, Alabama, to international fame in Oslo, Norway. Adversaries who snidely referred to him as "de Lawd" inadvertently acknowledged "the stature of the man and the force of his moral leadership." [32] Blacks no longer could be denied their rightful role and influence in the body politic. Although a significant achievement, it was only a first step. Consistent with his concept of the social gospel, King concentrated his remaining five years on adequate housing, fair employment, and proper nourishment for all citizens.

While charisma has on occasion been identified as the basis of his leadership, there is a more substantial explanation. King was a leader because he was literate in the highest sense of the term. In expressing the aspirations of his race, he could outspeak, outwrite, and outthink most of his contemporaries both black and white. The quality of King's oral and written discourses underscores the absurdity of Establishment denials of full citizenship rights to blacks. By contrast, it is doubtful that any official—Bull Connor, Albert Boutwell, Laurie Pritchett, Ross Barnett, George Wallace, Robert Kennedy, or even John F. Kennedy—could match King's unassisted command of the language. Confined within the hopeless atmosphere of a barren prison, he could produce eloquence on scraps of newspapers, and his was unmatched by those with elaborate speechwriting staffs. His rhetorical bibliography,

32. Simeon Booker, "America's Most Influential Negro?" *Ebony*, XVII (February, 1962), 31–37; "America's 100 Most Influential Negroes," *Ebony*, XVIII (September, 1963), 228–32; "Man of the Year," *Time*, January 3, 1964, pp. 13–27; C.W.T. [Charles Walker Thomas], Editorial, *Negro History Bulletin*, XXVIII (1964), 35.

stretching over a dozen years, remains impressive even when it is contrasted with the achievements of others who enjoyed much longer careers.[33]

Finally, for King, nonviolence and loving acts were not just commandments; they were practical instruments of power. The Holy Scriptures offered rhetorical examples that found their way into his expressions and actions. He provided a calibre of clerical leadership that attracted other effective ministerial colleagues to the SCLC—among them, Ralph Abernathy, Andrew Young, Jesse Jackson, Fred Shuttlesworth, Wyatt Walker, and Bernard Lee. While keeping his rhetoric hermeneutic, King succeeded in "detheorizing" the gospel. Whether he was euphoric or besieged by panic, he was able to siphon off those durable, appropriate, fundamental teachings. King's scriptural rhetoric gave to his constituents what they did not always have the power to give themselves—their self-respect, their sense of somebodiness—without subtracting comparable qualities from his white adversaries.

Militant Reactors

While Martin Luther King, Jr., was advocating "justice," "equality," and "love," Stokely Carmichael was screaming "Black Power!" accompanied by the clenched fist, and Malcolm X was declaring "It's the ballot or the bullet!" In the 1960s, the Stokelys and Malcolms seemed to increase in both number and stridency. However, probably as an eternal tribute to King's effectiveness, violence induced by blacks never became a feature of the southern social revolution. Nevertheless, functioning simultaneously at the time of King's most memorable rhetorical efforts, Malcolm X, Stokely Carmichael, and Eldridge Cleaver renounced passive resistance and urged more violent action.

Malcolm X, born Malcolm Little in Omaha, Nebraska, was the son of a reactionary, itinerant Baptist minister. With the father a dedicated organizer for Marcus Garvey's back-to-Africa movement, the family was a constant target of violence. Malcolm, un-

33. Brian A. Haggerty, "Martin Luther King, Jr.: A Chronological Bibliography," *Journal of Negro History*, LXVI (1981), 64–69; Sidney M. Willhelm, "Martin Luther King, Jr. and the Black Experience in America," *Journal of Black Studies*, X (1979), 3–19.

familiar with the South, grew up in the North and spent his adult years in Boston and Harlem. In his autobiography, he alludes to one brief visit to Atlanta with Muslim organizers. He had only an eighth-grade education, and later he became a thief, burglar, dope addict, dope peddler, pimp, and prison inmate. In the penitentiary, he converted to the religion of the "Nation of Islam" led by Elijah Muhammad. He was a man of quick intelligence and commanding personality who read widely and was introduced to academic debating while still behind bars.[34]

Malcolm's language was particularly bitter in opposing Christians and Christian clergymen, especially Martin Luther King, whose nonviolence he saw as disarming the blacks. He treated protest marches, demonstrations, and singing with derision: "You don't have a turn-the-other-cheek revolution. . . . Who ever heard of a revolution where they lock arms . . . singing 'We Shall Overcome'? You don't do that in a revolution. You don't do any singing, you're too busy swinging." He mocked the March on Washington as "that 'Farce on Washington.'" He advocated complete separation of blacks from whites in a geographical area within the United States. "For twelve years he taught the Negro not to love the white man but to see in him the devil incarnate." Then, in his last days, he mellowed, becoming something of an integrationist, even predicting a chance for a "bloodless revolution."[35]

Southern blacks likely found Malcolm X considerably more alien to them than were most whites they knew. Their repugnance would have been generated at the outset by his opposition to Christianity. His crime-filled ghetto life probably would have been received with utter disbelief, especially when he seemed to flaunt his tarnished background. Then the strange religion with its allegiance to Mecca in a distant part of the world would have been totally mysterious. If the southern black saw him in person with his light skin, tendency to freckle, and his reddish hair, perhaps

34. Alex Haley (ed.), *The Autobiography of Malcolm X* (New York, 1964); Robert Penn Warren, "Malcolm X: Mission and Meaning," *Yale Review*, LVI (1966), 164.

35. James L. Golden and Richard D. Rieke, *The Rhetoric of Black Americans* (Columbus, Ohio, 1971), 413–21; George Breitman (ed.), *Malcolm X Speaks* (New York, 1965), 9; Haley (ed.), *The Autobiography of Malcolm X*, 278; Samuel A. Weiss, "The Ordeal of Malcolm X," *South Atlantic Quarterly*, LXVII (1968), 53; Warren, "Malcolm X," 168.

even basic doubts concerning his "blackness" would have arisen. But, indeed, any hope of identity would have dissolved once they heard Malcolm's erudite speech that seemingly shunned the call-response soulful sounds of southern clergy. His militancy had no ready avenue into the minds and hearts of southern blacks.

Another new black voice did invade the South, causing a temporary flurry of agitation. Stokely Carmichael, an admirer of Malcolm X, swept through Mississippi with his fist clenched over his head and yelling "Black Power!" Listeners disagreed about the meaning of his discourse; however, the black power salute soon enjoyed official recognition as a symbol of anti-Americanism. Dick Gregory, addressing a predominantly white audience, declared that Stokely's action "scared the niggers worse than it did you." Handsome, flamboyant, and shrill, Carmichael could address an audience with stirring effect in fluent white, black, or ghetto speech as the occasion demanded. He was affiliated with the Black Panther party as well as SNCC, and his ideas were ultra–left wing. In an interview in Havana in the late 1960s, he reportedly declared that Fidel Castro "is the greatest man I have ever met." His anticipated speaking appearance usually drew early opposition and predictions of ensuing violence. Once he arrived, a media event followed that promised much and produced a dozen or two of his own personal bodyguards from SNCC and scores of policemen. Whitney Young, executive director of the National Urban League, calculated that Carmichael's following "amounts to about 50 Negroes and about 5,000 white reporters. . . . There is no organization; there is no following." [36]

Carmichael was momentarily entertaining for selected white listeners and television news editors, but once he had performed his initial act, there was little that endured. He had a natural affinity for the discourses of Malcolm X inasmuch as both recommended early in their speaking careers a "kill whitey" theme as the solution to all black problems. While studying in Africa, he

36. Dick Gregory, "Black Power and the Civil Rights Movement," phonotape, Colorado State University, October 26, 1967; Golden and Rieke, *The Rhetoric of Black Americans*, 534; Pat Jefferson, "The Magnificent Barbarian at Nashville," *Southern Speech Journal*, XXXIII (1967), 77–87; Elizabeth Flory Phifer and Dencil R. Taylor, "Carmichael in Tallahassee," *Southern Speech Journal*, XXXIII (1967), 88–92; "Racial Problems Ahead," *U.S. News & World Report*, April 22, 1968, p. 46.

"delivered" the dedication address *in absentia* at the opening of Malcolm X Liberation University in Durham, North Carolina. However, by that time, influential blacks saw him as something of a troublesome oddity. For example, in an Atlanta speech, a noted black psychologist allegedly numbered Carmichael among "the strutting Negro militants to be branded as quitters and accommodators of whitey." According to Eugene Patterson, when the black militants' "talking and their rioting is over and done, their phony fanaticism will have done nothing but lead the Negro people into a tragic retrogression to the separated life where white segregationists wanted to hold them all along."[37]

The Black Panther party, with its international mailing address in Algeria, listed only one southern chapter—Winston-Salem, North Carolina—and no black leaders in the South. The party subscribed overtly to Marx, Lenin, Stalin, Mao, and Ho Chi Minh, in direct opposition to King's Baptist Christianity. Although he was born in Wabbaseka, Arkansas, Eldridge Cleaver likely would have baffled southern audiences with his advocacy of a "violent revolution by the proletariat" just as Bobby Seale and David Hilliard would have repulsed many persons with their barracks language. Almost as if to seek confusion, the Black Panthers subscribed to the efforts of assorted other groups: Communist Party U.S.A., Socialist Workers' party, Progressive Labor party, Republic of New Africa, Students for a Democratic Society, Red Guards, Peace and Freedom party, Black Student Unions, Young Lords, American Servicemen's Union, Youth Against War and Fascism, White Panthers, Young Patriots, Los Siete de la Raza, Committee to Defend the Panthers, New Mobilization Committee to End the War in Vietnam, Venceremos Brigade, SNCC, and CORE. Internationally, the Panthers identified in varied degrees of intensity with groups in North Korea, Cuba, Algeria, France, West Germany, South Vietnam, Scandinavia, Mexico, Canada, Tanzania, Mozambique, Angola, South Africa, Haiti, and South America.[38]

37. Stokely Carmichael, "We Are All Africans," *Black Scholar*, I (1970), 15–19; Eugene Patterson, "Rap, Stokely and Booker T., A Document," *Journal of Negro History*, LII (1967), 325–26, reprinted from Atlanta *Constitution*, November 6, 1967, p. 4.
38. G. Louis Heath, *The Black Panther Leaders Speak* (Metuchen, N.J., 1976), 6–17.

Perhaps some southern readers were exposed to Eldridge Cleaver's popular *Soul on Ice*, his *Post-Prison Writings and Speeches*, and maybe even his *Playboy* interview; but it is unlikely that they ever acknowledged him as a black "leader." James Baldwin probably was perceived in much the same way. His various novels published in the 1950s and 1960s received some play in southern literary circles, but he was a northern writer preoccupied with alien themes and foreign places. Most southern folks of all races, as Flannery O'Connor observed, "innately distrusted . . . the northern liberal intellectuals." Whether they were older writers or SNCC youths, the relief following their departure was the same: "I'm glad they're gone . . . they had too high an opinion of themselves. . . . Very ignorant, but never silent." They probably shared a defect that Whitney Young saw in "the Stokely Carmichaels and the Rap Browns"—they were not "sophisticated."[39]

In general, the fire-eating rhetoric of black militants played no enduring role in the southern social revolution. These outsiders had numerous inherent liabilities that assured their estrangement from target audiences: they had no discernible religion, or one derived from a completely alien society; they had no apparent affinity for music, which silently suggested a lack of soul; they used northern ghetto speech, rapid, clipped, often profane, with its aggressive, threatening, arrogant delivery; they were sometimes attired in the costumes of distant African or black ghetto cultures; their values accepted a documented life of serious crime as an attribute of credibility; and they were devoted to other countries with a zeal that suggested treason.

The southern black could find considerably more security in dealing with the southern white rather than the black militant invader. With the former, the difference was merely one of race that all parties comprehended at the outset; with the latter, the difference was a confusing religious, cultural, axiological, and communicative mosaic. However, the militants' significance evolved "not from their numbers but from their importance as social barometers." Their rhetoric reflected an angry and frustrated "indictment of the white power structure . . . to which millions of American

---

39. Robert Coles, *Flannery O'Connor's South* (Baton Rouge, 1980), 9, 37; "Racial Problems Ahead," 46.

Negroes would subscribe."[40] Their strident calls for "Black Power" and overt force were rhetorical warning shots that eventually made King's nonviolent restraint even more appealing to the white community.

Evolving Southern Black Rhetoric

The final chapter conclusively describing all characteristics of the evolving southern black rhetoric must await the test of time for its completion. However, certain qualified conclusions or trends can be cited. The messages of black speakers are received cordially and respectfully. The intellectual substance and civil demeanor of their immediate predecessors, sometimes under the most intimidating conditions, have had a sobering effect on previous opposition. Language loaded with personal insults openly aimed at the black minority is practically a thing of the past. Rhetorical degradation is practiced routinely only in isolated professional hate groups, which are national maladies more than distinctly southern defects. The South now courts the potential business of anyone with purchasing power irrespective of race; thus, in a commercial sense, blacks have acquired somebodiness. This is not to say that blacks have achieved equitable opportunities in all business enterprises. But barriers to future growth certainly have been substantially removed, with the result that members of many races now are more visible in a variety of work environments, such as mass communications, where minorities were a rarity during the 1960s. With this change, the South has diminished its need to justify integration on commercial grounds and has discontinued much of the pseudo-optimistic sloganeering of the past.[41]

The black church continues as a vital training ground for dispensing soul in both music and rhetoric. Rhythm inherent in the amen corner, call-response, spontaneous improvisation, and subtle codes still convert erstwhile listeners into active participants in song and speech. When new racial challenges threaten,

40. W. Haywood Burns, "The Black Muslims in America: A Reinterpretation," *Race* [U.K.], V (1963), 31, 33.
41. For example, in the 1960s, one note of contrived optimism declared, "Big, bustling Atlanta—a city too busy to hate" (Coles, *Flannery O'Connor's South*, 45).

these potent forces can be pressed into action immediately. For example, as recently as 1982, about 450 demonstrators, mostly blacks, marched from a rally and news conference at a Baptist church in Greenville, South Carolina, to the gates of Bob Jones University. There, they knelt, sang, clapped, and prayed for a change in the university's segregation policies. Even in responding to contemporary issues, blacks continue to control essential elements of the rhetorical situation, collectively marshaling music and rhetoric in carefully orchestrated patterns. While there is no Martin Luther King, Jr., on the horizon, articulate rhetors remain active. Two of King's former associates in the SCLC, the Reverends Andrew Young and Jesse Jackson, ranked one and two on *Ebony's* 1980 list of the ten most admired black Americans.[42] Young gained international fame as Jimmy Carter's ambassador to the United Nations and was subsequently elected mayor of Atlanta. Jackson was appointed by King to Operation Breadbasket and later became the national president of Operation PUSH, an organization dedicated to economic generation and spiritual regeneration, prior to running for president in the 1984 Democratic primaries. Other black leaders, such as Benjamin Hooks, the president of the NAACP, continue to be practicing Baptist ministers.

Third on that "most admired" list was Barbara Jordan, former U.S. congresswoman from Houston and currently a professor at the University of Texas and hostess of the weekly "Crisis to Crisis" program televised nationally by the Public Broadcasting Service. Jordan's most noteworthy rhetorical achievement was her keynote speech before the Democratic National Convention, July 12, 1976, the first black female ever accorded such a distinction. Her address was assessed critically as "a rare accomplishment" free from "subterfuge," "pettiness," or "platitudes." As if to recall King's Washington sermon, she stated that "my presence here is one additional bit of evidence that the American Dream need not forever be deferred." In addition to Jordan, the ascendance of prominent black lawyers was marked nationally by such people as Thurgood Marshall on the Supreme Court and Constance Baker Motley, who battled southern segregation laws for

42. Fort Collins *Coloradoan*, February 7, 1982, Sec. A, p. 3; "The Ten Most Admired Black Americans," *Ebony*, XXXVI (November, 1980), 144–48.

twenty years, on the federal judiciary. More than 23 percent of *Ebony's* total selections over the years for most influential blacks are trained as attorneys. Next, at 10 percent, are the black ministers.[43]

History provides examples that may suggest some modest generalizations about southern black rhetoric. Frederick Douglass was optimistic, worked within the system, and emphasized racial justice. Booker T. Washington, despite his condemnation as an Uncle Tom by some blacks, offered a rhetoric of optimism within the system that clearly prevailed over the defiance of W. E. B. Du Bois. The success of Martin Luther King, Jr., followed the examples set by Douglass and Washington. None branded their adversaries publicly with the racial slurs and epithets that they were attempting to eradicate. Likewise, they separated themselves from those who advocated violence in any form. They attempted to free blacks from rhetorical degradation and physical abuse rather than respond in kind.

Ironically, new generations of practitioners sometimes must learn again those basic lessons from the past. Decades of change made it possible for Andrew Young to apply degradation humorously before five hundred members of the National Association of Black Journalists: "I didn't know there were this many niggers that could write." But he unwisely resorted to the racial slur, branding Walter Mondale's campaign staff "smart-assed white boys." Jesse Jackson, the first black candidate for president to execute a sustained campaign on the national level, seemed perpetually submerged in rhetorical pitfalls of his own making. He could not be excused for his racist labels for New York Jews or for failing to renounce immediately the intemperate statements of Louis Farrakhan, one of the leaders of the Black Muslims. Then he further damaged prospects for the so-called rainbow coalition by going to

43. Wayne N. Thompson, "Barbara Jordan's Keynote Address: Fulfilling Dual and Conflicting Purposes," *Central States Speech Journal*, XXX (1979), 272–77; "Barbara Jordan's Keynote Address: The Juxtaposition of Contradictory Values," *Southern Speech Communication Journal*, XLIV (1979), 223–32; all quotations from the Jordan speech are in *Congressional Record*, 94th Cong., 2nd Sess., Vol. CXXII, pt. 18, pp. 23261–62, and *Vital Speeches*, August 15, 1976, pp. 645–46; Minnie H. Freeman, "Blacks Making Their Mark in Legal Profession," *Negro History Bulletin*, XXXVIII (1975), 440–41; Charles P. Henry, "*Ebony* Elite: America's Most Influential Blacks," *Phylon*, XLII (1981), 125.

Cuba, embracing Fidel Castro, arranging the release of selected prisoners with suspicious backgrounds, evoking the wrath of the U.S. State Department, and stimulating editorial condemnation.[44] Nevertheless, the two former colleagues in the SCLC remain formidable spokesmen of black aspirations. Young served in high office, enjoys a national perspective that few blacks share, and is respected for his outspoken independence. Despite past blunders, Jackson can be eloquent in applying those traditional call-response rhythms of black preaching and its complementary supplement of black music. Unfortunately, his persona ebbs and flows from that of Du Bois to Washington to King. His escapades with Farrakhan and Castro are reminiscent of Du Bois; his call to train ghetto youths as glaziers, bricklayers, and carpenters is Washingtonian; and his stirring "It's time for a change" address at the Democratic convention, followed by the audience's swaying, hand-holding participation in Whitney Phipps's gospel rendition of "Ordinary People," was in the emotional tradition of King. George Will called that last event a "pentecostal moment," but some blacks were disappointed by Jackson's apparent "compromise" with the powers in the party. Even with a stable persona, an active minister is less likely to be accepted nationally in American politics. While their positions appear secure in the South, black clergy may need to abandon the profession or yield national leadership to those in other occupations.[45]

Black militants never fared well in the South, and there are no indications that their inflammatory rhetoric will be received favorably in the near future. For one thing, despite intermittent problems in the 1950s and 1960s, the general trend in the South has pointed consistently toward peaceful accommodation. Researchers at the National Opinion Research Center concluded in 1971 that in a thirty-year span, "the trend has been distinctly and strongly toward increasing approval for integration. For the most part the trend has not been slowed by the racial turmoil of the

44. Fort Collins *Coloradoan*, August 18, 1984, p. 1; *Washington Post Weekly Edition*, April 23, 1984, p. 24; Denver *Post*, July 13, 1984, Sec. A, p. 13, June 30, 1984, Sec. A, pp. 1, 20, July 1, 1984, Sec. C, pp. 1, 3.

45. Public Broadcasting Television Service, July 17, 1984; Denver *Post*, July 18, 1984, Sec. F, pp. 1, 2; Fort Collins *Coloradoan*, July 20, 1984, Sec. D, p. 1; *Washington Post Weekly Edition*, July 30, 1984, p. 26.

past eight years [1963–1971]."[46] This "turmoil" was manifested in rhetorical and dialectical confrontation, much of which received national television coverage. Black speaking, marked by calm restraint and a willingness to remain within the system during this period, deserves overwhelming credit for the positive results. As if to respond to any pockets of militancy that remain, Barbara Jordan emphasized in her 1976 address: "We cannot improve on the system of government handed down to us by the founders of the Republic, there is no way to improve upon that. But what we can do is to find new ways to implement that system and realize our destiny."

It is premature to label black southern oratory a "rhetoric of optimism" or even to state that it possesses a thematic devotion to "the South," as some have concluded about white southern oratory. At this point, it shows some optimistic tendencies. It has evolved from the social climate of the 1950s and 1960s in a state of both constancy and change. Blacks still have not achieved stable prominence. The *Ebony* roster of America's most influential blacks shows almost a two-thirds turnover rate in eight years. Also, few of those on the list "actually wield national power." With the exception of full-time ministers, most serve at the pleasure of white voters or white government officials. Thus, even among the *Ebony* elite, blacks do not share power in proportion to their number. With native-born southerners constituting 65 percent of those listed,[47] a rhetoric of black optimism apparently will come to the fore only when black leaders are full participants in those decisions that have an impact on their lives. Future signals are favorable. Jordan exuded considerable confidence in addressing national unity in a collective sense rather than separating black from white: "We [Americans] are a people in search of a national community. . . . We have a positive vision of the future founded on the belief that the gap between the promise and reality of America

46. Andrew M. Greeley and Paul B. Sheatsley, "Attitudes toward Racial Integration," *Scientific American*, CCXXV (June, 1971), 13–19. This report tended to substantiate an earlier projection made in a similar 1956 study and published by *Scientific American*.

47. For example, John D. Saxon, "Contemporary Southern Oratory: A Rhetoric of Hope, Not Desperation," *Southern Speech Communication Journal*, XL (1975), 262–74; Henry, "*Ebony* Elite," 123, 132.

can one day be finally closed. We believe that. . . . And now we must look to the future. Let us heed the voice of the people and recognize their common sense. If we do not, we not only blaspheme our political heritage, we ignore the common ties that bind all Americans."

In leading the section's social revolution, southern black speakers have persistently used conservative rhetoric. That is, their assertions evolved deductively from Establishment-sanctioned and revered authority. Except for his flirtation with disobeying unjust laws, Martin Luther King, Jr., and his followers never advocated taking more than what already was their legal due. They accepted a hierarchy of authority as well as a hierarchy of values. The radicals usually were their white adversaries who subscribed to unconstitutional policies of illegal suppression. Southern black speakers continue in this tradition of functioning strictly within "the system." Thus, the movement was no "revolution" in ideology or action, but simply the defeat of white reactionaries and black militants by black conservatives who successfully applied effective rhetoric to a series of communication crises.

Ralph McGill's Moderate Campaign for Racial Reform

Calvin M. Logue

W hen Harvard University conferred an honorary degree on Ralph McGill, the citation praised his "steady voice" in a "troubled" South.[1] Indeed, the South from 1946 to 1969 was a place of great social upheaval, changing publicly from a racially segregated to a substantially integrated society. As editor and publisher of the Atlanta *Constitution* from 1946 until his death in 1969, McGill spoke and wrote for the rights of blacks while most whites remained hostile to or silent about any change in the social status of blacks. McGill's support for equal citizenship for blacks is studied here under six divisions: his potential audience (hostile and silent), his resolve, his underlying rhetorical strategy of public instruction, his discourses from 1946 to 1954 and from 1954 to 1969, and a conclusion.

After this essay had been written for *A New Diversity in Contemporary Southern Rhetoric*, the Louisiana State University Press provided permission for the chapter to be published in Calvin M. Logue (ed.), *No Place to Hide: The South and Human Rights* (2 vols.; Macon, Ga., 1984). "Ralph McGill's Moderate Campaign for Racial Reform" is a revised version of the essay published in *No Place to Hide*.
    1. New York *Times*, June 16, 1961.

Potential Audience: Hostile and Silent

Until the 1960s the white South was largely hostile to any consideration of racial reforms. The few moderates who dared oppose
racial segregation risked immediate social ostracism, loss of job,
verbal abuse, and physical harm. Ministers, journalists, professors, students, and others willing to congregate in public with
blacks or question unfair policies and practices met ridicule and
bombs. In 1941, Lillian Smith told of a threat she received after
speaking against racism. In the 1950s, Virginia Durr warned that
"social and economic ruin" awaited social reformers and that persons harmed by racists would have "no recourse in law." Because
McGill sat with blacks on speakers' platforms and criticized the
"shame" of racial injustice in the South, haters poured garbage on
his lawn, made abusive telephone calls, mailed threatening letters, demonstrated outside his office, shot holes in his mailbox
and window, and denied him a hall in which to speak and an official religious publication in which to write.

Because of the dominance of segregation and dangers associated with attempting to change that system of inequities, most
moderates remained silent until well into the 1960s. Clearly no
public market existed among whites in the region for talk of equal
citizenship for blacks. McGill chided so-called moderates for leaving a rhetorical "vacuum" for Ku Klux Klan–types to fill. McGill
urged business leaders, educators, clergy, and journalists to explain obedience to laws as an alternative to extremists' practices.
If fair-minded men and women failed to offer clear and reasonable
counsel, argued McGill, southerners would be left with "a vast
mythology of confusion and distortion."[2]

A Reformer's Resolve

Although doing so was hazardous, some citizens challenged racial wrongs in the South. The Southern Regional Council, of which

2. Ralph McGill, *The South and the Southerner* (Boston, 1964), 251–52; in Calvin
McLeod Logue (ed.), *Ralph McGill: Editor and Publisher* (2 vols.; Durham, 1969):
"Cooper Union Lincoln Day Address," II, 161, 165, "DePaul University Address,"
II, 366–67, "South in Transition Speech," II, 359, "Rochester City Club Speech," II,

McGill was a charter member, was founded in 1944 to assist blacks, but not as a force of "mass appeal." Virginius Dabney of the Richmond *Times-Dispatch* argued for equal and separate facilities. Sociologist Howard Odum praised the South's culture and values and worked for increased opportunities for blacks. Rather than attempting to integrate blacks and whites, Dabney and Odum worked for improvements in education, the job market, and voting rights within a segregated society. Lillian Smith and Aubrey Williams, on the other hand, criticized the "gradualists" and demanded that the cruel system of discrimination be replaced by equal opportunities for blacks.[3]

Studying the evolution of McGill's efforts for civil rights for blacks helps explain the resolve of moderates, the moral and political choices with which they grappled, and the persuasive strategies they employed. In the 1940s and 1950s, when neither legal opinion nor public morality was on his side, what motivated Ralph McGill to risk social status and physical harm to help deprived citizens? In his determining goals to reach and methods to use, what caused him to ignore criticism from both the Klan and liberal professors? Why was he more teacher than crusader?

McGill's resolve originated primarily from within. To him, satisfying self was the only certain promise of correct choice. With Thoreau and Emerson as guides, McGill found spiritual strength and direction apart from the social and political fray, no easy task for a daily columnist and prolific speaker. Being fiercely independent, McGill refused to be "tamed" by any cause or group, whether segregationist or social activist. If he joined an organization with a special cause, he might be hesitant to criticize the group's actions. Because he exercised his intellectual independence when discussing blacks, racists called McGill "nigger lover," and liberals sometimes dismissed him as a "former liberal" and a "practical" journalist. McGill chose to be liberal in his views rather than to be what he called a "professional" reformer, and took pride in his

347, "Harvard University Law School Speech," I, 226; Atlanta *Constitution*, October 16, 1958, December 11, 1953.

3. Morton Sosna, *Southern Liberals and the Race Issue: In Search of the Silent South* (New York, 1977), 55–56, 119, 121, 167–78, 184, 226.

public pragmatism. He joined only the Democratic party—an "arena" for debate—and the Masons, a group committed to brotherhood.[4]

To steer private judgments, McGill drew from universal virtues several premises. McGill's writings and speeches reveal stock values that guided his choices and actions. These were honor, integrity, intellectual honesty, decency, human dignity, common justice, civil liberties, opportunity, and promise. From these and from long experience communicating with the public, McGill formed assumptions about what social changes one can reasonably achieve and how best to accomplish those goals. By balancing strongly held values and personal experiences, McGill developed six basic beliefs that influenced the advice he offered concerning race relations to an angry and suffering South: individuals and governments should pursue policies that are feasible; laws should be obeyed; free individuals have a moral responsibility to oppose wrong; education is requisite to individual and community progress; all persons should be granted the rights and privileges of full citizenship; and southern states should ensure the rights and privileges of their own citizens.[5]

McGill wrestled with these conflicting beliefs when speaking and writing on controversial social issues. To McGill, issues of race were complex. He resisted simplistic answers and doubted individuals and groups who claimed a monopoly on morality. But sometimes the stands he took on social issues appeared to supporters and critics to be inconsistent. On one hand, for example, for many years McGill opposed federal antilynching laws because he felt that southerners should stop the violence and could do so most effectively. On the other hand, when a person or group harmed an individual, a church, or a synagogue, McGill took a strong moral stand against the violence. If impatient with the conclusions of others, McGill was also seldom satisfied with his own

4. In Logue (ed.), *Ralph McGill*: "Institute for Education By Radio and Television Speech," II, 170–71, "University of North Carolina Commencement Address," II, 249; Atlanta *Constitution*, November 4, 1946, February 27, 1949.

5. In Logue (ed.), *Ralph McGill*: "Mercer University Inauguration Speech," II, 232–35, "Cranbrook School Commencement Address," II, 175–76, "Harriet Elliott Social Science Forum Speech," II, 197, "*Arkansas Gazette* Pulitzer Winners Speech," II, 103, "West Georgia College Honors Day Speech," II, 137.

assessment of causes and solutions. Consequently his under-standing of and position on civil rights evolved with changing times and choices. Once when pausing to reflect upon his own perspective on society, McGill concluded: "I expect always to be found in the middle of the road, just a little left of center, highly idealistic about life, but knowing that progress in government comes by politics and that they are practical problems." McGill claimed the right to "call" his own "shots" and to "aim where" he decided a round would be most helpful.[6]

What distinguished McGill from most moderates was not his in-tegrity and sense of justice but his insistence that personal creed be consummated in wise deed. Personal conviction and self-direction can be no cover for apathy, indecision, or cowardice. The intellectually honest person cannot hide behind moral truths, re-ligious dogma, legal interpretation, or fear. Concealed belief is im-potent. Private values should propel one to social action. Moral conviction finds strength and success only in participation. Mc-Gill explained that productive citizenship is found in the fusion of "moral considerations with social inventiveness." Specific values that combine articles of faith and social involvement are enthusi-asm, plain unselfishness, realism, insight, self-comprehension, self-sacrifice, chivalry, ambition, wisdom, kindness, gentleness, stubbornness, unity, good will, and plain speaking.

Certainly McGill had the promise of a social activist, however reluctant he was to assume the role of crusader. He worried about individuals and groups being exploited by more powerful citi-zens, whether the abused was penniless artist, individual family member in the Ku Klux Klan, or descendant of slaves. He was a "dreader and a fretter" and hated to lose. By personality McGill was "partisan" and had an "almost narcotic" fascination with politics. He enjoyed the "maneuverings" of a public fight and was confounded by persons who avoided controversial problems.[7] But

6. Atlanta *Constitution*, February 29, June 24, 1948.
7. In Logue (ed.), *Ralph McGill*: "Oberlin College Commencement Address," II, 295, "Philadelphia Award Speech," II, 479, "Elijah Parish Lovejoy Convocation Ad-dress," II, 190, "Ford Teenage Press Conference Speech," II, 151–52; Atlanta *Con-stitution*, September 1, 1942, January 1, April 23, June 29, July 19, December 12, 1946, February 18, November 4, December 25, 1947, February 29, June 13, August 22, 1948, January 28, February 27, 1949, January 2, 1950, August 10, 1955.

rather than crusade emotionally for social causes, McGill invented a persuasive strategy more suitable to the classroom than to the pulpit.

Persuasive Strategy of Public Instruction

In numerous speeches across the South and beyond and in a widely read newspaper column, McGill often followed a form of advocacy more in the genre of teaching than of selling. When reacting to the bombing of a church or the ravings of a racist, McGill was appropriately blunt in his criticism. But McGill was compassionate toward the mass of whites threatened by racial change. He attempted to nudge their thinking forward by explaining why the South separated blacks and whites, why there was conflict, and what had to be done to remedy problems. This effort to educate the general public was particularly appropriate for the 1940s and 1950s, when McGill prepared southerners for enormous changes in race relations he forecast the Supreme Court would demand. After the 1954 ruling against segregated public schools, McGill increasingly stressed a unified southern society with liberty and justice for blacks as well as whites. McGill's advice for the region balanced the ideals of democracy and the realities of a volatile situation, evidencing a distinctive blend of intellectual honesty, gentleness, and stubborn independence. This Georgian's advice for southerners consisted of three parts: study the issues, participate in the discussion and the decision making, and communicate informatively.

McGill insisted that southerners study critically their history, biography, economics, agriculture, literature, population distribution, and social structure. He believed that specialized knowledge of the nature and causes of racial conflict enables one to avoid overly simplistic claims and "glib" promises. By distrusting false remedies concocted by extremists—in either direction—one can find feasible and worthy solutions to frustrating problems. In his own work McGill read a variety of books and periodicals, traveled to scenes of disturbances, interviewed diverse groups of witnesses, and weighed alternatives critically. McGill urged citizens to discuss social problems and to share in society's decisions. To him, communicative involvement was a means of public education and social advancement. Although democracy could be "awkward and inefficient," he advised, community policy should derive from the "clamour of the marketplace." Freedom could not be "restrained" or "regimented," he stated, with policy handed down by a silent few. Workable and wise programs depend upon a vigorous debate among persons of different experiences and judgments. The more diverse the opinion the greater the revelation. A fair and acceptable plan for equal citizenship for blacks would come only after prolonged and agonizing debate by an enlightened public.[8]

McGill prescribed a special brand of speaking and writing, one that he said "informed" rather than "inflamed." His own communication was a laboratory for inquiry, in which he coaxed audiences to think and to act responsibly for themselves rather than be forced into decisions by new laws. For more than twenty years McGill sparred with listeners and readers. At his speeches and in response to his radio talk shows, for example, individuals asked about miscegenation. In addition, readers responded to his daily Atlanta *Constitution* column with letters to the editor. Some respondents supported his moderate views on race, but most were hostile; nevertheless, they all listened in their own way. In his discourses, McGill often was as much concerned to persuade auditors to think carefully about a topic as he was to convert them to his particular belief.

In his assessment of the South's treatment of blacks, McGill admitted the section's mistakes, attacked racist actions, and suggested reasonable explanations and feasible solutions. He provided wide-ranging analyses of the causes of conflict and discrimination. So important to McGill was historical context that in speeches he often wandered for thirty minutes or more over periods of slavery, the Civil War, Reconstruction, and the 1920s, leaving little time for application to current issues. When an act of raw racism occurred, McGill criticized the actors harshly as "crackpots," "fanatics," and "lunatic fringe." Cruel abuses of blacks and whites McGill called "evil and wicked," "cold-eyed, cruel, calcu-

8. In Logue (ed.), *Ralph McGill:* "St. Paul's Church Speech," II, 100, "Reynolds Lecture," II, 472, "University of Arkansas Address," I, 135–36; Atlanta *Constitution*, March 23, December 25, 1947, June 7, 9, 1949, March 1, 1950, November 20, 1951, February 16, 1955, January 2, 1959.

lated, rapacious exploitation," and "shameful perversion of justice by Southern juries." "To the Kluxer mentality," McGill judged, "the Christian communion cup must be a Dixie cup." Although McGill could be devastating in his evaluation of racism, most of the time he tried to negotiate with white southerners for fair choices.[9]

Discourses on Blacks' Rights, 1946–1954

McGill's campaign for blacks came in two stages: from 1946 to 1954, when he advocated equal and separate rights, and from 1954 to 1969, when he increasingly supported full citizenship for blacks within a racially integrated society. During the first period McGill, though reprehended by some liberals, saw equal—if separate— rights as an honorable and workable strategy for helping blacks. McGill was correct in the 1940s in perceiving himself as "a voice crying in the wilderness." Continuing in the language of the Bible Belt, he "cried aloud" the economic, political, and judicial abuses in the South. Unlike many persons who held blacks captive by a separate-but-equal lie, McGill applied that formula literally to comply with federal law and to improve the living conditions of blacks. Stressing equal treatment within separate arrangements allowed McGill to support blacks and accommodate whites' fears. For example, McGill stated on one occasion: "Believing . . . in separation of the races as the best and only workable system, it is possible to make a few comments." This equation he employed as license to develop a variety of arguments. McGill, for example, combined loyalty to region with his audiences' sense of fairness and desire for economic security: "Thousands of good Christian men and women" want blacks to have employment and "still not have to mix with other workers; equal opportunity for education, without mixing in school." Industries, he insisted, would not locate in a state marked by "violence and hate."

The dangerous situation required McGill to confront threats and clarify confusion created by politicians such as Eugene Tal-

9. In Logue (ed.), *Ralph McGill*: "Japan Newspaper Publishers and Editors Speech," II, 280, "Hartford *Courant* Speech," II, 332; Atlanta *Constitution*, July 14, May 8, 1946, November 18, 1947, October 22, 1949, September 21, 1950, March 24, 1954, September 16, 1957, January 21, 1958, December 10, 1960.

madge. Some officials claimed that change in the status of blacks inevitably meant social equality and intermarriage. Because so many whites feared mixing the races, McGill confronted that topic directly—before 1954 and after—promising in the 1940s that there would be no black policemen arresting whites, no integration of the schools, and "no social equality measures, now or later." What blacks wanted, insisted McGill, were good schools, equitable pay, and a fair opportunity for education. Part of his syllabus for public instruction was a "primer of Southern thinking." The fundamental lesson was that southerners should solve their racial problems at home without pressures from outside the region. Southerners had in fact been "dishonest" in promising equal "educational, travel, recreational and other facilities" and not providing them. If the federal government and activist groups would just "let us alone," southerners had claimed, "we would do the job." Yet whites had failed to fulfill promises. McGill asked if the South could find "moral courage" to correct the problem. In a continuous stream of moral maxims, McGill proclaimed what southerners should do: demonstrate "honest facing up to facts as facts"; avoid "cowardly retreating into dishonest refuges of phony values"; accept that "the issue is entirely a moral one—and not political"; and recognize that "the only supremacy which will endure is the supremacy based on justice."[10]

In compensating for his call for equal opportunities with a promise of continued separation, McGill invited criticism from racists and liberals. After speaking to a racially integrated audience at Spelman College—an act unacceptable to most whites—McGill explained that he felt like a "sacrificial lamb" and why he favored a realistic course based on historical awareness and southern determination rather than on an ideal and federal law:

> The critics on one side damn you as supporting the Claghorn type of congressman. The Ku Klux type mind hollers that you talk to audiences with Negroes in them. Your mail reflects both criticisms. . . . While believing without reservation in human and civil rights, I cannot bring myself to be intellectually dishonest enough to oversimplify it as awaiting only the panacea of another law added to many others. . . .

10. Atlanta *Constitution*, June 12, August 3, October 9, 1946, September 27, 1947, January 22, 1948.

Here in the South there are old customs, traditions and walls of thought built by warfare, religion, economics and the forces of history. . . . We cannot remove them by a law. . . . The answer is within us, and it can be answered only from within the Southern pattern. . . . I want the South to do what is right. . . . This, I know, satisfied no one—not even me. But, not being beholden or in politics, I can say it.

Between 1946 and 1954 in speeches, newspaper columns, and periodicals, McGill publicized how blacks had been "standing at the end of the line" in matters of law, education, employment, voting, and housing and social services. In the 1940s, McGill insisted on a fair trial for blacks and "full" justice "without regard to color," challenging the powerful sheriffs in the region. He asked that the citizenry correct law enforcement that had become a "mockery" of human justice and demanded that blacks be made "safe" from prejudiced policemen. McGill matched his criticism with the severity of the deed, attacking "lynching murders," "mob violence," and "corrupt county governments."[11]

While unequivocal in his stand for basic rights, McGill perplexed liberals by his independence in criticizing federal laws designed to correct southern wrongs. For some years, for example, he opposed a federal antilynching bill because he wanted to maintain contact with southern whites and because he was convinced that local enforcement could work best. In 1947, McGill recalled having "long ago" debated Mark Etheridge on the value of the antilynching bill. At that time he had taken the negative side "and lost." Eventually McGill changed his mind, concluding that southerners would not protect blacks. He and others could no longer with integrity oppose federal intervention as long as "lynch-murders" continued in Walton County, Georgia. During the late 1940s, McGill urged the passage of a federal antilynching law, but with the qualification that the bill not include "police power," for that was within the province of states.[12]

McGill expressed "passionate" faith in education, defining public schools as the "foundation of America." While believing that

11. McGill, "Southern Labor Conference Speech," in New York *Times,* May 13, 1946; Atlanta *Constitution,* March 10, April 9, 1946, July 23, 1947, March 1, 1948, February 20, 1950, July 14, 1951.
12. New York *Times,* June 27, 1949; Atlanta *Constitution,* August 23, 1946, January 7, 1947, May 30, 1948, June 27, 1949, July 14, 1951.

legitimate private schools served an important function, this Georgian argued that no system of private education could meet the needs of all the region's students. McGill insisted that blacks were not receiving a "square rattle" in a school system that even failed whites, but once again McGill preferred that southerners solve their own problem by providing blacks their "due in education" rather than waiting for federal authorities to mandate equality. McGill repeated economic threats, warning that only persons receiving an adequate education would survive in the new industrial South. All southerners would "pay a heavy price" for unequal opportunities in education. Early in the 1940s, McGill avoided identifying separate facilities as a cause of discrimination. Later, however, he linked the two: "The school system is a segregated one and the Negro pupils and teachers have suffered by discrimination." [13]

Blacks were relegated to the "least rewarding" jobs, and the results of these economic practices were "substandard" incomes, poverty, and an inability to pay taxes and to buy goods and services often provided by whites. McGill's solution was precise— provide for blacks work based solely on "skills and ability." Appealing to self-interest, McGill reminded whites how they were "carrying on" their backs the burden of unemployed and underemployed blacks. Only when southerners of every race could afford to "trade at the stores" would the region prosper.

For a time, McGill opposed the federal Fair Employment Practices Commission (FEPC) as an instrument for providing blacks jobs. In 1947 he maintained that the pending legislation for the FEPC was "not a sound bill" because it was "largely political" and would "create as many abuses" as it corrected. To merely transfer cases of job discrimination from the "county courthouse to the federal building" was no remedy. McGill, however, threatened southerners with passage of the FEPC bill if they refused to treat blacks fairly. Denying blacks "skilled" employment would only give supporters of the FEPC "a whip hand." By 1950, McGill had

13. Ralph McGill and Thomas C. David, *Two Georgians Explore Scandinavia: A Comparison of Education for Democracy in Northern Europe and Georgia* (Atlanta, 1938); New York *Times*, January 5, 1947; Atlanta *Constitution*, March 20, 1946, September 27, 1947, February 19, 1948, November 13, 1949, October 22, 1950, July 14, 1951; Daytona *Sunday News Journal*, March 20, 1946.

conceded that southern states would not provide equal employment for blacks, and he labeled the FEPC "a fair and equitable law
which will have public acceptance."[14]

In the 1940s, McGill cautiously advised whites to accept blacks
as participants in the political process. McGill apparently anticipated a negative response and thus declared, "I do not at all mean
to discuss here the pros and cons of Negro voting." However, he
then proceeded to do just that. He assured whites they could out-
vote a few blacks, and by this argument, he attracted criticism
from liberals who charged that he was at best only one step ahead
of his contemporaries on matters of race relations. "Shall we be
fooled," he continued, by the fact that one black "voter can out
vote" ten whites? To further appease whites, McGill advocated
strict qualifications for voters. He insisted that the vote not "be
given to the unqualified," particularly persons "not literate enough
to know the issues." Specifically McGill "vigorously" opposed
giving "uneducated" blacks the vote. To implement this restriction, he stated, literacy tests should be administered to protect
the "white majority."

While McGill's warranty of white political dominance seems to
have echoed moderate conservative attitudes more than challenged them, he did attempt to persuade whites to allow blacks to
vote. "It would be political folly," he explained, "once the court
decision is final, to bar those who are qualified." By 1949, McGill
advocated eliminating restrictions, particularly the poll tax. In
1954, less cautious in his support of black participation, McGill
predicted that "within four years" there would be two million
black voters. Through the vote, blacks would achieve "a sounder
basis of citizenship."[15]

When speaking for black needs, McGill voiced appeals ranging
from accommodating pleas to sarcastic indictments. To help with
housing, he wrote an informational pamphlet entitled *The Housing Challenge* for the Atlanta Housing Authority. Chiding whites

14. McGill, "Manufacturers Industrial Congress Speech," in Atlanta *Constitution*, December 10, 11, 1949; New York *Times*, May 13, 1946, January 5, 1947, February 19, 1948; Atlanta *Constitution*, December 3, 1946, June 22, July 23, 1947, February 19, 1948, June 7, 1949, March 1, 1950, July 15, 1951.
    15. In Logue (ed.), *Ralph McGill*: "Daytona Beach Speech," II, 46–51; Atlanta
Constitution, March 31, 1946, June 23, 1947, February 19, 1948, June 7, 1949.

who would keep blacks in substandard housing, McGill said scornfully: "I suppose it is very bad of Negroes that they don't dig holes in hillsides and live in them. But, for some reason, they like to have a roof, even if it is leaking." McGill extended his campaign to all social services, asking on behalf of blacks for their portion of tax dollars for parks, paved streets, public health, and sewers.[16]

Precursor of Desegregation

Although few whites took his prophecy seriously, McGill in the late 1940s and early 1950s warned of the traumatic social changes to come. On March 20, 1949, McGill chided southern leaders for not creating "machinery" to implement Supreme Court rulings. Regional newspapers, clergy, business, and labor had also remained silent, he explained. Without necessary planning, there would be "chaos and disorder." Trying not to stampede audiences, McGill patiently explained what the region was "up against." While personally desiring that rulings "be delayed," he warned that the Court was poised to decide the future of segregated schools in the South. McGill accurately predicted "violent talk or worse" following judicial mandates and he warned that "the law would remain."

By the early 1950s, McGill challenged segregation of public education as being too expensive for states that could barely afford even one school system. Because of the great economic burden of dual school systems, the South would find ways of reducing the "rigidity of school segregation." By 1950, four years prior to the Supreme Court's historic decision, McGill represented discriminatory school policies as unconstitutional. No "honest person," he contended, could defend "compulsory segregation" as a democratic institution. By 1953, McGill declared that "segregation by law no longer fits today's world." The new challenge was "how to live with the change."[17]

16. In Logue (ed.), *Ralph McGill*: "Ohio Northern University Address," II, 435; New York *Times*, January 5, 1947; Atlanta *Constitution*, November 10, 1946, September 27, 1947, May 30, 1948.
17. New York *Times*, May 13, 1946; Atlanta *Constitution*, April 13, December 3, 1946, July 23, 1947, January 22, September 2, 1948, March 20, November 13, 30, 1949, February 20, 1950, July 14, 1951, April 9, December 1, 1953, January 3, 1954.

Discourses on Desegregated Public Schools, 1954–1969

Whereas McGill in the 1940s and early 1950s discussed a variety of rights owed to blacks, his human rights discourse after 1954 centered on public education. During this dangerous period of social revolution McGill, a veteran of many racial battles, calmly explained the South's difficult predicament. "The world," he advised, was experiencing a time when "change has been cranked up" and southerners were caught in the turmoil. Citizens could no longer ignore social forces engulfing them. Every parent and schoolchild would have to choose between moderation and extremism.

Alarmed that sound judgment was being "drowned out" by radicals on all sides, McGill urged responsible clergy, media people, and business persons to offer "sane" leadership. Confronting a situation filled with hate and fear, McGill spoke in a voice of moderation. In Augusta, Georgia, though there was "considerable objection" to his speaking, McGill's 1959 address on human rights and open schools "started some discussion" among moderates in that city. In 1961 in Birmingham, Alabama, a city under siege, McGill reduced the choice for whites to obedience to law or violence. Race relations, he told the Birmingham Rotarians, were "never going to be as they were before." Responsible citizens of Birmingham and throughout the South must be flexible to adjust to the new social status of blacks.[18]

This analysis of McGill's role in the changing South between 1954 and 1969 includes the social setting, McGill's advice for speakers, his defense of the Supreme Court, the importance of public schools, his opposition to violence, his exposing myths, and his view of the historical causes of social conditions.

Social Setting

Two years after its 1954 ruling against segregated public schools, the Supreme Court extended its ban to tax-supported colleges. Then came judgments against discrimination in public transpor-

18. In Logue (ed.), *Ralph McGill*: "Fayette County [Kentucky] Bar Association Speech," II, 228, "Sidney Hillman Foundation Speech," II, 132–33, "Augusta Rotary Club Speech," II, 120–30, "Birmingham Rotary Club Speech," I, 212–22.

tation, swimming pools, courthouse cafeterias, voting, employment, jury trials, and public accommodations. To enforce laws,
President Dwight Eisenhower sent troops to Arkansas, and President John Kennedy federalized troops in Mississippi and Alabama. Ten years after the historic decision, the Supreme Court
ordered the public schools in Prince Edward County, Virginia, to
reopen as racially integrated institutions. In 1965, the Atlanta
School Board was ordered to increase desegregation to two grades
a year, beginning that fall with kindergarten and completing the
process by September, 1968.[19]

White opposition to desegregated schools was swift. Governor
Herman Talmadge of Georgia said he did "not recognize" the ruling as legal, labeling the act "judicial brainwashing." On June 11,
1954, twelve southern states planned legal strategies for circum-
venting the Supreme Court's order. In 1956, bills were introduced
in the state senate of Georgia to defend segregation. That same
year, Virginia voters, by a two-to-one margin, approved state
money for tuition grants to private schools. Virginia proposed a
pupil placement act, the "cornerstone of the massive resistance"
to school desegregation, but in 1957 the Court ruled it unconstitutional. In 1958, the Court nullified Little Rock's attempt to lease
four public high schools for private academies. The state legislature of Mississippi authorized its governor to close the public
schools if necessary. In 1960, the Court upheld integration of New
Orleans schools. Until 1962, Florida law required total segregation
of public schools.

Coercive efforts employed to prevent racial integration consisted of demonstrations, parades, catcalls, bombings, and murder. Angry whites threatened newspapermen in Clay, Kentucky,
where two blacks attempted to enroll in school. Whites tried to
stop three blacks from registering at Texarkana Junior College.
Approximately 570 white children left a desegregated elementary school in Weaverton, Kentucky. Explosions damaged schools
in Clinton, Tennessee, and Atlanta. In an Athens dormitory,

19. Houston *Post*, July 3, 1964; Detroit *Free Press*, December 13, 1960; New York
Herald Tribune, May 26, 1964; Atlanta *Constitution*, March 6, April 24, 1956, April 2,
September 25, October 22, 1957, September 30, 1958, January 10, 20, 1959, April 22,
1960, January 7, 1961, September 29, 1962, May 13, 21, June 12, September 11, 1963,
September 1, 1964, April 2, 22, 30, July 7, August 10, 1965.

windows were broken when Charlayne Hunter enrolled at the University of Georgia. Arsonists burned black churches associated with desegregation activities in southeastern Georgia, and dynamite killed four black children in a Birmingham church. Amid the violence, all words and actions were carefully observed and instantly labeled as segregationist or integrationist. No middle ground was allowed, though McGill attempted to walk a path of moderation. Tension was so great that in 1959, Harry Ashmore questioned whether Emory University could continue an evening forum on the crisis of the schools. However, McGill addressed that conference and many others, giving other moderates valuable encouragement and insight.[20]

Advice for Speakers

As tension escalated, individuals and groups asked McGill how they could defuse violence and save public schools in their own communities. Having spoken to many hostile audiences and written to angry readers for a number of years, McGill had specific advice for moderates. Preserving schools and restoring order depended upon the cooperation of four "elements" of society: clergy, media, business, and labor. Acknowledging that some ministers had justified racism with Scripture and that others had lost their pulpits because of moderate sermons preached on human relations, McGill insisted that clergymen use one advantage they had over politicians. Many ministers possessed a pulpit from which to speak of change, whereas political leaders could only mirror the masses. Preachers should employ the forum available to them to explain that "Christianity is not a private club" and that blacks were citizens too. Editors also enjoyed a certain independence, and McGill criticized "spineless newspapers" that chose profit over influence in the community. Business and labor leaders, according to McGill, too often remained aloof from discriminatory practices, leaving extremists to "defy" the law. Responsible citi-

20. New York *Times*, May 17, 1955; Richmond *News Leader*, January 22, 1958; Atlanta *Constitution*, June 7, 11, 1954, January 10, 20, April 11, September 8, 10, 1956, September 28, 1957, October 6, 1958, January 12, 13, 1961, September 10, 21, 1962, September 5, 16, 1963, March 26, April 26, May 7, 1965; Richard Barnett and Joseph Garai, *Where the States Stand on Civil Rights* (New York, 1962), 12–13.

zens should "chart a way out of chaos and deterioration." Only an "unrelenting determination" would preserve the South's safety and the public schools.[21]

Abandoning his inquiring style when he spoke to audiences, McGill prescribed step by step how persons could fight for public schools. In a highly personal response to southerners who asked for advice after the formal portion of his speeches, McGill emphasized the importance of selecting proper cities and planning appropriate communicative strategies. McGill suggested that they avoid hostile environments. In Georgia, he instructed, moderate spokespersons could not discuss desegregation in Echols, Baker, and Clinch counties. But forums on desegregated public schools could be held in Atlanta, Macon, Columbus, and other cities. Any person planning a meeting to discuss race should be extremely cautious, realistic, and judicious. In some locales, planners should be "almost secretive" and "meet quickly." In making arrangements, one should invite the "political leadership" to participate, but do so "carefully and quietly" and only after having evaluated the mood of the community. When the session begins, McGill continued, speakers should "stand quietly," speak "calmly" and "forthrightly," and "explain the depth of our dilemma" and the "agony of our situation." During a question-and-answer period after a speech in 1959 during Ministers Week at Emory University, McGill recommended a format that he had followed for more than a decade:

> Anytime a Christian church or leader or community can carry out by discussion, information programs, all to the good. I think that if you can get them out of the process of debate you will do better. Unhappily, a lot of people don't want to hear the truth. . . . But if you could have somebody who could project the real dilemma or have just a discussion, have both sides, but let it be talked; the important thing is that it will be discussed. I think we have been in a position where we have been almost afraid to discuss this until the last few months. It was a subject that was taboo. . . . Now people are beginning to talk about it and debate is beginning, and I think that will be healthy.[22]

21. McGill, *The South and the Southerner*, 231; in Logue (ed.), *Ralph McGill*: "Ministers Week Speech," I, 163–79, "Sigma Delta Chi Speech," II, 451, "Birmingham Rotary Club Speech," I, 217–19.
22. In Logue (ed.), *Ralph McGill*: "Ministers Week Speech," I, 163–79.

While instructing others on how to hold public discussions, McGill continued his campaign to save the public schools. He defended the Supreme Court, emphasized the importance of public schools, opposed violence, exposed false myths, and explained the historical roots of change.

Defense of the Supreme Court

At a time when billboards across the South asked that Chief Justice Earl Warren be impeached, McGill refuted politicians who asserted that Supreme Court rulings were not binding. The Court "has not violated the Constitution because it can't," argued McGill. Citizens could oppose judicial decisions but should not "delude" themselves about the results. The order against racial segregation in public schools was "final" and had to "be accepted, acceptable or not." The Court that supported blacks' rights was a "shield and buckler" for all races against "domestic tyranny." Charging Governors George Wallace and Ross Barnett with "practiced deceit," and holding obstinate officials responsible for discrimination against a "generation of children," McGill warned "podium prancers" that there would be no heroes in this "lost cause."[23]

Importance of Public Schools

Worried that the southern states would close schools before desegregating them, McGill urged listeners to weigh carefully the devastating consequences of that action. Because many states proposed to change schools from public to private, McGill countered that private education could not satisfy demands of the region. In addition, southern states could not afford to pay for new schools when existing school systems were inadequate. McGill quoted the National Education Association to demonstrate the poor quality of the section's schools. The curriculum in many communities failed to prepare students for universities. Low faculty salaries drove teachers to other areas. "To destroy" even the poor-quality

23. Atlanta *Constitution*, May 30, 1968; in Logue (ed.), *Ralph McGill*: "Elijah Parish Lovejoy Convocation Address," II, 183.

schools available, McGill argued, was an action "too fantastic to be believed." McGill attempted to frighten white citizens into conformity with the Court by using threats of monetary losses. Companies employing specialists would not move to a town or state with inadequate schools. To sacrifice the children "would be irreparable." Even if some schools were closed for a period, McGill refused to believe that responsible persons would allow them "to remain shut." "While public education may be crucified on a cross of willful destruction," he proclaimed, "it will rise again out of the wreckage." [24]

Opposition to Violence

Appalled by the violence, McGill once stated that he preferred closed schools to "ruthless brutality," "filthy abuse," and "murder." Even though he risked personal harm in saying so, McGill refused to allow "violent haters" to become the "voice" of the South. If he could prevent it, Georgia and surrounding states would not wear a "criminal's mask." McGill criticized bombings and "frownings" with a bluntness different from his familiar teaching posture. Frustration, worry, and affection distended into metaphoric argument. He compared University of Mississippi students with "Nazi black shirts" and condemned their "grotesque show." As for their governor, Ross Barnett, "not all the perfumes of Araby will wash clean" his "political hands." Persons endangering students and education in the South were "politically chained to the rock of prejudice" and "pecked and shrilled at by the vultures of fanaticism." McGill also diagnosed the highly contagious nature of violence. No one could at the same time both "preach" and "restrict" destruction. "When the wolves of hate are loosed" on blacks, no white would be safe. The "bitter-enders" were "trampling out the vintage where the grapes of wrath are stored." Something is lost in a community torn apart by hate and violence. "The wages of violence," McGill continued, "is a sort of death." [25]

24. In Logue (ed.), *Ralph McGill*: "Philadelphia Award Speech," II, 485, "Reynolds Lecture," II, 469; "Massachusetts Council Speech," in Boston *Daily Globe*, January 24, 1959; Atlanta *Constitution*, September 22, 1955.

25. In Logue (ed.), *Ralph McGill*: "Rochester City Club Speech," II, 347, "Mas-

Exposing Myths

Southern thought was controlled by blind obedience to values of the Old and New Souths. Segregationists, McGill argued, were more loyal to "this never-never land" than to public schools. The "curse" of these attitudes obscured reality and imprisoned holders in the "song and myth" of the South of the past. McGill explained how perceptual distortions prevented social change. He exposed several "threadbare myths." First, he denied the existence of a Solid South. Actually, people in the region held different attitudes, beliefs, and positions; they were not "all of a piece." Second, McGill challenged the assumption of the sovereignty of states. Southerners had for years been controlled by a "deadly oratory" of statism. This "holy" rhetoric confused any serious discussion of school desegregation and discouraged obedience to court rulings. A third image McGill corrected was whites' perception of blacks: There were not as many blacks in the South as whites believed, all blacks were not "dirty" and "inferior," blacks were not "happy" living in tenant shacks, and blacks were not primarily concerned with marrying whites. To refute these allegations, McGill explained why whites could deceive themselves with a stereotype of blacks being subhuman. Separation of the races and a lack of meaningful communication between the races had prevented whites from learning what the black "community wants, thinks, or feels." In a similar fashion, many whites had not given themselves a chance to know "a cultured, educated Negro."

McGill also decoded linguistic techniques used by spellbinders to market regional fantasies. He refuted potent myths by disclosing the prejudices implied in the segregationists' speeches and pamphlets. Defenders of racial segregation were merely "retelling" misconceptions, opening "old wounds," and "parading prejudices." Opponents of desegregated schools, for example, selected language intended to "arouse the church burners." Extremists packaged phrases with emotional promises of sacrifice, heroics, and the Lost Cause. Here are some sentiments that McGill disclosed: "We won't stop fighting until we drop to our knees; the Confederate guns speak to us from the past; our heads are

sachusetts Institute of Technology Speech," I, 240–42; Atlanta *Constitution,* January 18, 1957, August 31, 1962, October 2, 1962.

bloody but unbowed; we will never surrender." Out of these defensive regional maxims came the doctrine of white superiority, a segregated society, and social evils only now being explained. McGill warned that these "follies" were "leaks in the dykes of civilization," and that the only defense was people's willingness to refute mistaken views, to provide constitutional rights to all, and to view a black person as a fellow human being.[26]

Historical Causes of Social Conditions

To understand the present state of the South, McGill looked to the past. Recurring themes in his speeches and articles were "what made us 'Southern'" and the "South in transition." For the region to change for the better, citizens must know the "'why' of the happenings" and the "great forces" that had molded the mind of the South. Using biblical passages familiar to many southerners, McGill preached about experiences peculiar to the section that had "touched us all stopping at every door, passing over none." That past, he said, can "paralyze" the present. McGill explained citizens' loyalty to the South and their dislike of outside criticism. He reviewed the "fogs of prejudice" and values left from the Civil War and Reconstruction; how cotton, rice, tobacco, and the climate "demanded a slave labor" and thereby "set us apart"; the "seating" (1876–1877) of Rutherford B. Hayes that separated the South from the agrarian West; statutory segregation; white supremacy; decline of the "cotton South" (1919–1920); effects of World War II; elimination of the white primary; a two-party system of politics; and court decisions.

McGill stressed the social and economic implications of the migration of blacks and whites from the farm to the factory. The South was changing from an agrarian society to a new "urban regionalism" symbolized more by a "test-tube" than a cotton farm. Sadly, however, a population of uneducated and unskilled men

26. In Logue (ed.), *Ralph McGill*: "Civil Liberties Union Speech," II, 319, "Massachusetts Historical Society Speech," II, 399, 402, "Alfred M. Landon Lecture," II, 427, 429, "Cooper Union Lincoln Day Address," II, 162–64, "Carney Hospital Speech," II, 312, "American Association of School Administrators Speech," II, 453, 458, 462, "Rosenwald Centennial Speech," II, 288.

and women were being moved by "great engines of war" to "semi-unemployment" in the cities—from rural to urban poverty. Also, agrarian values were carried into urban areas, including prejudices, belief in separation of the races, and assumption of paternalistic relationships. McGill told how persons employed in the cotton mill and timber plant were in a situation similar to that of the sharecropper and the tenant on the cotton plantation. But the face of the South was changing—only one in ten blacks was a farmhand. It was migration to cities, not the work of Communists and aliens, that brought the new racial "patterns" and "characteristics," he stated.[27]

McGill reconstructed the past more skillfully in articles than in speeches, since in the latter, there was never enough time for him to piece all the elements together. Apparently he edited printed words more carefully than he prepared oral discourse. But he was gifted in using the language. For example, I heard McGill speak without notes to more than six thousand delegates to the National Education Association meeting in 1966 in Miami Beach, and he captured poetically the scene of southerners leaving farms: "I can remember how the cotton sharecroppers and tenant cabins emptied, some of them burned, leaving the chimneys there like silent sentinels representing something gone never to return. I saw . . . their wooden windows sagging, the doors sagging . . . the roof broken in, the old hearth places where people had dreamed and thought and perhaps sorrowed, and turned over, animals moving in through the buildings—1920."[28]

The South after 1954 was ripe for racial conflict and change. As long as blacks were kept subservient, there was little opportunity for improvement in their social status. But when white primaries and segregation of schools, transportation, and public accommodations were ruled unconstitutional and blacks began demanding changes, whites fought to defend their social and political dominance. But the region would never be the same, as more blacks

27. In Logue (ed.), *Ralph McGill*: "Hartford *Courant* Speech," II, 332, "Crisis in Schools Speech," I, 180, 189–92, 205, "South in Transition Speech," II, 349–60, "United Negro College Fund Speech," II, 236–39, "Georgia Teachers Education Association Talk," II, 485–86, "Jewish Education Alliance Speech," II, 77, 80.

28. In Logue (ed.), *Ralph McGill*: "National Education Association Speech," I, 246, 248, 250.

and whites addressed old problems and new opportunities. McGill advised that change, though difficult, was morally right and regionally profitable.

Conclusion

While scathing in his criticism of irresponsible leaders and violence, McGill refused to "accuse" average citizens for their fears. Even after 1954 he called for tolerance among southerners, maintaining that no "fixed opinion" would "fit" problems of race. Confessing that he did not "know all the answers," McGill refused to speak with "dogmatic finality." On a number of occasions in 1959 and after, he claimed no "program" or "policy of integration," though he might define one if asked. As blacks and whites integrated schools, McGill accommodated citizens' concerns by stating that sitting in a classroom was not a social arrangement, an argument he had created in the 1940s to win basic rights for blacks. Still convinced that social progress would come slowly, McGill asked for more time. He wanted legal suits delayed until a few border states could desegregate schools as an "example" for the Deep South. Increasingly in the 1960s, McGill demanded final resolution of racial conflicts and the school problem. "Segregation is dead," he pronounced. "What remains" is the "effort to delay interment." The year before he died, McGill stated: "I am weary of the old hanging on of the dual school systems and the excuses and the evasion." A country that could place a person in space should not argue where a black "child shall go to school." In the last newspaper column he saw in print, he called segregated schools "viciously unjust . . . a disease that weakened all education."

The day he died, in 1969, he talked informally to students at Booker T. Washington High School in Atlanta of the "nonsense of supremacy" and "separation." No longer concerned about accommodating conservative whites, McGill asked that people "speed up the process of acceptance of what must be done morally . . . and what ought to have been done long ago without all the pressures." He exhorted citizens who for too long had "listened to lies and political bombasts" to accept desegregation. A person's "rights cannot be compromised." "Law is not enough," he maintained.

"The heart also must listen." McGill supported the sit-ins as a necessary mechanism for bringing to the "fore a moral issue heretofore obscured by politics and lawyers." Demonstrators involved in acts of civil disobedience would "win," he predicted, because they are morally right and because they are protected by the Constitution. The demonstrations redefined plantation perceptions that whites had of blacks.

In the final days of his life, McGill was evaluating means of effecting constructive change. Assessing the need for street demonstrations, for example, he asked: "Has this policy . . . played its limit? Has it attained what it can? And now is there need for another policy?" The day he died, a young black student asked his opinion of the "black separatist movement." When he answered, McGill must have thought back over the long struggle to expose the separate-but-equal sham: "I don't think this will work," he advised. "You can't separate yourself from the world . . . from your fellowman." [29]

Ralph McGill was a crusader with common sense and, as the New York *Times* judged, "a sense of humor." [30] The problems of people who were exploited bothered him. McGill addressed those concerns directly in his writings and speeches, but with compassion for most and with limited expectations. Convinced that social progress moves slowly, he assumed the role of teaching critic, instructing readers and listeners in basic lessons of southern history, social science, social change, civil rights, and responsible citizenship. In searching with audiences for causes of conditions, he was inspiringly poetic and—as he said—"hodgepodgingly" organized. For years he often angered segregationists and disappointed integrationists. But always he acted with courage and considerable charisma in exhorting southern audiences to look beyond the racism of their region. Persons who shared his dream of equality for all found encouragement and strength in his oral and written instruction. During the difficult period from 1946 to 1969, McGill offered southerners an alternative to apathy, vio-

29. In Logue (ed.), *Ralph McGill*: "Ministers Week Speech," I, 163–68, "Editors View the South Speech," I, 143–62, "Augusta Rotary Club Speech," II, 129–30, "Birmingham Rotary Club Speech," I, 219, "Booker T. Washington High School Speech," II, 503–506; Atlanta *Constitution*, February 3, 1959.
30. New York *Times*, February 5, 1969.

lence, and racial discrimination. For his pronouncements he was verbally abused, physically threatened, and awarded a number of prestigious prizes. Refusing to bow to extremists on any side, McGill believed that the only certain reward for an independent and honest spokesman was the "inner satisfaction of being able to face one's self." Staying a middle course, he spoke the truth as he perceived it by insisting that civilized persons have a duty to oppose wrong. In doing so, McGill personally helped blacks in their efforts to achieve equal citizenship in the South and in the nation.

Fulbright and Ervin
Southern Senators with National Appeal

David Zarefsky

T he Ninety-third Congress of the United States adjourned late in December of 1974. Leaving the Senate for the last time were two southerners whose appeal had long since transcended their native region. One achieved a national audience during the 1960s with his persistent dissent from the course of American foreign policy; the other, during the 1970s with his defense of the Constitution at the time of Watergate. Between them, J. William Fulbright and Sam Ervin had served fifty years in the Senate.

Fulbright reached Congress after a brief career in academe. He was born in 1905, received his early education in Fayetteville, Arkansas, and then attended the University of Arkansas. On the casual recommendation of one of his professors, he applied for and received a Rhodes scholarship in 1925. After law school and several years in Washington, he and his family moved back to Arkansas in 1936. Fulbright joined the faculty of the University of Arkansas Law School and from that position was elected president of the university at the age of thirty-four. But after he had been in office only a year, the Arkansas governorship was won by Homer Adkins, against whom Fulbright's mother had editorialized in the family-owned newspaper. When Adkins took office, a majority of the university's board of trustees resigned. They were replaced with Adkins appointees, and the reconsti-

114

tuted board, without cause, fired the president. Soon thereafter, Fulbright was approached by the area congressman, one of his former law students, who was preparing to resign from the House in order to run for the Senate. After some hesitation, Fulbright decided to run for the vacant House seat, which he won in 1942.

Two years later he successfully ran for the Senate, winning the seat held for twelve years by Hattie Caraway and—in a proof that revenge is sweet—defeating Governor Adkins in the primary. The campaign was vicious: Fulbright was accused of having evaded the World War II draft, of having voted for a "nigger" (though he supported the white primary and opposed equality of the races), and of being the political stooge of organized labor. It was the last difficult campaign Fulbright would face until his final two races for the Senate.

Fulbright quickly developed a reputation as a critic of presidents. In the 1946 congressional elections, the Republicans won control of both houses of Congress. Concerned about the possible deadlock when the executive and legislative branches were controlled by different parties, the senator proposed that President Harry Truman appoint a Republican as secretary of state and then resign. (Since the vice-presidency was vacant, the secretary of state was next in line of succession.) Even in his later years, Fulbright never disavowed the proposal that quickly drew Truman's ire. In a widely quoted off-the-record remark, the president referred to the senator as an "overeducated Oxford S.O.B."[1] During the Eisenhower administration, Fulbright became a more vocal critic of American foreign policy, charging Eisenhower and John Foster Dulles with aimlessness and apathy. He also criticized aspects of foreign policy under Presidents John Kennedy, Lyndon Johnson, and Richard Nixon.

In 1968, for the first time, Fulbright faced serious opposition in his race for reelection, but not only because of his criticism of the war in Vietnam. His primary opponent, James D. Johnson, accused the senator of being "soft on communism." He charged "Chairman Fulbright" with openly aiding the Communists and insisted that the incumbent had been "endorsed by the official

1. Haynes Johnson and Bernard Gwertzman, *Fulbright: The Dissenter* (Garden City, N.Y., 1968), 105. Senator Joseph R. McCarthy had a different epithet; he referred to Fulbright as "Halfbright."

communist organ in this country." Fulbright's reponse was to conduct a "low-key folksy campaign"—his attire included boots and checked sport shirt. As for Vietnam, Fulbright only mused about what could be done to develop rural Arkansas were it not for "that wild goose chase to fight in a poor, little country 10,000 miles away." Fulbright won the primary, but with only 53 percent of the vote. In the general election, Republican Charles T. Bernard echoed the "soft on communism" theme and added two others. Bernard portrayed himself as a racial moderate, openly wooing the black vote and stating that he would have voted for some of the civil rights bills that Fulbright opposed. And he charged that Fulbright's involvement in foreign affairs had caused him to lose touch with his Arkansas constituents. "The man is definitely vulnerable," Bernard said immediately after the primary. "He's lost contact with the people."[2] But Bernard's dual appeal to blacks and to white conservatives was not found credible by either, and Fulbright was reelected to a fifth term.

In 1974, though, he faced a far stronger primary opponent in the popular governor, Dale Bumpers. Bumpers capitalized on his youth, on the low public regard for incumbents in Washington as a result of the Watergate scandal, and on his own reputation as governor. The appeals were summed up in Bumpers' argument that "a Senator who had been in Washington 30 years must somehow be part of the mess." Bumpers also appealed overtly to the state's black population. Fulbright, in his defense, stated that he had stopped voting against civil rights bills around 1965—which, as one local newspaper editorialized, was about the time they stopped being introduced.[3] But Bumpers never attacked Fulbright directly, never even mentioned his name. He told the press that he agreed with the incumbent more often than not, and refused to answer Fulbright's public accusations. This studied silence deprived Fulbright of a response, and he became more desperate and shrill—which in turn suggested that he was out of touch with Arkansas and its people. Although the race was expected to be close, the governor won the primary by a margin of almost two to one.

2. New York *Times*, July 22, 28, 31, August 1, 1968.
3. New York *Times*, May 29, 1974; *New York Times Magazine*, May 26, 1974.

Sam Ervin also left Congress in 1974, but he returned to his home in Morganton, North Carolina, through voluntary retirement rather than electoral defeat. Ervin was born in 1896. At the age of sixteen he entered the University of North Carolina at Chapel Hill and, upon completing his studies there, enlisted as an infantry private during World War I. Having apprenticed in his father's law office, Ervin was admitted to the North Carolina bar in 1919. But, desiring formal legal education, he entered Harvard Law School, where he began with the third-year course. He explained that he had a hometown sweetheart, Margaret Bell, and that he was unsure their relationship would survive his long absence in Cambridge. So he took first the courses in which he was most interested. At the end of the year he reappraised the situation and decided it was safe to return for the second-year course, and then the following year for the first. He received his law degree in 1922 and two years later married Margaret Bell.

Ervin began a law practice, though he also served for three terms in the North Carolina General Assembly. In 1935 he was appointed a county court judge and in 1937 a superior court judge, a position he resigned six years later because of a bleeding ulcer. Ervin's brother Joe, a member of the U.S. House of Representatives, committed suicide in 1946, and Ervin was named to serve the remainder of his brother's congressional term. He then returned to North Carolina, where in 1948 he advanced to the state supreme court.[4]

In June, 1954, Ervin was appointed to fill the Senate seat left vacant after the death of Clyde R. Hoey. He was sworn in by Vice-President Richard Nixon, who asked Ervin to pledge to uphold the Constitution. That fall, Ervin won a special election to fill the remaining two years of Hoey's term, and then he was reelected in his own right in 1956, 1962, and 1968.

Barely six weeks a senator, Ervin was one of six appointed to a committee to investigate the conduct of Joseph R. McCarthy. He most likely was selected because of his judicial experience. Like Fulbright, he came out strongly against the junior senator from

4. For details of Ervin's life, see especially Paul R. Clancy, *Just a Country Lawyer: A Biography of Senator Sam Ervin* (Bloomington, Ind., 1974); Bill M. Wise, *The Wisdom of Sam Ervin* (New York, 1973).

Wisconsin; unlike Fulbright, however, Ervin was not prepared to support censure in advance of a committee investigation. Named to the Judiciary Committee, Ervin in 1957 was placed on its Subcommittee on Constitutional Rights. In 1961 he became chairman. Later, he also chaired the newly created Subcommittee on Separation of Powers. Perhaps because of his long experience with such issues, Ervin spoke mostly about constitutional rights and procedure during the 1960s. He had little to say about Vietnam, the dominant issue of the decade. He seldom spoke on foreign policy matters at all.

Perhaps because his issues were not those gripping the nation, Ervin passed nineteen years in the Senate in relative obscurity. He quickly became a celebrity, however, in February of 1973, when the Senate voted unanimously to establish a select committee to investigate improprieties in the 1972 presidential election and Ervin was named to chair the committee. The Senate leadership decided to create a special committee because the two standing committees to which the investigation might have been assigned— Judiciary and Government Operations—were both large, making an efficient investigation difficult. And since each committee included past or future Democratic presidential aspirants, it would likely be accused of partisan political motives. A small select committee could avoid these pitfalls. As for why Ervin was named chairman—a decision made by Senate Democrats while Ervin was icebound at his home in North Carolina—three reasons were offered. Ervin was the Senate's leading expert on constitutional law; he was regarded as "the most nonpartisan Democrat in the Senate"; and at the age of seventy-six, he clearly harbored no ambitions for a higher elective office.[5] In the Senate debate over the resolution to create the select committee, most speakers assumed that Ervin would be named chairman. Indeed, the desirability of the committee was ultimately bound up with the assets Ervin would bring to it as chairman. The committee's nationally televised hearings during May and June of 1973 introduced Americans to the appeal of a man who has been described as the Senate's outstanding constitutional lawyer and as its leading raconteur.

5. Sam J. Ervin, Jr., *The Whole Truth: The Watergate Conspiracy* (New York, 1980), ix.

This essay investigates the public discourse of Fulbright and Ervin. For each man, what were his recurrent themes and appeals?
With what values did he identify? How did he achieve national
stature despite his opposition to civil rights legislation? And what
role did his southern heritage play in his rhetoric?

Fulbright of Arkansas: The Legislator as Teacher

Foreign Policy

Young Congressman Fulbright soon demonstrated that he was
most interested in international issues. Barely two months into
his term, he introduced a resolution supporting the establishment of a postwar international organization. The Fulbright Resolution, as it was quickly called, was the first public declaration that
America did not intend to repeat the isolationist course followed
after World War I.

In the Senate, though not originally appointed to the Foreign
Relations Committee, Fulbright immediately sought to make his
mark in foreign affairs. With fifteen cosigners he sent a letter to
President Roosevelt urging vigorous action to create the United
Nations. In the fall of 1945 he introduced a bill to establish what
came to be known as the Fulbright scholarships, which financed
the international exchange of students in education, science, and
culture. During 1947 and 1948 he spoke frequently in favor of the
political unification of Western Europe, a result that Fulbright saw
as the logical consequence of the Marshall Plan and the North Atlantic Treaty Organization.

The Arkansas senator's discourse on foreign affairs became
more prominent after he became chairman of the Senate Foreign
Relations Committee in 1959. He held the chairmanship until his
defeat in 1974, longer than any senator in history. It was widely
reported that Fulbright would have been named as John F. Kennedy's secretary of state but for his stance on civil rights; it is not
known whether Fulbright would have been seriously interested in
the post. He soon developed a close relationship with the new
president. Nevertheless, he was a strong critic of American involvement at the Bay of Pigs, arguing that as long as the Soviet

Union used Cuba only as a political and not as a military base, it was "a thorn in the flesh; but . . . not a dagger in the heart."[6] The following year, however, believing his proviso violated, Fulbright advocated American invasion of Cuba in response to the Soviet Union's emplacement of missiles on the island. During this period Fulbright spoke of the need for a strong and activist presidency, a position that he attenuated if not recanted in his final Senate speech.[7]

Fulbright looked forward to an even closer relationship with his old friend Lyndon Johnson when the Texan became president. When he delivered his most famous speech, "Old Myths and New Realities," to the Senate in the spring of 1964, he did not believe that he was saying anything revolutionary. Nor did he break with the administration; as he viewed things, the administration was engaged in precisely the reexamination of American foreign policy for which he called. Although Johnson reportedly was annoyed by the speech, he stopped speculation about a rift by asking Fulbright to take on a personal diplomatic mission to Greece and Turkey and by having the senator second Johnson's nomination at the 1964 Democratic convention. Fulbright campaigned enthusiastically for the president in the fall and was credited with a major role in Johnson's winning Arkansas.

Although Vietnam was the object of Fulbright's greatest doubts, his initial break with the Johnson administration came because of America's 1965 intervention in the Dominican Republic, an act the senator saw as a throwback to earlier attempts at American hegemony in the Western Hemisphere. Talk about unproven Communist infiltration in Santo Domingo was jingoism and not compatible with the goal of building bridges between East and West. In July, Fulbright's committee held hearings on the intervention, and on September 15 the senator delivered a speech sharply critical of both the administration's policy and its underlying premises. His close relationship with Lyndon Johnson was broken.

From there it was but a short distance to Fulbright's public dissent over Vietnam. The senator's doubts about the wisdom of

6. Johnson and Gwertzman, Fulbright, 175. I am indebted to Bruce B. Auster for assistance in researching the speeches of Senator Fulbright.
7. Congressional Record, 93rd Cong., 2nd Sess., 41076, 91st Cong., 2nd Sess., 19178, 92nd Cong., 1st Sess., 40171, 93rd Cong., 1st Sess., 42766.

American policy grew during the fall of 1965, when the military strategy shifted from protecting enclaves to conducting search-and-destroy operations. In January, 1966, Fulbright announced that his committee would hold hearings to provide the first searching congressional examination of the wisdom of Vietnam. Featured were such eminent authorities as George Kennan, former U.S. ambassador to Moscow, and General James M. Gavin, as well as representatives of the Johnson administration. The prestige of these speakers, and of the Foreign Relations Committee itself, lent credibility to a previously scattered and ineffectual antiwar dissent. These hearings were followed by another set that reexamined American policy toward mainland China, again raising questions about some of its most basic assumptions.

Fulbright's most severe criticism of American foreign policy was delivered after these hearings. In a series of lectures at Johns Hopkins University, he introduced the term *arrogance of power* and pleaded with his audience to follow a "higher patriotism" rather than give unconditional support to current American foreign policy. He also defended dissent as having a positive influence—and he thereafter was known as a dissenter.[8]

During his final term the Arkansan was preoccupied with the Vietnam War and the need to reappraise America's traditional hostility toward China. In the context of Vietnam he began to argue for limitations on presidential power, contrary to his earlier views. He opposed the nomination of William H. Rehnquist to the Supreme Court because Rehnquist supported a "sweeping doctrine of executive privilege." During the 1973 Yom Kippur War, Fulbright alienated many Jews by suggesting that the United States reappraise its attitude toward the parties in conflict and that multilateral action by the United Nations was the most appropriate response to the situation. He had begun to speak on the Middle East in 1970, and was one of the first to argue that Israel should trade territory for peace. He saw Israeli intransigence as the main obstacle to peace, spoke favorably of an "imposed"

8. *The Vietnam Hearings* (New York, 1966); J. William Fulbright, *The Arrogance of Power* (New York, 1966); *Congressional Record*, 93rd Cong., 2nd Sess., 41076. In his farewell address, Fulbright denied the intention to be known as a dissenter, but added, "When things go contrary to your highest hopes and strongest convictions, there is nothing you can do except dissent—or drop out."

Middle East peace, and at one time publicly identified himself with the Arab position, though he insisted he was not "anti-Israel" but "pro-balance."[9]

Four aspects of Fulbright's discourse on foreign affairs are especially noteworthy. First, his statements reveal an explicit recognition of the rhetorical dimension of foreign policy, a sense that diplomacy is the enactment of rituals and routines in order to convey a message to various audiences. As he put it in 1966, "Words are deeds and style is substance insofar as they influence men's minds [and] behavior." In his early years, he defended the United Nations on the grounds that its creation would send a clear signal to would-be aggressors. Symbolically, it would convey a united will to resist, thereby overcoming the miscalculation that led Hitler to war.[10] To his later embarrassment, Fulbright in 1964 supported the Gulf of Tonkin Resolution, largely because it too sent a clear signal. The resolution, he said, "is designed to shatter whatever illusions our adversaries may harbor about the determination of the United States to act promptly and vigorously against aggression." Fulbright also described America's Vietnam policy as an attempt to *persuade* China "of our determination to remain in southeast Asia." He felt, however, that this policy would not work and that China instead would be convinced that Americans "will sooner or later withdraw their support from an unsupportable commitment and abandon southeast Asia to the unchallenged hegemony of China."[11]

Second, Fulbright's discourse on foreign policy reflects the paramount position of the myth/reality pair. Repeatedly Fulbright separated a foreign policy problem into what was "mythical" and what was real, urging audiences to reject the former and pursue the latter.[12] This opposition between myth and reality was the

9. *Congressional Record*, 91st Cong., 2nd Sess., 19173, 92nd Cong., 1st Sess., 5231–34, 45791, 42884, 93rd Cong., 1st Sess., 36479, 42765, 16263.

10. *Congressional Record*, 89th Cong., 2nd Sess., 6749 ("The Two Americas," Brien McMahon Lecture, University of Connecticut), 78th Cong., 1st Sess., A3862 (American Bar Association speech), 78th Cong., 2nd Sess., A413 (United Commercial Travelers speech), 81st Cong., 1st Sess., 9584.

11. *Congressional Record*, 88th Cong., 2nd Sess., 18400, 89th Cong., 2nd Sess., 4382.

12. This is an example of a "philosophical pair," useful in dividing a seemingly unitary concept into parts. See Chaim Perelman and L. Olbrechts-Tyteca, *The New*

motif of Fulbright's "Old Myths and New Realities" speech, but it had been developed throughout his career. He began his maiden Senate speech, discussing the United Nations, with the words, "Mr. President, myths are one of the greatest obstacles in the formulation of national policy." In criticizing John Foster Dulles, Fulbright distinguished between truth and "a delusion which, if it pierces the human mind, does so because of a small truth it twists." With respect to the intervention in the Dominican Republic, Fulbright maintained that the United States had responded to myth. Concerning China, Fulbright declared that the "most immediate need" was "a concerted effort to dispel myths with realities." Fulbright retained the myth/reality pair in his later years, delivering in 1970 a reprise of his 1964 speech. Furthermore, he referred to the "myths" and "realities" of the Middle East and to the "myths" of the military budget, and he complained that—official protestations notwithstanding—the United States had not abandoned the myth of monolithic communism.[13]

Clearly, the myth/reality pair defined Fulbright's god and devil terms. A policy could be most soundly criticized if it was based in myth; it deserved support if it reflected reality. When Fulbright took issue with policies for which there was widespread support, he frequently did so through dissociation, relying on the myth/reality pair to divide each notion into two different parts.

Third, Fulbright's public discourse reveals a tension between supporting and challenging the orthodox position in foreign affairs. In several cases the senator began by endorsing an "official" interpretation of events, only to reverse himself later. For example, in the late 1940s and early 1950s he shared the prevailing view that the Soviet Union, guided by implacable Communist ideology, was bent on dominating the world. He supported applying the Truman Doctrine to aid Greece and Turkey as a step "to coun-

---

Rhetoric, trans. John Wilkinson and Purcell Weaver (Notre Dame, 1969), 411–59; *Congressional Record*, 88th Cong., 2nd Sess., 6227–32 ("Old Myths and New Realities" speech).

13. *Congressional Record*, 79th Cong., 1st Sess., 2896, 84th Cong., 2nd Sess., 3370, 89th Cong., 1st Sess., 28374, 89th Cong., 2nd Sess., 6752, 91st Cong., 2nd Sess., 10150–57, 29796–813, 93rd Cong., 1st Sess., 10503; J. William Fulbright, *The Crippled Giant: American Foreign Policy and Its Domestic Consequences* (New York, 1972), 91.

teract the apparently unlimited expansion of communism." And at the time of the "Great Debate" of 1951, Fulbright characterized the Soviet Union as "an adversary who accepts no rules, and has no honor, no moral code, no respect for word or conduct; who ridicules religion and believes that any means justifies the end." By the end of the 1950s, however, he was more cautious. At the time of the 1958 intervention in Lebanon, he foreshadowed the later "arrogance of power" thesis in a critique of the Eisenhower administration. "Let something go wrong," he said, "—whether it be in China or Nigeria—and we have had a ready answer. The Soviet Union was behind it." He went on to charge that "the spectre of Soviet communism" was being used "as a cloak for the failure of our own leadership." In "Old Myths and New Realities," Fulbright carefully distinguished between communism as an ideology and the Soviet Union as a sovereign nation. The United States, he insisted, need be concerned only with the latter: "We must deal with the Soviet Union as a great power, quite apart from differences of ideology." [14]

Nowhere was the tension between the orthodox and the heterodox more apparent than in Fulbright's tortured statements on Vietnam. In the 1950s he cited the experience of South Vietnam as "the first defeat inflicted on communism in Asia with entirely political weapons." And in 1964, Fulbright accepted the Johnson administration's thesis that North Vietnam had committed aggression against the South. Subversion, he insisted, was aggression, "a modernized specialized kind of aggression" perfected by Mao Tse-tung. He accepted the administration's view of the incidents in the Gulf of Tonkin, calling the North Vietnamese attack on American destroyers "without any doubt a calculated act of military aggression." And he insisted that discussion about the wisdom of America's original involvement was not helpful because it was not useful in stating what should be done next. But Fulbright later revised his position on most of these matters. By 1966 he was calling on scholars to investigate the origins of the war. He now characterized Vietnam as "not an international conflict but an in-

14. *Congressional Record*, 80th Cong., 1st Sess., 3137, 82nd Cong., 1st Sess., 521, 85th Cong., 2nd Sess., 16318, 88th Cong., 2nd Sess., 6228 ("Old Myths and New Realities" speech).

surrection in one part of a divided country supported by the other part."[15]

Torn between the orthodox stance of administration supporter and the iconoclastic stance of critic, Fulbright frequently began by supporting the president on an issue. Then he would wonder. Then, after some time passed, he would redefine his position. The myth/reality pair facilitated this progression by enabling Fulbright to dissociate concepts. The orthodox position could be characterized as the "myth" of communism, for example, or of Vietnam. By contrast, the critical position was the "reality." The critique of official views gave him the means to modify his own: what Fulbright attacked were often positions that he had previously supported.

A fourth recurrent theme in Fulbright's discourse on foreign affairs was the need for proportion. Means should be appropriate to ends; specific actions should be appropriate to more general policies; policies should be appropriate to the facts of the world and to human nature. For example, while defending the Gulf of Tonkin Resolution, Fulbright urged that Vietnam be kept in context. The overriding objective was détente with the Soviet Union; Vietnam must not be allowed to loom so large as to threaten this central objective.[16] He repeatedly made the same argument about Cuba, urging that Fidel Castro be viewed as a minor irritant rather than a major threat to the security of the United States. Moreover, American foreign policy should be proportionate to human nature and the facts of the world. Human nature showed that man was imperfect, so it was a mistake of proportion to predicate nuclear deterrence on the absence of human error. And the paramount fact of the world was change; it was an error of proportion for foreign policy to be inflexible and not adaptable.

It was easy for Fulbright to criticize policies of which he disapproved as lacking proportion and hence as deviations from guiding principles. "Many of our most vexatious problems," Fulbright declared, "have grown out of the occasional lapses and departures from the philosophy that has inspired our policies." He

15. *Congressional Record*, 89th Cong., 2nd Sess., 16808.
16. *Congressional Record*, 86th Cong., 1st Sess., 18333, 88th Cong., 2nd Sess., 18402, 14793, 18399, 18407, 18400.

cited as examples the 1950s posture on neutralism, the 1956 cancellation of the Aswan Dam, John Foster Dulles' statements on massive retaliation, and the assumptions that led to the debacle at the Bay of Pigs. Likewise, his critiques of American policy in Vietnam often argued that America's interests were not proportionate to its actions and commitments. And the extent of American support for Israel was deemed out of proportion to true national interest. The cause for these lapses was not hard to find—the distorting effect on public discourse of oversimplified moralism and ideology in foreign affairs. He decried the familiar tendency for Americans to view themselves as the chosen people, insisting that "it is not possible to reshape the world in the American image." [17]

Throughout his thirty-year career in the Senate, Fulbright distinguished himself principally in the area of foreign affairs. His public discourse on that subject was marked by a recognition that foreign policy has a major rhetorical dimension, by the prevalence of the myth/reality pair, by the tension between supporting orthodoxy and becoming a critic, and by the appeal that foreign policy retain or regain a sense of proportion. These themes surfaced in Fulbright's statements on international organization, communism, the Soviet Union, China, Latin America, Vietnam, and the Middle East. He articulated a set of principles that characterized an informed and enlightened outlook on the place of the United States in the modern world.

Civil Rights and Education

How, liberals often wondered, could Fulbright reconcile his enlightened stance on world affairs with his consistent opposition to civil rights? He signed the Southern Manifesto of 1956 (though only after it had been rewritten so as not to condone illegal resistance). He participated actively in filibusters against the Civil Rights Acts of 1957 and 1960, spoke in the early 1960s against the constitutional amendment to ban the poll tax and against restric-

17. *Congressional Record*, 87th Cong., 1st Sess., 11703, 90th Cong., 1st Sess., 1223 ("Meet the Press" transcript), 93rd Cong., 1st Sess., 16263, 86th Cong., 1st Sess., 18773, 89th Cong., 1st Sess., 316, 89th Cong., 2nd Sess., 9329 (Johns Hopkins University address), 91st Cong., 2nd Sess., 10157; "The American Agenda," in *Vital Speeches*, June 15, 1963, p. 524 (William L. Clayton Lecture, Tufts University).

tions on the literacy test, and—albeit in a more restrained way—
opposed the Civil Rights Act of 1964. A study of Fulbright's method
of argument may help to explain this seeming paradox.

If one looks at his Senate speeches, Fulbright was no racist. His
statements contain no protestations of black inferiority—or, for
that matter, fixed opposition to integration. In fact, the Arkansas
senator frequently expressed his broad *support* for the principle of
civil rights. As early as 1946, while opposing a bill for a permanent Fair Employment Practices Commission, Fulbright stated, "I
think all of us from the South agree, and all of us who oppose this
bill agree, that it is a perfectly proper objective that no person
should discriminate, either in his business or in any other way,
against those who are good law-abiding, Christian people." In
1964 he was even more explicit: "I do not argue . . . as to the ultimate objective; I only disagree as to the best way to proceed toward it and as to the rapidity with which changes can be made—
especially by means of a statute." So civil rights was not a question of ends, but "only" one of means. Focusing his opposition in
this way enabled Fulbright both to disarm his antagonists—they
hardly could call him racist if he professed his support for civil
rights—and to give emphasis to the particular grounds of his dis-
agreement. This choice also conveniently permitted him to focus
his arguments on the *stasis* of place, or procedure—a focal point
that preempts substance. An issue not addressed in the right
place or manner was moot until the proper forum was secured.

Fulbright repeatedly insisted that civil rights proponents had
committed procedural violations. For example, complaining about
the absence of committee hearings on the 1964 civil rights bill,
Fulbright charged that supporters were "so imbued with the idea
that they know the answer to the difficult problem of race relations that they are impatient with our established principles." As
he saw it, they were trying to short-circuit "procedures which
have been established throughout the centuries to deal with basic
human rights."

Deviations from normal Senate procedure were not mere tech-
nical niceties. As Fulbright argued, they contained the potential
for far greater abuse. If orderly process is to be ignored when legislation of one type is under consideration, why cannot the same
result ensue when other types of bills are at stake? The only pro-

tection against this risk is to elevate procedure to a matter of principle. This transformation is even more evident in some of Fulbright's other objections to civil rights. The literacy-test proposal of 1962, as he saw it, violated the explicit constitutional provision that each state was empowered to set its own qualifications for voting. Trample on one constitutional guarantee and what other guarantee was safe? In 1964, Fulbright argued for jury trials in all cases of criminal contempt arising under the proposed civil rights bill, charging that unless the bill were so amended, the right to trial by jury, guaranteed in four places in the Constitution and Bill of Rights, "would most certainly be impaired in the most drastic way." The unspoken part of the argument, of course, was that if one guarantee was surrendered, then no constitutional protections were safe. Fulbright frequently employed a "slippery slope" argument, predicting dire consequences, often in unrelated fields, of the surrender of procedural safeguards. In debate over the 1957 civil rights bill, he argued that its passage would lead to the erosion of the right to jury trials for other crimes. Given the principle of that bill, the Arkansan said, "we could go a step further and give the court the authority to enjoin all citizens of the United States from committing murder. Any time anyone committed murder, all the court would have to do would be to exercise the contempt power, throw him in jail and keep him there without a trial by jury, simply because the person violated the court's order." Likewise, federal regulation of literacy tests would start the country down a slippery slope, since "there is no end to the insatiable demands of minority groups who want a special legal status in our society." Fulbright speculated, "Once the door is opened it will be impossible to prevent passage of other measures to homogenize the States."[18]

Sometimes Fulbright's objections were based on the second-order results the laws would produce. In the course of pursuing civil rights—admittedly a laudable objective—other consequences would be sufficiently damaging as to make the venture on balance unwise. The nature of these other results varied. For instance,

18. *Congressional Record*, 79th Cong., 2nd Sess., 500, 88th Cong., 2nd Sess., 95, 8699–8700, 8701, 8704, 11534, 87th Cong., 2nd Sess., 7280, 7283, 85th Cong., 1st Sess., 11081.

Fulbright sometimes assumed that to extend rights to some necessarily meant taking them away from others. Since rights gained
were offset by rights lost, legislation was not justified. Anticipat-
ing arguments of the later 1960s, Fulbright charged that this approach to civil rights actually led to reverse racism, which was
unacceptable. The equation of equal opportunities with equal results was disdained by Fulbright, who charged that with the 1964
Civil Rights Act "a movement for legal equality has become a
crusade for economic success." On other occasions, Fulbright
charged that the second-order results of civil rights laws would
impair some other value more important than civil rights. National unity was one such value, especially in light of the psychology of the cold war. In 1960, for example, Fulbright warned, "We
are faced with a threat to our existence. The Russians, I am sure,
are taking great delight over the sectional struggle taking place in
this country. Any force which tends to divide our people and de-
ter us from attention to the common enemy sacrifices our national
interests to the advantage of our adversaries." The clear implication was that whatever the merits of civil rights legislation, it
ought to wait until some presumably more tranquil time.

Another value violated by civil rights laws, Fulbright thought,
was the spirit of compromise. In 1957 he charged that the proponents risked succumbing to a self-righteous absolutism that accorded their adversaries' judgment no respect. "I would suggest,"
he told his colleagues, "that where men depart from the processes
of compromise they depart also from the processes of democracy." In an *amicus curiae* brief submitted to the Supreme Court at
the time of the Little Rock school integration crisis, the senator
made a similar argument in behalf of the principle of gradualism.[19]

Many of the senator's arguments against civil rights remained
constant throughout his career, but it would be inaccurate to say
that his position underwent no change. In the 1940s he had favored the white primary, yet by the 1960s he claimed not to object
to measures that would increase black voting, particularly since
he thought that Negroes voted freely in Arkansas. In the early

19. *Congressional Record*, 87th Cong., 1st Sess., 17339, 86th Cong., 2nd Sess.,
3980, 3978, 88th Cong., 2nd Sess., 9587, 85th Cong., 1st Sess., 12548, 85th Cong.,
2nd Sess., 19853.

1950s he cited the establishment of a hospital in which facilities for blacks and whites were segregated within the same building as a sign of racial *progress*; it is unlikely that he would have made the same statement two decades later. Nor, perhaps, would he have remained silent as he did at the time of the Little Rock integration crisis. And he might not have participated vocally as he did in the filibusters of 1957, 1960, and 1964. Following the lead of President Johnson, Fulbright tried during the 1964 election campaign to minimize the significance of the issue to the white South. And in a 1970 Senate speech on education, Fulbright acknowledged that though he had voted against many civil rights acts, he would "now accept them as the law of the land," adding, however, that he still thought it unwise "to approach the problem as it was approached."[20]

A discussion of *how* Fulbright opposed civil rights legislation, however, still leaves open the question of *why* he did so. The senator claimed simply that he had voted his conscience. In an interview for *Saturday Review* upon his retirement, he stated, "Well, I voted my convictions at the time. That seemed to me then the only way to vote, for various reasons—the most effective way, even from the point of view of bringing about the integration of black people into our society." Those convictions no doubt included the southerner's respect for place and order, manifest in Fulbright's consistent concern for means and procedure. There is another explanation for Fulbright's votes, though. In his first term in the Senate, he delivered a lecture titled "The Legislator" at the University of Chicago. In this speech, to which he often referred in later years, he described the tension between a legislator's duty to his constituents and to his conscience. Sometimes the tension was resolved in favor of constituency; sometimes, in favor of conscience. "The average legislator, early in his career," Fulbright explained, "discovers that there are certain interests, or prejudices, of his constituents which are dangerous to trifle with. Some of these prejudices may not be of fundamental importance to the welfare of the Nation, in which case he is justified in humoring

20. *Congressional Record*, 88th Cong., 2nd Sess., 9596, 82nd Cong., 1st Sess., A6542–43 (Crittenden Memorial Hospital speech, West Memphis, Ark.), 91st Cong., 2nd Sess., 2906.

them, even though he may disapprove." In other cases, however, if the prejudice concerned "fundamental policy affecting the national welfare," the legislator was obliged to override his constituents' wish.[21] In this lecture, Fulbright used the poll tax as an example of the former case and isolationism as an example of the latter, but in his behavior he applied the principle more broadly. Civil rights laws were not "of fundamental importance," since matters of morality and interpersonal relationships could not be legislated. By contrast, national unity in foreign policy was vital. Consequently, Fulbright would satisfy the wishes of his constituents on civil rights, in order thereby to have the freedom to follow his own lights in foreign affairs.

Some evidence that Fulbright held this position may be found in the contrast between his views on racial and sex discrimination. Whereas he consistently opposed civil rights acts, he early supported the Equal Rights Amendment—even though some of his arguments against civil rights also could be applied against the ERA. Nevertheless, in 1972 he stated, "I have actively supported and co-sponsored this measure for many years," and added that it "will not be forcing social change, but rather we will be helping to provide the legal framework for change that is both just and responsive to the needs and requests of a majority of American citizens." The senator did not seem to notice the apparent double standard in his criteria for support. Perhaps sex discrimination did not affect the voters of Arkansas as immediately as did the topic of race, so that Fulbright was free to vote his own convictions. Alternatively, though, this seeming discrepancy may indicate how Fulbright's own convictions began to change in the years after 1965.

Probably some mixture of personal conviction and political calculation explains Fulbright's motive. One possible explanation, however, can easily be set aside. Southerners sometimes were accused of using procedural objections merely to mask their substantive opposition, so that they spoke in code. They always praised the end but opposed the means—*any* means. That criticism does not

21. Russell Warren Howe and Sarah Trott, "J. William Fulbright: Reflections on a Troubled World," *Saturday Review*, January 11, 1975, p. 19; *Congressional Record*, 79th Cong., 2nd Sess., A1285 ("The Legislator," University of Chicago address, February 19, 1946).

apply to Fulbright. He consistently proposed education as the path to civil rights. Since prejudices were learned, they could be unlearned, and in the fullness of time a harmonious relationship between the races would come about. It could not, he felt, be accomplished by legislative fiat. Again and again Fulbright returned to this theme. Discussing the literacy test, Fulbright argued, "Problems in this delicate area of human relationships can be solved only through education and the slow conversion of the human mind and heart," and added that there were limits to a legislature's wisdom and ability to act. In a lecture at Tufts University, he was explicit about the relationship between education and civil rights. "Education," he insisted, "is the *precondition*, the indispensable precondition, for the resolution of problems of race. It is axiomatic that prejudices and injustices relating to race are the product of ignorance. Only through the processes of education can men of different races learn to live together in harmony and in full respect for each other's rights." For this reason, it was a special tragedy that the civil rights movement had focused so much of its energy on school integration. "By making our public schools the arena for the highly emotional issue of race," he maintained, "we have generated unnecessary passions and animosities which aggravate race relations and at the same time add an enormous obstacle to our efforts to improve public education." Having said that education was the appropriate means to achieve the goal of civil rights, Fulbright consistently supported federal aid to education, often citing the inadequate expenditures of the southern states, despite their substantial tax rates, as a justification for federal aid.[22]

It was not only in the context of civil rights that Fulbright spoke of the value of education. Indeed, if *myth* was the key devil term in his hierarchy, then *education* was the key god term, the value he championed most. It was important not only to civil rights but to foreign affairs as well. We cannot act responsibly on the world

22. *Congressional Record*, 92nd Cong., 2nd Sess., 9550–51, 87th Cong., 2nd Sess., 7283, 80th Cong., 2nd Sess., 3949–50; "The American Agenda," 525. Fulbright spoke of the tragedy in 1964: "The very process upon which progress is dependent has been disrupted and distorted by the unwise policy of using the schools as a medium to force integration" (*Congressional Record*, 88th Cong., 2nd Sess., 5637).

scene if we are ignorant of the culture and history of other lands. Likewise, education was for Fulbright the primary solution to the problem of poverty: "Only education can give hope to young people in very low-income families whose futures are otherwise bleak."

There is ample evidence that Fulbright placed education at the top of a hierarchy of government functions. Citing Jefferson, he attributed to the Founding Fathers the preeminence of the public's interest in education. But Americans had somewhere gone awry and abandoned this basic commitment. Consequently, Fulbright's task was to reassert the primacy of education. His most explicit statement on this issue was in a 1963 Senate speech: "The highest priority need of America in the 1960's is the expansion and improvement of public education." So important was education that Fulbright was one of a small number of senators who opposed the space program in its heyday, on the grounds that it diverted national resources from the more pressing needs of education. Similarly, in a 1972 book, Fulbright discussed education as the best and perhaps only hope for avoiding nuclear holocaust and suggested that we must "use whatever respite a new balance of power provides to try to expand the boundaries of human wisdom, sympathy and perception."[23]

Explicit statements are not the only evidence of the priority Fulbright assigned to education. An examination of his metaphors reveals that objects often were evaluated positively by being described as educational. For example, in a 1959 lecture the Arkansan labeled Congress "an educational institution" with respect to foreign affairs. Foreign policy itself was viewed as an educator. The major lesson of Vietnam, Fulbright hoped, would be "a new appreciation of the power of nationalism in southeast Asia and, indeed, in all of the world's emerging nations." Particularly as he became a critic of the Lyndon Johnson administration's policies, Fulbright made increasing use of the "teaching" metaphor. In both "The Arrogance of Power" lecture and a separate 1966 speech on Latin America, the senator observed that Haiti, the Dominican Republic, and Cuba, "the countries which have had most of the

23. *Congressional Record*, 88th Cong., 2nd Sess., 16761, 88th Cong., 1st Sess., 19763; "Space and National Priorities," in *Vital Speeches*, November 1, 1963, p. 43; Fulbright, *The Crippled Giant*, 274.

tutelage in democracy by U.S. marines are not particularly democratic." Fulbright concluded sarcastically, "Maybe, in the light of this extraordinary record of accomplishment, it is time for us to reconsider our teaching methods." The 1966 hearings on Vietnam by the Senate Foreign Relations Committee were sometimes referred to as "Bill Fulbright's Teach-Ins"; the chairman himself called them "an experiment in public education."[24] The nation was suffering from inadequate understanding of a problem; a congressional committee would serve as educator so that the nation could be better informed; understanding was presumed to prompt the right actions. In a very real sense, Fulbright's speeches incorporated the popular American belief that education can contribute powerfully to solving all ills.

Sometimes, however, Fulbright complained that America was learning the wrong lessons. In 1961 he acknowledged that "many Americans, including some whose judgment is generally good," were drawing the wrong conclusions from the Soviet success in placing a man in space, from the debacle at the Bay of Pigs, and from the deteriorating situation in Laos. Fulbright called the idea that the United States should never hesitate to commit its military strength to the defense of its policies "dangerous doctrine," adding that "nothing would please Communist leaders more." But what were the "right" lessons? Fulbright referred to two. One was that the United States should strive to teach by the power of example rather than by active involvement in other nations. In "The Arrogance of Power," he complained that American intervention, among its other faults, was "denying the world the example of a free society enjoying its freedom to the fullest." Employing the teaching metaphor, he added, "This is regrettable indeed for a nation that aspires to teach democracy to other nations." The other lesson to be learned was the need for flexibility and adaptation to change. That lesson was the central theme of "Old Myths and New Realities," in which Fulbright urged his countrymen to "cut loose from established myths and to start thinking some 'un-

24. "Our Responsibilities in World Affairs," in *Vital Speeches*, June 15, 1959, p. 531 (Columbia University lecture); *Congressional Record*, 89th Cong., 1st Sess., 13657 (Fulbright was still supporting Johnson at this time), 89th Cong., 2nd Sess., 6753, 10807 ("The Arrogance of Power" speech), 6439 ("Higher Education and the Crisis in Asia," National Conference on Higher Education address).

thinkable thoughts'—about the cold war and East-West relations, about the underdeveloped countries and particularly those in Latin America, about the changing nature of the Chinese Communist threat in Asia and about the festering war in Vietnam."[25] But this need for adaptability was a frequent appeal in the senator's public discourse. Fulbright's explicit statements and implicit metaphors made clear that he regarded education as a supreme value, more important than such ephemeral interests as space exploration, and the key ingredient in a successful foreign policy and the solution to such domestic troubles as poverty and race.

Fulbright's Rhetorical Method

Throughout his public speaking career, Fulbright made a set of choices that collectively defined his rhetorical method. These choices involved his overall persona, the material for his arguments, and the nature of his appeals.

The persona Fulbright often adopted was that of the academic. He tended toward abstraction, theoretical speculation, and careful documentation. He sought critical appraisal rather than unthinking acceptance of propositions. He was alert to paradoxes, ironies, and careful distinctions. As an academic, Fulbright welcomed controversy; he believed that airing differences was essential to making sound decisions. Defending his actions in criticizing the Johnson administration's policy in the Dominican Republic, the senator complained that consensus which conceals differences is a violation of democracy. "I think," he went on, "we Americans tend to put too high a value on unanimity . . . as if there were something dangerous and illegitimate about honest differences of opinion honestly expressed by honest men. . . . [We] tend to be mistrustful of intellectual dissent, confusing it with personal hostility and political disloyalty." Although Fulbright welcomed controversy, he himself played the part of the reluctant critic, driven to opposition only as a last resort. In 1956 he prefaced a critique of John Foster Dulles with two paragraphs acknowledging the difficulties of the secretary of state and eschewing any attempt at par-

25. "United States Foreign Policy," in *Vital Speeches*, August 1, 1961, p. 616; *Congressional Record*, 89th Cong., 2nd Sess., 10808 ("The Arrogance of Power" speech), 88th Cong., 2nd Sess., 6227–28 ("Old Myths and New Realities" speech).

tisan vilification. On Vietnam, he held back his dissent for many months and, as late as June, 1965, ingratiated himself by praising President Johnson's "wisdom and vision," his "steadfastness and statesmanship," saying that Johnson was "providing the leadership appropriate to a great nation." Fulbright apparently preferred the role of senior scholar, engaging in reporting and pronouncement rather than heated controversy.

As befits the academic, Fulbright maintained a generally skeptical outlook. He was skeptical, for example, about whether the heavy burden of defense spending really represented the will of the people: "It may be that the people and their representatives are making a carefully reasoned sacrifice of welfare to security. It may be, but I doubt it. The sacrifice is made so eagerly as to cause one to suspect that it is fairly painless." He was skeptical about cultural exchanges as a propaganda tool. "Of course we are concerned with men's minds," he acknowledged, "but by the very nature of our view of the world we cannot be a party to any effort to capture those minds or convert them to a thesis which is not freely acceptable to the independent exercise of a man's judgment." He was skeptical of détente even as he supported it: it would not "lead to a grand reconciliation that will end the cold war and usher in the brotherhood of man." And he even was skeptical of the prominence given to foreign policy "because it diverts a nation from its sources of strength, which are in its domestic life."[26]

Of course, Fulbright's academic persona was most evident in his Senate speeches and public lectures. When campaigning in Arkansas, however, Fulbright adopted a quite different stance. The dualism between the international statesman and the local politician led Daniel Yergin to charge that Fulbright had been "two things to two sets of people. To the people of the world, he was the urbane peace prophet J. William Fulbright, of the furrowed brow, the three-piece suit, the dignified mien. . . . To the folks

26. *Congressional Record*, 89th Cong., 1st Sess., 28373, 84th Cong., 2nd Sess., 3369, 89th Cong., 1st Sess., 12732, 13656, 88th Cong., 2nd Sess., 7094 ("The Cold War in American Life," University of North Carolina speech), 87th Cong., 1st Sess., 11400, 88th Cong., 2nd Sess., 6229 ("Old Myths and New Realities" speech), 89th Cong., 2nd Sess., 10804 ("The University and American Foreign Policy," Center for Democratic Institutions speech).

down home in Arkansas, he was plain old Bill Fulbright, shirt sleeves rolled up, baggy pants held up by suspenders and collar open at the neck, talking to them about the price of cotton and chickens."[27] Clearly, then, the Fulbright persona was influenced not only by the senator's sense of himself and his mission but also by astute audience analysis.

What of Fulbright's manner of argument? His most typical approach was seemingly deductive: to state a broad thesis as a general proposition, and then to sketch out its implications for the specific subject at hand. "Old Myths and New Realities," for example, began with the statement that "there is an inevitable divergence, attributable to the imperfections of the human mind, between the world as it is and the world as men perceive it."[28] The general thesis was taken as true; the argument then applied, explained, or extended it. The thesis functioned as Fulbright's "doctrine" and enabled him to proceed as if arguing from self-evident truths.

Frequently Fulbright argued from historical experience and precedent. In his early speeches, he cited the frustrating peace settlement after World War I as reason not to wait for war's end before developing an international organization. The successfully negotiated peace of 1815, contrasted with the demands for total victory in 1918 and 1945, furnished a valuable lesson for Americans concerning Vietnam. The history of Prohibition was sometimes cited as proof of the futility of civil rights legislation. These arguments from historical experience established strong presumptions about what actions should be taken, as long as one assumed that the current situation was basically similar to its precedent. Fulbright was quick to make this assumption—too quick, in the judgment of some of his critics. Henry Fairlie charged in particular that the historical examples cited in "The Arrogance of Power" were "debatable" and that the links between America's

27. Daniel Yergin, "Fulbright's Last Frustration," *New York Times Magazine*, November 24, 1974, p. 14.

28. *Congressional Record*, 88th Cong., 2nd Sess., 6227 ("Old Myths and New Realities" speech); "Foreign Service Needs Young People," in *Vital Speeches*, November 1, 1944, p. 42; *Congressional Record*, 83rd Cong., 2nd Sess., 12915, 86th Cong., 2nd Sess., 12915 (American Bar Association address); "The American Character," in *Vital Speeches*, January 1, 1964, p. 164; *Congressional Record*, 89th Cong., 2nd Sess., 10806 ("The Arrogance of Power" speech).

current condition and ancient Athens, Napoleon's invasion of Russia, or the Spanish-American War were less than perfect.[29]

Occasionally, though far less often, Fulbright argued from analogy. He compared the national ego to that of an individual, suggesting that both could profit from psychiatric analysis. Advocating an international organization, he drew a parallel between world conditions in 1943 and the United States when Abraham Lincoln proclaimed that the nation could not survive half slave and half free. In his maiden Senate speech, refuting Clare Boothe Luce, he compared freedom of the skies with freedom of speech and religion. Eisenhower's 1960 admission that the United States was conducting U-2 flights over the Soviet Union was likened to the parable of George Washington and the cherry tree, to prove that the president always should tell the truth. None of these analogies is fresh or well developed—evidence, perhaps, that Fulbright did not wholly subscribe to the belief that analogy can be the most potent means of persuasion.

In addition to the development of a general thesis, the use of historical precedents, and analogies, Fulbright occasionally supported his position by argument from residues. This form consists of identifying a finite number of possible positions and then excluding all save one that survives by default. Arguments of this type were used frequently by Lyndon Johnson to defend his Vietnam policy. But the same mode of argument was used sometimes by Johnson's chief critic on the Senate Foreign Relations Committee. Discussing the situation in the Dominican Republic, Fulbright identified only three options for the United States and then ruled out two. Likewise, he defended attempts at détente with the Soviet Union "not because this approach is inherently more desirable than one of total victory for American interests but because there is no acceptable alternative in the nuclear age."

In his public speeches, Fulbright appealed to his audiences primarily by the force of the arguments themselves—again consistent with the persona of the academic. Certainly his delivery was not a major cause of his influence. Charles Seib and Alan Otten contrast the extended amount of time Fulbright spent preparing

29. *Congressional Record*, 78th Cong., 1st Sess., A477, 89th Cong., 2nd Sess., 4380, 88th Cong., 2nd Sess., 9597; Henry Fairlie, "Old Realities and New Myths," *Reporter*, XXXIV (June 16, 1966), 20.

his speeches with the manner of their presentation. The delivery, they conclude, "has the dead beat of a metronome, and [Fulbright's] extemporaneous remarks are not only uninspiring but sometimes confusing."[30] Nonetheless, some key elements of Fulbright's appeal had little to do with the substance of his arguments. Of these elements the most prominent was sarcasm.

The Arkansas senator combined an awareness of irony, an appreciation of the comic, and a recognition that a barb delivered with a disarming smile can nevertheless injure. Fulbright's sarcasm was at its most caustic in an otherwise insignificant speech in 1965, in which he responded to criticism by Congressman John V. Lindsay of New York that no blacks were registered to vote in Newton County, Arkansas. He began his reply, tongue in cheek, by noting, "Occasionally we are called to account by some of our younger colleagues who stand up for the right no matter what the price." He then related the charge, which had been backed up in a "poignant and moving editorial" in the New York *Times*. Then he launched into his response. "It is laudable that it matters not," he began, "that no more than two nonwhites of voting age reside in Newton County out of a total nonwhite population of eight and that there is some question in the collective mind of the Census Bureau as to whether either of them is a Negro." He went on: "Some of us might wonder how successful Federal registrars would be in signing up even 50 percent of the nonwhite population of voting age inasmuch as the hills and gullies of Newton County, which lie deep in the Ozark Mountains, have often shielded residents of the area from Federal officers who in the past have sought to aid the local populace in computing their excise tax liabilities." And what if the two blacks were registered and the electorate rose from 2,680 to 2,682? "It is true that in many counties in Arkansas, and Newton County is no exception, elections are sometimes close and perhaps these new voters would hold the balance of power. Who can foresee the totally new political climate which might come?" Finally, he noted that "this example of adherence to principle is an inspiration to me, as I am

30. "The Synthesis of Both Liberty and Unity," in *Vital Speeches*, October 1, 1960, p. 739; *Congressional Record*, 78th Cong., 1st Sess., A478, 86th Cong., 2nd Sess., 14736, 89th Cong., 1st Sess., 28375, 316; Charles B. Seib and Alan L. Otten, "Fulbright: Arkansas Paradox," *Harper's*, CCXII (June, 1956), 61.

sure it is to all Members of Congress and indeed to the country as a whole."[31]

This speech revealed the varied uses to which Fulbright's sarcasm could be put. The speech was a strong though gentle attack on a "knee-jerk" liberal who drew conclusions without checking the facts. It attributed to the northerner a smug self-righteousness while the more mature southerner appreciated the comic discount. It took advantage of the resources of understatement and irony, and it trivialized the issue about which Lindsay was concerned.

Fulbright's sarcasm was equally evident in speeches in which it was not the central motif. Noting that Congress was reluctant to cut defense spending but eager to slash foreign aid appropriations, the senator observed "how astonishingly the forces of economy had picked up strength between the debate on the $50 billion Defense appropriation and the $4 billion foreign aid bill." Referring to administration pledges to maintain a presence in Asia to defeat aggression, Fulbright wondered "whether the Asian doctrine will reap for the United States as rich a harvest of affection and democracy as has the Monroe Doctrine" and "whether China will accept American hegemony as gracefully as Cuba and the Dominican Republic have accepted it." Secretary of State John Foster Dulles was described as a man "who greets the dawn with a boast about his triumphs, and meets the dusk with scare words of panic, saying that the Nation will be ruined unless it unites to ratify the mistakes he made during the day."

Fulbright's other modes of appeal tended to vary far more from speech to speech. Although he usually understated his case, he permitted himself occasional use of hyperbole, as when he described the Eisenhower administration as "a leadership that is at once aimless and feeble, and a bureaucracy so fearful of change that it clings desperately to the ancient pillars of policy even as they rot away under the pressure of irresistible international developments." He seldom employed the device of the anti-authority, but he responded to Jacob Javits' defense of the 1957 civil rights bill by exclaiming, "The Senator from New York is entitled to approve the bill if he so desires. The people in Russia, in the Kremlin, approve this kind of procedure. It was approved in Germany."

31. *Congressional Record*, 89th Cong., 1st Sess., 6542.

He seldom engaged in personal attacks, but in 1972 he rebuked Senator Henry M. Jackson of Washington, charging that Jackson, by consistently supporting high levels of defense spending, had "done more than any other Senator to destroy the fiscal responsibility of our country."[32]

In sum, then, Fulbright's persona was primarily that of the academic. He welcomed controversy and thought that it gave rise to careful analysis, yet he was skeptical of most conclusions. His arguments developed a general thesis and then applied it to the specifics of the case at hand, though he occasionally used other forms of argument. And to the degree that Fulbright had a characteristic mode of appeal, it lay in his use of sarcasm. These patterns, taken together, describe Fulbright's overall rhetorical method.

Fulbright and the South

Particularly when discussing foreign affairs, Fulbright seldom made reference to his southern roots. It was as if the region of his birth was irrelevant to the part his country should play on the world stage. Occasionally, however, he suggested that the southern heritage shed light on a contemporary problem. In talking about the economic reconstruction of Vietnam, he disclaimed the goal of turning Third World nations into staunch American allies. He argued by analogy: "It was not many years ago that politicians in the American South were automatically suspect in the eyes of their fellow southerners if they cozied too closely with rapacious 'Eastern interests.'" In the same manner, Fulbright reasoned, "it is demeaning in the eyes of proud and sensitive peoples in the less developed countries if their leaders stand in too well with a rich and powerful America." The common point of the analogy is the symbolism created by economic aid—it conveys acknowledgment of a superior-subordinate relationship. America's own "arrogance of power" made its people insensitive to this symbolic dimension, but reference to the history of the South should awaken them to it. In another example, describing the American attitude toward China as irrational, Fulbright spoke of the harm that can come

32. *Congressional Record*, 88th Cong., 2nd Sess., 7095 ("The Cold War in American Life"), 89th Cong., 2nd Sess., 16808, 85th Cong., 1st Sess., 1856, 85th Cong., 2nd Sess., 11844, 85th Cong., 1st Sess., 11085, 92nd Cong., 2nd Sess., 27940.

from basing policy on faulty perceptions. "Perhaps we souther-ners," he said, "have a sensitivity to this sort of thing that other Americans cannot fully share." The reason was the South's experi-ence of "both the hot-headed romanticism that led to Fort Sumter and the bitter humiliation of defeat and a vindictive Reconstruc-tion." Fulbright also maintained that the South's history made it easier for Americans to understand the Third World. Explaining the fanaticism of the Vietcong, Fulbright said, "Well, coming from the South, with all its memories of Reconstruction, I think I can understand. They've been put upon, and it makes them so fanati-cal they'll fight down to the last man." To a delegation of visiting Africans, Fulbright insisted that he understood their problems, because "you're about where we were 30 years ago in Arkansas."

These few examples virtually exhaust Fulbright's appeals to his native region when foreign affairs were of concern. In contrast, appeals to the South loom far larger in Fulbright's repertoire when domestic policy was at issue. To start with, Fulbright insisted that the South was misinterpreted, partly because of its treatment by the press and partly because of northern prejudice. The press in-sisted on caricaturing "those of us who believe in adhering to traditional procedures of this body as obstructionists and fili-busters," so that there was no hope of "fair treatment for the southern viewpoint in the northern press." If the South stood accused of prejudice against blacks, Fulbright turned the tables: the real prejudice was that which northerners held against the South.[33]

Fulbright's speeches reveal a well-constructed southern vision in which the region is under siege by a northern conspiracy bent on passing civil rights laws to gain some transitory political ad-vantage at the South's expense. Having expressed his own oppo-sition to the bills, Fulbright needed some explanation of why others would favor such perverse legislation. The obvious answer was to assert that civil rights was but a means to political self-aggrandizement at the South's expense. Because Fulbright ac-cepted this southern vision, he was quick to see conspiratorial de-

33. *Congressional Record*, 89th Cong., 1st Sess., 12733, 89th Cong., 2nd Sess., 5145, 89th Cong., 2nd Sess., 10810, 10812 (reprint of Brocke Brower, "The Roots of the Arkansas Questioner," *Life*, May 13, 1966), 87th Cong., 1st Sess., 17338, 88th Cong., 2nd Sess., 5637.

sign in the actions of the North. In 1949, opposing a proposal to raise the minimum wage for workers in small businesses, Fulbright asserted that the bill was the work of northerners who wanted to offset the South's advantage in labor costs and thereby hinder its economic development. In 1948, when President Truman nominated a Pennsylvanian to a seat on the Federal Reserve System's Board of Governors that had previously been held by a southerner, Fulbright protested that he saw "the beginning of a determined effort on the part of the great financial institutions of the East to take over the control of our monetary and banking system." The 1960 Civil Rights Act was "part of a scheme to prescribe moral standards for human conduct toward a minority race. The North has arrogated unto itself the position of supervising human relations in the South." The proposed civil rights bill of 1964 was "designed to humiliate a proud and sensitive section of our country."

Sometimes Fulbright was more philosophical, attributing southern difficulties to the impersonal forces of history. In 1958, pleading for delays in integration and defending a policy of gradualism, Fulbright submitted a brief to the Supreme Court stating, "The whites and Negroes of Arkansas are equally prisoners of their environment," for they shared a pathology inherited from the experience of Negro slavery. A nearly identical theme was struck during debate on the 1964 civil rights bill. And Fulbright was ready to acknowledge the problems of the South. He probably made fewer references to his home state than is common, but when he did refer to Arkansas, it often was as an example of southern economic troubles, whether inadequate spending for public education or the persistence of poverty. Fulbright also, of course, could speak of the South with pride, praising twentieth-century achievements in arts and letters and extolling developments that made the South the nation's "new economic frontier."[34]

Fulbright's long Senate tenure is at least partly attributable to the one-party system of the Solid South. Within the Senate, however, his success depended very little on his southern ties, and it

34. *Congressional Record*, 81st Cong., 1st Sess., 12569–71, 80th Cong., 2nd Sess., 4319, 86th Cong., 2nd Sess., 7732, 88th Cong., 2nd Sess., 5636, 81st Cong., 1st Sess., 5593, 88th Cong., 2nd Sess., 16762, 87th Cong., 1st Sess., 11403, 84th Cong., 2nd Sess., 6625.

may well be for this reason that his appeals to regional pride or loyalty are relatively infrequent. With the exception of the civil rights issue during the period from 1956 to 1964, Fulbright was not an active spokesman for southern interests. The references to the South that emerge in his public statements were more often examples or analogies, drawing on the southern experience to make a broader point rather than arguing directly in the South's behalf.

Not particularly dependent on ties to the region, Fulbright may have been relatively insensitive to changes occurring across the South in the early 1970s. Widespread economic development had brought in its wake a group of governors who sought to transcend the race issue altogether by offering an appealing vision of a bright future under enlightened leadership. This vision sought to remove what C. Vann Woodward has called "the burden of southern history"[35] and to overcome the traditional southern pessimism about the prospects for improving the human condition through public action. When the economic signs are positive, it is an attractive vision, and it was appealingly espoused in 1974 by Governor Bumpers of Arkansas.

Ervin of North Carolina: The Lawyer as Storyteller

Civil Rights

Besides his service on the McCarthy investigating committee, Sam Ervin first developed a Senate reputation for his opposition to civil rights laws. He was even more vocal than was Fulbright. He signed the Southern Manifesto of 1956, participated in the filibusters of 1957 and 1960, and spoke against both the Civil Rights Act of 1964 and the Voting Rights Act of 1965. Like Fulbright's arguments, however, Ervin's took a slightly unusual direction and eschewed overt racism. Whereas the Arkansan had grounded his opposition to civil rights laws in faith in the gradual contribution of education, the Tarheel grounded his in the sanctity of the Constitution.

35. C. Vann Woodward, *The Burden of Southern History* (Rev. ed.; Baton Rouge, 1968); John D. Saxon, "Contemporary Southern Oratory: A Rhetoric of Hope, Not Desperation," *Southern Speech Communication Journal*, XL (1975), 262–74.

To be sure, particularly in his earlier years Ervin defended segregation. In a 1955 interview, he insisted that "men segregate themselves in society according to race in obedience to a basic natural law, which decrees that like shall seek like." In the same interview, denying that integration was a religious imperative, Ervin explained, "Although He knew both Jews and Samaritans and the relations existing between them, Christ did not advocate that courts or legislative bodies should compel them to mix socially against their will." Explicit defenses of segregation were rare, however, and Ervin specifically proclaimed that his opposition to civil rights was not prompted by racism: "I have no prejudice in my mind or heart against any man because of his race. I love men of all races. After all, they are my fellow travelers to the tomb." And, in a more expansive moment, he declared, "My stand is unequivocal. No man should be denied the right to vote on account of race; no man should be denied the right to seek and hold any job, the right to live by the sweat of his own brow; no man should be denied the right to have a fair and impartial trial by a jury of his peers; no man should be denied the right to a decent education or to enjoy any other basic human right." [36]

But the proposed laws were never the proper means to secure these rights, Ervin argued, because they did violence to the Constitution. This constitutional grounding for his objections made him what one writer described as the "most formidable obstacle" to the passage of civil rights laws. The North Carolinian based his position on a strict interpretation of the document he regarded as "the finest thing to come from the mind of man" and the nation's only bulwark against tyranny. In 1957 he explained, "I oppose the civil rights bill simply because I love our constitutional and legal systems, and desire above all things to preserve them for the benefit of all Americans of all races and all generations." He opposed the 1965 Voting Rights Act on the grounds that Article I, Section 2, of the Constitution explicitly gave to the states the power to determine qualifications for voting. He was an early and

36. "Compulsory Integration is 'Fundamentally Wrong,'" *U.S. News & World Report*, November 18, 1955, pp. 90–91; *Congressional Record*, 90th Cong., 1st Sess., 24584; James M. Naughton, "Constitutional Ervin," *New York Times Magazine*, May 13, 1973, p. 85. I appreciate the assistance of Carol Miller-Tutzauer, Frank E. Tutzauer, and Cheryl M. Zeken in researching the speeches of Senator Ervin.

vocal opponent of mandatory busing, claiming that it violated the equal protection clause of the Fourteenth Amendment by treating people differently on the basis of race.

Sometimes Ervin's constitutional argument was based on a specific clause or amendment. More generally, he argued that the judiciary, in assuming an activist role, had defiled the Constitution and usurped the powers of the legislature and the people while forsaking its assigned function. Judicial activism was particularly serious—self-restraint was the only real check against abuse of power, which was not the case with the other two branches of government. Ervin was particularly concerned about a growing trend toward judicial activism. He defined "judicial activists" as "judges who undertake to amend the Constitution or the laws while professing to interpret them." Opposing Thurgood Marshall's nomination to the Supreme Court, Ervin explained, "The Founding Fathers intended that the Constitution should operate as an enduring instrument of government whose meaning could not be changed except by an amendment" and rebuked his critics by stating that "the contention to the contrary is necessarily founded on the assumption that George Washington and the other good and wise men who fashioned the Constitution were mendacious nitwits who did not mean what they said." [37]

In other words, laws or Court decisions not in keeping with the original intent of the Constitution were indefensible; the Constitution was not intended to be a changing document for changing times. Ervin always identified how civil rights measures did violence to the Constitution. He took special delight in arguing that the equal protection clause of the Fourteenth Amendment was being trampled upon, since this clause was widely used to *justify* civil rights and was especially popular among liberals. He stated that busing violated the clause in two different respects: all students were not permitted to attend their neighborhood schools, and this selection was made on the basis of race. Warming to his subject, he also declaimed, "The Supreme Court of the United

37. John Herbers, "Senator Ervin Thinks the Constitution Should Be Taken Like Mountain Whisky—Undiluted and Untaxed," *New York Times Magazine*, November 15, 1970, p. 107; E. W. Kenworthy, "Southern Attack on Vote Bill Fails," New York *Times*, May 7, 1965, p. 27; *Congressional Record*, 85th Cong., 1st Sess., 10992, 91st Cong., 2nd Sess., 3074, 3075, 3080, 90th Cong., 1st Sess., 24586.

States and other judges have piled so much judicial and intellectual rubbish on top of the equal-protection clause of the Constitution that you can't even see it anymore." An antibusing constitutional amendment, according to this view, would restore the true intent of the equal protection clause. Earlier, he had implied that the 1954 *Brown* decision itself jeopardized equal protection because it represented a "constitutional somersault," repudiating the interpretation of "due process" and "equal protection" approved for more than eighty years.[38]

Interestingly, however, Ervin's attack changed with time. Originally he had opposed both the *Brown* decision and the 1964 Civil Rights Act, but in the late 1960s and early 1970s he seemingly accepted both of these documents and drew on them to support his opposition to busing. The 1954 decision, he claimed, had been interpreted "to give each child the right not to be excluded from any school operated by a State for which he is otherwise eligible on the basis of race." This very ruling, he charged, was now being distorted by *requiring* that children be assigned to schools on the basis of race. The Civil Rights Act of 1964, both in text and legislative history, was also cited as opposing busing, as was the Elementary and Secondary Education Act of 1965. When federal bureaucrats and judges ignored these laws and judicial decisions (most of which Ervin originally had opposed), they were violating the law, just as a murderer or a thief did.

The other major argument Ervin developed against civil rights laws was that they denied rights to some in order to extend them to others. Like Fulbright, he assumed that the "supply" of rights was finite, so that a zero-sum game was involved: to extend civil rights to blacks was to deprive others of their rights, and redistribution of rights was not the federal government's proper business. Ervin denounced the 1960 civil rights bill as "based on the strange thesis that the best way to promote the civil rights of some Americans is to rob other Americans of civil rights equally as precious and to reduce the supposedly sovereign States to meaningless zeros on the Nation's map." On another occasion, he said, "We will not fool history as we fool ourselves when we steal free-

38. "Invasion of Privacy—How Big a Threat?" *U.S. News & World Report*, March 6, 1972, p. 45; "Compulsory Integration is 'Fundamentally Wrong,'" 95–96.

dom from one man to confer it on another." This line of argument enabled Ervin to deny any racist sentiment and to deplore violations of civil rights while effectively arguing that the proposed cure was worse than the disease. It would violate not only federal law but also the Constitution, permanently defiling the "greatest and most precious possession of the American people."[39]

It is worth noting that Ervin opposed the civil rights laws on precisely the same grounds that another southern politician appealed for *support*. Lyndon Johnson, knowing that white southerners despised civil rights but revered the Constitution, tried to reconcile them by arguing that the laws were but the fulfillment of a constitutional obligation. He employed this argument in campaigning in the South in 1964.[40] And, as if to preempt Ervin's approach, Johnson, in his March, 1965, speech appealing for the Voting Rights Act, stated that there was no constitutional issue because the command of the Constitution was plain.

The Constitutional Appeal

It was not only with respect to civil rights that Ervin appealed to the Constitution. Throughout his Senate career, his appeal to constitutional procedure was paramount, the key value in his hierarchy as was education in Fulbright's. The constitutional appeal unified Ervin's seemingly diverse positions on a range of issues.

Ervin assumed that "since the Constitution is a written instrument, its meaning does not change, unless its wording is altered by an amendment adopted in the manner prescribed by article V." From this assumption, it followed that the duty of the judge was to discern the true intent of the framers of the document and then to apply that intent to the case at hand. To do otherwise was, as Ervin put it, "merely [to] seek ostensible reasons to justify disobedience to the Constitution's commands and evasion of its prohibitions."

Ervin was a strict constructionist as to the ends permitted by

39. *Congressional Record*, 91st Cong., 2nd Sess., 3079–80, 85th Cong., 1st Sess., 10992; Naughton, "Constitutional Ervin," 85.
40. See Eric F. Goldman, *The Tragedy of Lyndon Johnson* (New York, 1969), 244; David Zarefsky, "Subordinating the Civil Rights Issue: Lyndon Johnson in 1964," *Southern Speech Communication Journal*, XLVIII (1983), 103–18.

the Constitution, but he construed broadly the means by which the goals might appropriately be achieved. Referring to what he called "the cliché that the Supreme Court should interpret the Constitution with flexibility," he indicated that if users of this cliché meant "that a provision of the Constitution should be interpreted with liberality to accomplish its intended purpose," they would discover him "in hearty agreement with them." So, for example, when the Nixon administration sought to subpoena an aide to Alaska Senator Mike Gravel to testify about the release of the Pentagon Papers, Ervin insisted that this act was an affront to the constitutionally protected freedom of speech and debate in the Senate. Ervin noted that the privilege is explicitly mentioned in the Constitution and that "the Supreme Court each time it considered the subject, has taken pains to state how broad is the privilege." Certainly, he thought, it should be construed broadly enough to encompass a senatorial aide. But that was quite a different matter from reading into the Constitution goals and objectives not explicitly provided there. Several implications follow from Ervin's belief that the meaning of the Constitution is clear. First, it becomes apparent why he objected to judicial activism: in the guise of interpretation, judges are actually rewriting the law, usurping the function of the legislature. In the wake of the 1966 decision in *Miranda* v. *Arizona*, Ervin made the distinction between courts and legislatures clear. "While Congress and State legislatures may enact statutes . . . which enlarge the right of an individual to have the assistance of counsel," he said in a Senate speech, "the Supreme Court is powerless to add to or take from the scope of the constitutional right . . . as such right is defined in the sixth amendment." Since that definition was clear, what the Court was really doing in *Miranda* was attempting by judicial fiat to change the meaning of the Sixth Amendment. In another address, Ervin noted that since Article III of the Constitution mentions only the judicial power of the Supreme Court, it therefore "denies the Supreme Court policy-making power in plain and positive terms." When Thurgood Marshall was nominated for the Supreme Court, Ervin went so far as to say that he would vote against *any* judicial activist proposed for that tribunal.[41]

41. *Congressional Record*, 90th Cong., 1st Sess., 24584, 24589, 92nd Cong., 1st

Ervin had a clear view of the motives of judicial activists. As he saw them, they "labor under the delusion that there was little, if any, wisdom on earth before their arrival. As a consequence, they lay the flattering unction to their souls that the amendments they usurp the power to make improve the Constitution and the laws." It was, he thought, a classic case of assuming that a noble end justifies ignoble means. Fortunately, for most of its history the United States had avoided the perils of judicial activism. But in the Warren Court, self-restraint was weakened. As Ervin explained, "Shortly before 1953, Supreme Court Justices began to substitute their personal notions for constitutional provisions." He singled out for criticism Chief Justice Warren and Justices Douglas, Brennan, Goldberg, Fortas, and Marshall, but added that Justice Black also "often aligned himself with the Justices of the Warren Court" and that even some of the other justices "joined the Warren Court on some occasions in handing down revolutionary decisions inconsistent with the words and history" of the Constitution.

There was a second implication of Ervin's belief that the meaning of the Constitution is clear: Proposed amendments also should be unambiguous. This belief, in large part, explained his strong opposition to the Equal Rights Amendment. He occasionally justified his anti-ERA position by reference to biological differences between the sexes and to the belief that women should not be drafted into the armed forces, but his most fundamental objection was that the measure was ambiguous. As he put it, "The House-passed equal rights amendment is shrouded in obscurity, and no one has sufficient prophetic power to predict with accuracy what interpretation the Supreme Court will place upon it." If the ERA were construed as desired by its most forceful advocates, the result would be "to nullify every law making any distinction between men and women no matter how reasonable such distinction may be." In fact, Ervin insisted, women would lose essential existing protections if the ERA were passed. He thought that such a course would be particularly unwise, since other existing laws

---

Sess., 20171, 20172 ("The Role of the Supreme Court: Policymaker or Adjudicator?" Walter F. George School of Law address, Mercer University, April 30, 1971), 92nd Cong., 1st Sess., 32446, 89th Cong., 2nd Sess., 21040.

and court decisions amply protected the interests of women far better than would the proposed ERA.[42]

Third, the belief that the Constitution's meaning is plain implies that the document must be construed according to the context in which the Founding Fathers drafted it. That context was one of suspicion of a strong government. From this premise Ervin inferred many of the libertarian conclusions he espoused. For example, in opposing the 1970 District of Columbia crime bill, Ervin attributed to the Founding Fathers "the abiding conviction that the supreme value of civilization is the freedom of the individual," which Ervin defined as "simply the right of the individual to be free from governmental tyranny." The context of the Founding Fathers is the one that should govern contemporary deliberation as well. Similarly, he opposed federal data banks in the belief that they would threaten "the protection and encouragement" of the people's participation in politics, a central objective of the First Amendment. Opposing preventive detention of suspected criminals, Ervin was explicit in his balancing: "Would it not be better for a few narcotic peddlers or a few narcotic addicts or a few criminals to escape justice than to destroy the proud boast of American law that every man's home is his castle?" The boast was so proud, Ervin might have added, because of the historical circumstances out of which it grew—a context to which we are obliged to defer in attempting to discern the Constitution's meaning.

Ervin noted that proposals which have the effect of abridging individual freedom are typically justified by the claim that circumstances make them necessary. The Tarheel senator was unimpressed by this defense and he always responded to it the same way. He quoted William Pitt in the House of Commons in 1783: "Necessity is the plea for every infringement of human freedom. It is the argument of tyrants. It is the creed of slaves."[43] And if

42. *Congressional Record*, 91st Cong., 2nd Sess., 3075, 92nd Cong., 1st Sess., 20171–72; "Invasion of Privacy," 45; Naughton, "Constitutional Ervin," 85; "Should Congress Approve the 'Equal Rights Amendment'?" *Congressional Digest*, L (January, 1971), 13.

43. "Is the Present Scope of Collecting Data on Private Individuals Necessary to the National Interest?" *Congressional Digest*, L (October, 1971), 233; *Congressional Record*, 91st Cong., 2nd Sess., 24837, 25444.

necessity were not sufficient grounds for restricting individual freedom, certainly social desirability was no grounds at all. Any restriction on individual freedom should be scrutinized carefully, Ervin argued, because of its potential for infringing on the freedom explicitly protected by the framers of the Constitution. Among his objections to a proposal to create federal data banks was his contention that they would have a chilling effect on freedom of expression. He regretted that "no longer can a man march with a sign down Pennsylvania Avenue and then return to his hometown, his identity forgotten, if not his cause"; that "no longer are the flamboyant words exchanged in debate allowed to echo into the past and lose their relevance with the issue of the moment which prompted them." Similarly, opposing political surveillance of American citizens by the government, Ervin again emphasized the chilling effect: "The knowledge of a citizen that he may be under surveillance makes him very chary about exercising his freedom of speech or assembly, especially if he deviates in his thinking." Elaborating on the dangers of political surveillance, he said, "This has all the trappings of a police state in its worst form. We are in an era where fundamental liberties are very much imperiled."[44]

The experience of the Founding Fathers was one of conflict with the overreaching powers of a strong central government. To avoid such a danger, they divided powers between the federal and state governments and then further separated them among the three branches of the federal government. Ervin was sensitive to the need to preserve this careful balance, and he saw the greatest threat to the equilibrium in the central government itself. As John Herbers wrote in 1970, "To this day, Sam Ervin knows one source of tyranny—the central government. . . . On almost every issue, he is on the side against giving more power to the Federal Government." Ervin's antipathy for a strong central government, Herbers explained, stemmed "from the stubborn pride of the mountain people and a reverence for the Constitution in its original form." And within the federal government Ervin was most concerned

44. "Is the Present Scope of Collecting Data on Private Individuals Necessary?," 233; James K. Batten, "Sam Ervin and the Privacy Invaders," *New Republic*, May 8, 1971, pp. 22, 19.

about the Supreme Court because of the difficulty of checking it against abuse. As he explained, the Warren Court had "impeded the President and his subordinates," had "undertaken to [abridge or to] stretch the legislative powers of Congress," and had "invoked the due process and equal protection clauses of the Fourteenth Amendment as *carte blanche* to invalidate all State action which Supreme Court Justices think undesirable." When Ervin saw such rampant interference with individual freedom, it was no surprise that he should despair for the future of the Republic. Concluding one speech that resembled a jeremiad, he promised, "Despite their perilous state, the dream of the founding fathers can be rekindled and the precious right of the people to constitutional government can be preserved if those who possess the power will stretch forth saving hands while there is yet time."[45]

Since Ervin had attracted little public attention prior to 1973—for example, he had held only three press conferences in nineteen years—the underlying consistency of his position was not widely appreciated. It was known that he was an expert on constitutional law and that he somehow had managed to oppose civil rights while championing civil liberties. But Ervin had not changed, and the same consistent strict constructionism guided him as he chaired the Senate committee investigating Watergate. Then, of course, it was directed at the allegedly strict-constructionist president who viewed the Constitution expansively insofar as presidential power was concerned. For his part, Ervin steadfastly insisted on a hierarchy in which the Constitution stood above the president. Referring to the Nixon administration, he wrote, "They had forgotten, if they ever knew, that the Constitution is designed to be a law for rulers and people alike at all times and under all circumstances. . . . On the contrary, they apparently believed that the President is above the Constitution." Ervin added, "I . . . reject this doctrine of the Constitutional omnipotence of the President."[46]

45. Herbers, "Undiluted and Untaxed," 112; *Congressional Record*, 92nd Cong., 1st Sess., 20172.

46. "Individual Views of Senators of the Select Committee," *The Final Report of the Select Committee on Presidential Campaign Activities*, 93rd Cong., 2nd Sess., No. 93–981, p. 1102.

When Nixon invoked the doctrine of executive privilege to prevent his aides from testifying, Ervin derided the notion as "executive poppycock" and asserted, "It's akin to the divine right of kings, which passed out of existence in America in the Revolution." When Nixon softened his claim to an absolute executive privilege, Ervin regarded it as "a victory for constitutional government in America." And he developed his constitutional theory in personal terms during his opening statement at the Senate hearings: "If the many allegations made to this date are true, then the burglars who broke into the headquarters of the Democratic National Committee at the Watergate were in effect breaking into the home of every citizen of the United States."

As was consistent with his belief about the Constitution, however, Ervin did not view the Watergate hearings as essentially political; he was not engaging in a witch-hunt against the administration. To the contrary, he had been selected to chair the special committee in part because it was widely known that he would not hesitate to support a Republican president if he thought him right. Indeed, Ervin began the investigation in the hope and belief that Nixon would be exonerated, and he appealed to his own judicial experience to assure the Senate of his impartiality: "I have no prejudgments about any of the activities connected with the matter; and I am sure that, by reason of my judicial experiences, anything I have read or heard in connection with these matters can be laid aside and that I can reach my conclusions solely upon the basis of what the evidence, in my judgment, discloses."[47] Although Nixon later maintained that he was driven from the presidency by partisan vindictiveness aided by the press, this charge was never made against Ervin's handling of the Senate special committee.

Ervin's Rhetorical Method

When Ervin became a celebrity during the Watergate investigations, however, it probably was less because of his closely reasoned constitutional theories than because of his distinctive rhe-

47. Ervin, *The Whole Truth*, xi, 36, 93; "Ervin's Opening Statement: Why the Senate is Investigating Watergate," *U.S. News & World Report*, May 28, 1973, p. 106; *Congressional Record*, 93rd Cong., 1st Sess., 3551.

torical method. Ervin actually was a blend of two personas, the legal scholar and the mountain storyteller.

Like Fulbright, Ervin employed a didactic form of address. Whereas the Arkansan taught world politics, the North Carolinian lectured about constitutional law. Fulbright's didacticism was that of the scholar, constantly questioning his premises and reopening the inquiry. Ervin's was that of the lawyer, making the best case he could for a position he never really questioned. Ervin articulated legal principles, traced them through the nation's history, and applied them to the situation at hand. At the outset of a speech he often previewed the issues he would develop. For example, speaking against the Equal Rights Amendment, he said, "Any rational consideration of the advisability of adopting the House-passed equal rights amendment raises these questions," and then enumerated the traditional *topoi* of ill, blame, and cure. In his final statement on Watergate, Ervin proposed to "ask and endeavor to answer these questions: What was Watergate? Why was Watergate? Is there an antidote which will prevent future Watergates? If so, what is that antidote?"[48] These questions then formed the organizing principles for his report.

Ervin also evidenced the lawyer's respect for precedent and history. He decried the 1954 *Brown* decision as a "constitutional somersault" in part because it overturned a long-standing precedent. He complained that the doctrine of *stare decisis* became a nullity at the hands of judicial activists. And he frequently harked back to the Founding Fathers to support his arguments. Speaking against the 1957 Civil Rights Act, he recited the circumstances that led the Constitution's framers to oppose grants of excessive power to the executive and to insist on the right to a jury trial. In opposing an amendment to reinstate prayer in public schools, he described the colonial experience of religious persecution and the framers' intended meaning of the "establishment of religion" clause in the First Amendment. To justify his opposition to Thurgood Marshall's nomination to the Supreme Court, Ervin explored the founders'

48. "Should Congress Approve the 'Equal Rights Amendment'?," 11; "Individual Views of Senators of the Select Committee," 1097. For a discussion of these *topoi*, see Lee S. Hultzén, "Status in Deliberative Analysis," in Donald C. Bryant (ed.), *The Rhetorical Idiom* (1958; rpr. New York, 1966), 97–123.

desire to limit the judicial power to interpretation rather than law making. When the issue was the no-knock provision in the District of Columbia crime bill—giving officers investigating drug cases the right to enter a dwelling unannounced—Ervin told of the experience of James Otis and the campaign against general search warrants.

Sometimes these references to history were brief and general. Introducing the Watergate hearings, Ervin referred simply to the Founding Fathers' distrust of tyranny. And during the 1957 Civil Rights Act debate, he referred obliquely to "the primary lesson taught by history, that is, that no man is fit to be trusted with unlimited governmental power." On other occasions, however, his historical discussions were extensive, filling pages of text and citing specific individuals, incidents, court cases, and decisions. These discussions, across the topics Ervin addressed, resemble a basic treatise in constitutional law. Although Ervin occasionally used relatively recent evidence, such as opinions of Supreme Court Justices George Sutherland and Robert H. Jackson, the preponderance of his references were to the era of the Revolution. This preference may reflect his own fondness for the eighteenth century—one of *Time*'s writers called Ervin "the last of the founding fathers."[49] A more basic explanation, however, is that Ervin was practicing the lawyer's craft of determining meaning by examining legislative history, and the legislative history of the Constitution obviously was to be found at the time of its creation.

Ervin also demonstrated his legal training in his skillful refutation. Reflecting an eighteenth-century world view, he was by nature suspicious of men's motives, and from this basic suspiciousness emerged one of his most frequently used devices, the thin entering wedge. This form of argument asserts that a particular action which might seem innocuous is in reality but a foot in the door, the first step toward a grander and more sinister design. Speaking on civil rights, Ervin insisted that the appetites of bu-

49. "Compulsory Integration is 'Fundamentally Wrong,'" 95; *Congressional Record*, 90th Cong., 1st Sess., 24585, 24586, 24587, 85th Cong., 1st Sess., 10992, 10993, 89th Cong., 2nd Sess., 23123–28, 91st Cong., 2nd Sess., 1162–63, 25445; "Ervin's Opening Statement," 106; "Defying Nixon's Reach for Power," *Time*, April 16, 1973, p. 11. The remark was attributed to *Time*'s congressional correspondent Neil MacNeil.

reaucrats and judicial activists would not be sated on the South. Taking a position similar to Fulbright's, in 1957 he said "to my friends who champion the bill": "If these provisions can be used today to make legal pariahs and second-class litigants out of southerners involved in civil rights cases, they can be used with equal facility tomorrow to reduce other Americans involved in countless other cases to the like status." In 1970 he was even more explicit: "When the judicial activists and crusading bureaucrats reduce the South to a state of vassalage, they will not sit down like Alexander the Great and weep because they can find no other worlds to conquer. They will turn their attention to the North, the East, and the West, take over and exercise the functions of their school boards."[50] This thin entering wedge was credible to Ervin precisely because of his abiding suspicion of human nature and motives, which only laws strictly interpreted could hold in check.

The other major method of refutation at which Ervin excelled was "turning the tables," making an adversary uncomfortable by using his own arguments against him. Such a maneuver accomplishes what Henry Johnstone defines as the purpose of the *ad hominem* argument: refuting an opponent by demonstrating that his position leads to contradictory or self-defeating results.[51] For that reason, it is a particularly difficult form of argument to rebut.

Ervin characterized the 1957 Civil Rights Act, which permitted the attorney general to seek injunctive relief, as "government by injunction"—the very phrase many of the bill's *supporters* had employed during the 1930s to oppose the use of the injunction against labor unions. He described busing as a violation of the equal protection clause, precisely that aspect of the Constitution used in 1954 to overturn school segregation. In another example, responding to senators who thought judges could predict which suspects should be preventively detained, Ervin pointed out that it was impossible to predict even how senators would vote on the bill, since it was paradoxically supported by the liberal Senator Joseph Tydings and opposed by the conservative Senator Ervin. Finally, in the discussion of the Pentagon Papers, Ervin derided the seem-

50. *Congressional Record,* 85th Cong., 1st Sess., 10992, 91st Cong., 2nd Sess., 3081.
51. See Henry W. Johnstone, Jr., *Philosophy and Argument* (University Park, Pa., 1959), Chap. 6.

ingly strict-constructionist Nixon administration for broadly con-
struing executive privilege while at the same time ignoring the legislative privilege explicitly identified in the Constitution itself.[52]

When Fulbright lectured, he was sometimes thought esoteric
and too removed from the people. With Ervin, it was different: his
exposition of constitutional law was leavened by anecdotes from
his native state, folksy analogies, and quotations from the Bible,
history, and poetry. The second aspect of his persona, the raconteur, complemented his legalistic exposition.

Ervin frequently developed his arguments by anecdote. During
the McCarthy investigation he lightened the mood with the tale of
old Uncle Ephraim, tortured by arthritis, who was "bent double
as he sat in church one Sunday. The mountain preacher asked
various members of the congregation what the Lord had done for
them." After all but Eph replied, the preacher asked him directly.
Then "croaked Uncle Eph: 'Brother, he has mighty nigh ruint
me.'" That, Ervin concluded, was what McCarthy had done to the
Senate. On another occasion he explained his belief that the Supreme Court was rewriting the Constitution by telling the tale of a
Louisiana lawyer who thought he had lost a case because he failed
to wear a necktie and told the judge, "That reason would have
been far better than any reason you give in your opinion, in deciding the case against my client." He told the story of Job Hicks who
had assaulted an incompetent preacher, of "Jim" who had been
killed accidentally in a railroad accident, and of a nineteenth-
century Carolina preacher who tried to invoke the gospel against
women wearing their hair in topknots.[53]

The relevance of the anecdotes was sometimes tenuous and the
moral ambiguous. Herbers wrote that "many of his stories are not
very funny . . . but Ervin tells them with such relish—his eyes
dancing and a wide grin on his face—that everyone usually
laughs." But even in print some of the anecdotes raise a chuckle.
In his book on Watergate, Ervin relates his experience with a late-

52. *Congressional Record*, 85th Cong., 1st Sess., 11001, 91st Cong., 2nd Sess.,
3073, 3074, 25444, 92nd Cong., 1st Sess., 32448.

53. *Time*, June 1, 1962, p. 20; *Congressional Record*, 86th Cong., 2nd Sess., 4515–
16; Russell Baker, "A New Raconteur Reigns in Senate," New York *Times*, May 13,
1956, p. 61.

night caller from Kentucky who claimed to have personal revelations from the Lord. The man asked that he be called as the Watergate committee's first witness, as the Almighty Lord instructed. Ervin "advised him I hated to disobey the Almighty's instruction, and we'd be delighted to welcome the Almighty as the lead-off witness, but we couldn't permit the informant to enact the role because he didn't know anything about Watergate except what the Almighty had told him and somebody might object to his testimony because it was hearsay."

These anecdotes did more than break tension. For the very reason that they were entertaining and disarming, they often enabled Ervin to prove a thesis far more conclusively by indirection. People laughed at the stories, they thought well of the storyteller, and they generalized this feeling to the storyteller's propositions. As Ervin himself put it in reply to one interviewer, "Ah have always found if you got a good stowry that sort of fits things, a good stowry is worth an hour of argument."[54]

Ervin was seldom without a "stowry," having learned so many in his youth while apprenticing with his father. Sometimes, however, instead of an anecdote, he would tell a true story, developing his case for or against a position on the basis of how it had affected one of his constituents. Opposing lie detector tests, he read letters from citizens describing the indignities to which they had been subjected during polygraph examinations required of prospective government employees. On another occasion, he read a letter from a father in Raleigh as evidence of the absurdity of forced busing. It is unlikely that these illustrative examples were typical, but in their unusual nature they provided the same "perspective by incongruity" afforded by an apt anecdote.

Ervin's folksy image was also achieved through his liberal use of simple analogies. The District of Columbia crime bill "was just as full of injustices and unconstitutional provisions as a mangy hound dog is of fleas." Relying on the Equal Rights Amendment to remove obviously discriminatory laws from the statute books was "about as wise as using an atomic bomb to exterminate a few mice." School boards complying with busing orders were required

54. Herbers, "Undiluted and Untaxed," 120; Ervin, *The Whole Truth*, 123; Naughton, "Constitutional Ervin," 86.

to "herd their children around like cattle and shift them about like pawns in a chess game."[55]

Ervin was also a storehouse of quotations, often recalled from years past. He quoted poetry, specializing in nineteenth-century mountain poets. Tennessee's Walter Malone wrote "To a Judge," which spoke of the duty to "judge thy fellow-travelers to the tomb," a line Ervin often repeated. He frequently quoted North Carolina poet Josiah Gilbert Holland's "The Day's Demand," with its opening line, "God give us men!" But Ervin's favorite poet, if frequency of quotation is a guide, was Rudyard Kipling. His poems were cited as inspirations to duty in the face of adversity. Supporting the antiballistic missile system, Ervin quoted "For All We Have and Are," which urged Britons to "stand up and take the war." Ervin drew the conclusion that "America must keep her heart in courage and patience and lift up her head in strength." Historical figures also were quoted, and again there were favorites. One was Daniel Webster's statement that "whatever government is not a government of laws is a despotism, let it be called what it may." Another was Webster's observation, "Good intentions will always be pleaded for every assumption of power. . . . There are men in all ages who mean to govern well, but they mean to govern. They promise to be good masters, but they mean to be masters." Yet another was Mark Twain's admonition, "Truth is precious. Use it sparingly," which Ervin repeatedly announced that he was going to disregard.[56]

And Ervin often quoted the Bible. He was regarded as an expert on the Scriptures as well as the Constitution, and he seemed to quote both sources with equal ease. Opposing the District of Columbia crime bill, he read from the fourth chapter of the prophet Micah. He took the seventeenth chapter of Luke as his text for a speech against busing. The ability of law enforcement officers to

---

55. *Congressional Record*, 92nd Cong., 1st Sess., 22005 ("Twentieth Century Witchcraft—The Lie Detector," Greensboro Bar Association address), 91st Cong., 2nd Sess., 3078, 3081, 24850; "Should Congress Approve the 'Equal Rights Amendment'?," 11.

56. Ervin, *The Whole Truth*, x, 30; "Individual Views of Senators of the Select Committee," 1103; "Ervin's Opening Statement," 106; *Congressional Record*, 91st Cong., 1st Sess., 22386, 92nd Cong., 1st Sess., 20170, 20172, 91st Cong., 2nd Sess., 3074, 3075, 90th Cong., 1st Sess., 24584, 90th Cong., 2nd Sess., 28571.

predict whether preventive detention was appropriate was ridiculed by allusion to the prophet Jeremiah. During the Watergate
hearings, Ervin made reference to the Bible. When he asked John
Ehrlichman about the parable of the good Samaritan and Ehrlichman replied, "I read the Bible, I don't quote it," Ervin probably
was thought by the television audience to have had the better of
the exchange.[57]

Ervin's style was what Richard Weaver would have called "spacious"; his language certainly was not compact. Rather than identify a man as dead, Ervin said he was "sleeping in the tongueless
silence of the dreamless dust." Rather than describe a conclusion
as obvious, he had it "as clear as the noonday sun in a cloudless
sky." Rather than refer to the indefinite future, he contended that
if the Nixon administration had its way, his committee would be
unable to discharge its task "until the last lingering echo of Gabri-
el's horn trembles into ultimate silence."[58]

Particularly when discussing civil rights, Ervin indulged in
hyperbole. The 1957 civil rights bill was "a queer concoction of
constitutional and legal sins" and "as drastic and indefensible a
legislative proposal as was ever submitted to a legislative body
in this country." Its consequence would be to reduce southerners
"to a constitutional and legal status inferior to that of murderers,
rapists, robbers, thieves, smugglers, counterfeiters, dope peddlers, and parties to the Communist conspiracy." Over a decade
later, Ervin described busing as meaning that children "are being
made helpless and hapless subjects of a bureaucratic and judicial
tyranny."

The spaciousness of Ervin's rhetoric was also the result of repetition. Sometimes it was in successive phrases: "I love the Constitution. I love the Constitution with all my mind and all my heart.
I love the Constitution with all my mind and all my heart because
I know it was fashioned to secure to all Americans of all genera-

57. *Congressional Record*, 91st Cong., 2nd Sess., 3073, 24851, 25444; J. Anthony
Lukas, *Nightmare: The Underside of the Nixon Years* (New York, 1976), 386.
58. Weaver maintained that public discourse of the early nineteenth century
had this characteristic. See Richard Weaver, "The Spaciousness of Old Rhetoric,"
in his *The Ethics of Rhetoric* (Chicago, 1953), 164–85. "Individual Views of Senators
of the Select Committee," 1099; Ervin, *The Whole Truth*, 27; *Congressional Record*,
91st Cong., 2nd Sess., 1163, 3076, 25445.

tions the right to be ruled by a government of laws rather than by a government of men."[59] Sometimes within the same speech an idea, an example, or even a cliché would show up more than once. And often the same basic idea and even phrasing would recur from one speech to another.

Ervin and the South

In contrast to Fulbright, Sam Ervin seemed in many ways the stereotype of the southern politician. With Ervin in mind, New York *Times* columnist John Herbers wrote of "a filibustering, storytelling, legalizing Southerner of the older generation" with "white hair, heavy jowls and dark, bushy eyebrows which sweep up and down like a crow's wings as he . . . inveighes against some new tyranny that is threatening the foundations of the Republic." He was also humble and unpretentious—"just an old country lawyer," as he said of himself during the Watergate hearings. Like the fabled southern gentleman, he was courteous to a fault, and he was such a model of integrity that his critics hesitated to take him on.[60]

J. Anthony Lukas has described Ervin's reverence for the Constitution as "quintessentially southern." Perhaps so: the penchant for strict construction is obviously akin to the literalism that characterizes fundamentalist religion, particularly strong in the South. Furthermore, reverence for the original Constitution of 1787 calls to mind an aspect of the southern myth that sees the "golden age" in the past and denies that the course of history has been generally a path of progress. Indeed, the frequency with which Ervin willingly championed losing positions is reminiscent of the myth of the Lost Cause. And Ervin's overriding concern with constitutional procedure is not unlike traditional southern veneration for *stasis* in place—the same category of argument which would give the question of states' rights such great importance, and on which Fulbright also relied. While not conspicuously championing the cause of the South, and seldom even identifying himself as an ad-

59. *Congressional Record*, 85th Cong., 1st Sess., 10991, 10992, 10997, 91st Cong., 2nd Sess., 3073, 90th Cong., 1st Sess., 24591.
60. Herbers, "Undiluted and Untaxed," 51.

vocate for his region, Ervin no doubt reflected southern values and visions in his rhetoric.

For those who observed Ervin, his stylistic choices may have reinforced his stereotype as the southern politician who was spacious in expression but who could be bested in the thrust and parry of argument. Nixon's attorney, John Dean, purportedly had said that "Ervin, away from his staff, is not very much, and I think he might just give up the store himself and lock himself in." And Lukas surmised that "Ervin's drawling Tarheel accent, rustic mannerisms, cracker-barrel jaws, and eyebrows which flap like blackbirds' wings may have lulled the White House into believing he could be handled."[61] But anyone who so judged Ervin reckoned without his dual persona. He was *both* raconteur and lawyer, and—particularly as an antagonist or critic—he could be incisive.

Ervin did not vacillate or shift with the winds; with few exceptions his views during the 1970s were the same as those he expressed during the 1950s. How, then, did the segregationist of 1957 become the liberal folk hero of 1973? The answer probably is that liberals disliked strict constructionism when applied in the 1950s to civil rights but supported it in the 1970s when applied to presidential power. Perhaps the nature of the issues was different; perhaps it was simply a matter of whose ox was being gored. But Ervin was consistent throughout, grounding his arguments in his understanding of what the Constitution meant to those who wrote it. Rather than shifting with the times or the issue, he staked out his ground and held to it. His career bears out Richard Weaver's dictum that a man's method of argument is a truer index of his political philosophy than is his explicit profession of principles.[62] By that standard, Ervin clearly was a conservative.

Conclusion

This analysis of Fulbright and Ervin has focused primarily on the matter and manner of their argument. Although there are obvious differences between the two southern senators, there also are striking similarities. Both opposed civil rights, yet both eschewed

61. Lukas, *Nightmare*, 386.
62. Weaver, *The Ethics of Rhetoric*, 112.

racist appeals in so doing. Rather, they argued that however desirable the end, the means were wrong. They both contended that to grant new rights to some would of necessity impair the rights of others. They both spoke of the importance of proper procedure, they both opposed affirmative action, and they both believed that civil rights laws were but the first step in a campaign to deprive the people of their liberties. Both, however, left blacks in an impossible position, doomed by the senators' logic to await God's good time for an answer to their plight.

Fulbright spoke most often about foreign policy; Ervin, about constitutional procedure. Yet each was disposed to view current problems as lapses, departures from a norm and tradition he wished to restore. For Fulbright, the tradition was one of proportion between means and ends in foreign policy; for Ervin, it was a judiciary that confined itself to interpretation rather than law making. Each senator was able to characterize his interest as restoration of an older tradition.

Some methods of argument were shared by the senators. Both made frequent appeals to history, precedent, or experience. Both were adept at turning the tables on their opponents. Both invoked the procedural *stasis* and thereby preempted the substantive ones. And both argued as strict constructionists, a stance that gave their arguments the appearance of deduction as they took a seemingly certain general premise and applied it to the case at hand. Both were hard to classify as liberal or conservative; both were sometimes described as men of the eighteenth century.

Of course, an argumentative perspective necessarily offers an incomplete account of a rhetor's appeal; it focuses primarily on choices embodied in messages. Yet each man's Senate speeches were often heard by only a small number of his colleagues, and speeches outside the Senate were seldom widely reported. One might suggest that both men achieved their influence simply through the positions they occupied as chairmen of Senate committees at propitious times. There is something to such a suggestion, yet surely it is incomplete. Most committee chairmen achieve neither the prominence nor the influence of Fulbright and Ervin. Another factor is at work. Each man, while occupying the committee chair, emerged as a major critic of the president of the United States. Since conflict is the stuff of drama and "politics above all is drama," that fact alone might explain the prominence of these two southerners. But not their influence: the critic, lest he seem merely to be carping, must be able to appeal to an alternate vision of what could and should be. That vision is developed through public discourse, both in the identification of themes and in the recurrence of rhetorical choices.

Fulbright was most influential during the 1960s; Ervin, during the 1970s. There is much of chance in this difference, but it also may be important for the image each man projected of his native region. Particularly during the early 1960s, the South was on the defensive, largely because of the civil rights issue. It was appropriate, therefore, for Fulbright to de-emphasize his roots; if anything, to compensate for them with his urbane manner, his intellectual approach, and his concern for foreign affairs. By the early 1970s the South was again in favor. Commentators claimed to have found another "New South," and some even regarded the South as harbinger for the rest of the nation.[63] With such renewed interest in the region, Ervin's emergence—however coincidental—as a southern folk hero was also appropriate. It is hard to imagine Ervin attracting the same interest and support had he been on center stage ten years before, or to view Fulbright in the 1970s as still able to adopt one stance in Washington and another in Arkansas. The appeal of both Fulbright and Ervin, then, was a blend of the vision to which each appealed, the arguments and their manner of presentation, the role each occupied, the stance each took as a critic, and the appropriateness of the actor to the scene.

63. John Egerton, *The Americanization of Dixie; The Southernization of America* (New York, 1974).

The Rhetoric of States' Rights and White Supremacy

Harold Mixon

The concepts of states' rights and white supremacy have always played a key role in southern racial ideology. "States' rights" is a political construct that expresses the idea that under the United States Constitution certain powers are reserved exclusively to the states. Essentially a sociological concept, "white supremacy" asserts the superiority of the white race over the black race. Before the Civil War, southern advocates used the ideas to defend slavery in the region. After the Civil War, southerners turned to the same theories to bolster racial segregation.

In the mid-1950s, legal challenges threatened one of the South's most visible bastions of racial segregation. On Monday, May 17, 1954, the United States Supreme Court ruled in the case of *Brown* v. *Board of Education* that the South's dual system of schools for whites and blacks was unconstitutional, and one year later ordered the dismantling "with all deliberate speed" of segregated education in the region. The "Black Monday" decision, as it was first christened by Mississippi's United States congressman John Bell Williams, posed a major threat to racial segregation in the South. Carefully nurtured by southern tradition and provided the aura of legal sanction by the *Plessy* v. *Ferguson* decision in 1896, separate but equal schools symbolized racial segregation in Dixie.

Predictably, the threat produced an immediate response. Through legal maneuvers, attorneys for local school boards challenged the court order. The Ku Klux Klan spoke for the radical resisters. However, the most significant response was in the activities of the Citizens' Councils.

Born in the small Mississippi Delta town of Indianola, the Council movement developed largely from the efforts of a thirty-one-year-old plantation manager named Robert Patterson. Seven months before the fateful "Black Monday" decision, in November, 1953, Patterson, "having nothing better to do," attended a meeting at the local school. There he heard a speaker predict that the Supreme Court might soon order schools to integrate. Deeply disturbed by the prediction, the former Mississippi State University football star and army paratroop major began a letter-writing campaign aimed at generating resistance to desegregation. However, the attempt met with little success, and even after May 17, 1954, Patterson's efforts to mobilize his friends and neighbors generated no enthusiasm. He enlisted the support of D. H. Hawkins, who managed the town's cotton press. On July 11, 1954, fourteen men—a planter, a farmer, a dentist, the mayor, the sheriff, a lawyer, a gin operator, a farm implement dealer, two auto dealers, the town banker, a druggist, and a hardware dealer—met in Hawkins' home and established the first Citizens' Council. Patterson, who held membership card number one, was elected secretary. The banker became president and the city attorney vice-president, with Hawkins serving as treasurer.[1]

Through Council speeches and literature, a rhetoric of states' rights and white supremacy emerged which articulated southern opposition to school integration and, by extension, to any breach in racial separation. Representing middle-class white southerners, Council spokesmen developed the rhetorical strategies by which the South attempted to defend racial segregation.

I

Several excellent studies have examined in detail the history of the Citizens' Councils, and the purpose of the present essay is not to duplicate those efforts.[2] However, in order to understand the

1. John B. Martin, *The Deep South Says "Never"* (New York, 1957), 1–4.
2. See Numan V. Bartley, *The Rise of Massive Resistance: Race and Politics in the South During the 1950s* (Baton Rouge, 1969); Hodding Carter III, *The South Strikes Back* (Garden City, N.Y., 1959); Martin, *The Deep South Says "Never"*; Neil R.

rhetoric of Council discourse, it is important to understand the nature of the movement. That objective requires a brief look at the history of the movement.

Outside of Mississippi, the movement experienced diverse levels of success, never quite reaching the popularity achieved in the parent state. Next to Mississippi, perhaps most successful was Alabama, followed by Louisiana, South Carolina, and Virginia. Though never achieving elsewhere the intensity enjoyed in these five states, the Councils were active in varying degrees throughout the South. Perhaps most surprising was the case of Georgia, a Deep South state where the existence of a large black population would likely indicate a strong potential that Citizens' Councils would succeed. Yet in spite of prominent state officers and the support of Herman Talmadge, the Georgia group never won a large membership.

In the peripheral South, the movement likewise achieved mixed success. In North Carolina, Arkansas, Texas, Florida, and Tennessee, the Council attracted small memberships in local organizations. Its inability to enlist the support of either middle-class whites or the political leaders in the states' Black Belts contributed to its failure. Consequently, the white supremacists in those states failed to show significant membership.

A number of independent resistance organizations appeared across the South, most limited to one state. Such organizations emerged in Virginia, Georgia, North Carolina, Florida, and Tennessee. In most instances, these groups eventually coalesced with the developing Citizens' Councils, though in a few cases the local organizations continued to compete with the Councils. However, the most pervasive organized resistance movement was the Citizens' Councils, which by the end of 1955 had become the focus of white resistance to school desegregation.

The Councils launched impressive multimedia propaganda campaigns to promote the segregationist cause. Friendly stations aired radio tapes and television films. An extensive pamphlet campaign carried the segregation message in print all over the South. However, much of the resistance rhetoric took the form of

---

McMillen, *The Citizens' Council: Organized Resistance to the Second Reconstruction, 1954–64* (Urbana, 1971); Francis Wilhoit, *The Politics of Massive Resistance* (New York, 1973).

speeches. Leading political figures, such as George Wallace, Ross Barnett, John Bell Williams, and Lester Maddox, joined lesser-known persons in attacking the integrationists while urging the faithful on to even greater efforts in protecting southern racial separation.

From its beginning, the Council recognized the potential value of public discourse in spreading the segregationist gospel. Suggesting the importance the organization attached to persuasion, an early issue of *Citizens' Council* listed names and addresses of recommended speakers and urged interested groups to arrange for these individuals to speak in local communities.[3]

Two occasions provided special opportunities for speakers. One was the organizational meeting for a local Council. In August, 1956, *Citizens' Council* gave instructions for communities interested in establishing a Council. The procedure bears reviewing here, since it indicates a concern with enlisting the support of prestigious figures in the community and with structuring the setting for the organizational meeting in order to achieve maximum rhetorical impact.

One or two local leaders should call a meeting of fifteen to twenty community leaders; a state representative might be invited also. These men should discuss the advantages and disadvantages of a local organization. A temporary chairman should be selected and a steering and nominating committee appointed. A date should be set within two weeks for a large community meeting. The steering-nominating committee should publicize the meeting, prepare a charter and bylaws or articles of incorporation, and make nominations for a permanent chairman, a vice-chairman, a secretary, and a board of directors. In the latter case, "care should be taken to invite representatives of major business, agricultural, labor and industrial interests, as well as representatives of religious and social groups, to membership on the Board of Directors."[4] The order of business for the organizational meeting should be: an opening prayer, the temporary chairman's explanation of the initial meeting and the preparatory work of the steering committee, an address by a guest speaker, questions from the floor, and a vote on whether to organize. If the vote was favorable,

3. *Citizens' Council*, April, 1956, p. 2.
4. *Citizens' Council*, August, 1956, p. 4.

the charter and other documents prepared by the steering committee should be presented. Finally, the nominations for officers and the board of directors should be considered. The address by a guest speaker occupied a central place on the agenda, and its location indicated the importance of the address in creating support for the proposed Council.

A second occasion for persuasion was the mass meeting or rally sponsored by the Councils. Carefully staged, these rallies featured one or more speakers with known reputations for devotion to segregation. John B. Martin describes one such rally held at the Coliseum in Montgomery, Alabama, in 1956. His account is analyzed to demonstrate the emotional atmosphere that surrounded such occasions. The crowd in Montgomery was large and diverse. More than ten thousand people came "from everywhere" in "pickup trucks, old Fords, and Jaguars." The "well dressed" audience was distinctive in that persons from different backgrounds met on common ground to oppose racial integration. There were "millionaires," "farmers," men and women "with eager looks on their faces like people going to a Billy Graham revival." When they entered the Coliseum, "hundreds" of the participants demonstrated their commitment to racial segregation by stopping "at two long tables to sign up as Council members and put their money in cigar boxes and pick up literature."

The Montgomery meeting was a combination "pep rally and a political convention," with popcorn and the sounds of "Dixie." The mood of the meeting was skillfully orchestrated to enhance listeners' involvement. The Confederate flag was marched before the throng under "red, white and blue bunting." Among the crowd were "30 Alabama political leaders" and others from Georgia, including Sam Engelhardt, Robert Patterson, and Eugene Cook. The politicians pledged to "resist desegregation to the end." They praised "Alabama's courageous stand, and as each spoke he received a standing ovation and thunderous cheer." Senator James Eastland of Mississippi delivered "the main address," proclaiming: "Thank God the State of Alabama has started the offense; from this day, the direction is forward."[5]

One other speaking occasion should be mentioned. Council

5. Martin, The Deep South Says "Never," 40–41.

spokesmen were asked occasionally to speak to audiences outside the South. For the most part, these invitations came to speakers who achieved some degree of national recognition through media coverage of Council activities. For example, Governor George Wallace of Alabama and Judge Tom P. Brady of Mississippi addressed groups in California, and William J. Simmons, executive secretary of the Citizens' Councils of America, spoke in the Midwest and Northeast.

II

Council speakers came from a variety of backgrounds. Some were business and professional people who made themselves available to groups seeking speakers. As a service to Mississippi Councils, the April, 1956, *Citizens' Council* published the names and addresses of thirty-four Mississippians ready to speak at Council activities. On the list, four or five had achieved national or at least regional prominence as segregationists. The remaining individuals were four clergymen, five attorneys, five judges, and several businessmen, including bankers and industrialists. One professor of political science and two newspaper editors rounded out the cast. The publication suggested that these people were excellent representatives of the cause.

Always available were "professional" Councilors, men who held high office in their respective states. Robert Patterson, organizer of the first Citizens' Council at Indianola, Mississippi, traveled widely, in Mississippi and across Dixie, speaking at organizational meetings and mass rallies. William Simmons, the articulate executive secretary of the Mississippi Councils, frequently spoke at southern Council rallies as well as at meetings in other parts of the country. Other Council speakers emerged in neighboring states. Alabama produced Sam Engelhardt and Asa ("Ace") Carter, founders of rival Council organizations, who presented sharply contrasting styles, and Selma sheriff James Clark, who occasionally spoke outside his own state.

However, some of the best-known speakers were the political figures, who used the integration controversy to promote their own popularity. Alabama's George Wallace was much in demand, both in the South and outside the region. Mississippi's Ross Barnett and United States Senator James Eastland became featured speakers, as did South Carolina's Strom Thurmond and Mendel Rivers. In Georgia, Herman Talmadge and Lester Maddox attacked desegregation; in Louisiana, influential state senator William M. Reinach and Leander Perez, Sr., vehemently advocated racial separation.

Two men deserve special mention for their unique role in Council rhetoric. Mississippi's Tom Brady, born in New Orleans, was a graduate of the University of Mississippi Law School. Beginning his law practice in Brookhaven, Mississippi, he chaired the States' Rights Democratic party's speakers' bureau.[6] Early he became the primary spokesman for the emerging movement, and in his "Black Monday" speech, Brady laid down the principal lines of argument that later speakers followed.

A second figure, Carleton Putnam, is significant because of his efforts to enhance the intellectual respectability of the white supremacy arguments. Putnam's credentials were ideally suited to the image the Council wished to project. He was born in New York City and was a graduate of Princeton University and the Columbia Law School. In 1932, in the depths of the depression, he started Pacific Seaboard Air Lines, which eventually merged with Delta Air Lines, and Putnam became chairman of the board. He was widely known and respected as a businessman.[7] Because of his background, Putnam could hardly be cast in the role of the stereotyped provincial southerner with respect to his racial views.

In addition, Putnam brought academic credentials to his role as Council spokesman. In 1948 he began a biography of Theodore Roosevelt, the first volume of which appeared in 1958 and was acclaimed by reviewers and professional historians alike. His letters to the president of the United States and the attorney general regarding the racial question were published and widely distributed. The resulting popular interest led him to write *Race and Reason*, the definitive statement of prosegregation ideology, articulating virtually every argument that supported the "scientific"

6. McMillen, *The Citizens' Council*, 17.
7. W. D. McCain, "Who Is Carleton Putnam?" *Citizen*, November, 1961, pp. 9–11.

claims of white racial superiority. Putnam was also much in demand as a speaker.

Newspaper accounts provide relatively little information about how these speakers performed on the platform. Reporters focused on the size of the audience, excerpts and summaries of the speeches, and indications of audience response. Of the thirty-seven speeches by sixteen speakers located for this study, the majority were given by the better-known figures, such as James Eastland, John Bell Williams, Ross Barnett, Tom Brady, and George Wallace. Perhaps what the critic most misses is a record of what local people said in local meetings—their remarks were not afforded press coverage and are consequently lost. The speech texts that are available convey an impression of sameness, repeating the basic ideas and supporting materials. Indeed, numerous references scattered throughout issues of *Citizen*, the official Council publication, suggest that followers were encouraged to use outlines and materials supplied by the central organization. This uniformity facilitates generalizations about the rhetorical strategies of the speakers.

III

In analyzing the discourse produced by the segregationists, we must understand the assumptions that both speakers and audiences brought to the speaking occasions. Generalizing about those assumptions, a 1971 study concluded that by the 1950s, "the burden of proof of Negro inferiority had gradually shifted from the black man to the white racists themselves."[8] In the same vein, other writers have suggested that in the 1954 desegregation crisis, segregationist leaders faced audiences skeptical of the traditional arguments in support of white supremacy. This skepticism is held to stem in part from experiences of southerners in the military and in educational institutions outside the South that had eroded long-held southern racial stereotypes.[9]

However, there is evidence to suggest that such a view is overly

8. McMillen, *The Citizens' Council*, 163–64.
9. For example, James McBride Dabbs, *Who Speaks For The South?* (New York, 1964), 319ff.

optimistic. In the mid-1950s, aspiring gubernatorial candidates in the South recognized a powerful political issue when they saw it, and many rode white supremacy to governorships in southern states.[10] The saliency of the racial issue at the time is underscored by the oft-quoted remark Wallace allegedly made after his defeat in a gubernatorial race by a hard-line segregationist: "No one is ever going to out-nigger me again."

Many audiences adhered to the mythology of white supremacy that was fashioned in the antebellum South and that enjoyed an unbroken succession through Reconstruction down to the *Brown* decision. Thus, the segregationist speakers often addressed friendly listeners. In the discourse examined for this study, speakers repeatedly identified apathy as the cause of the region's racial problems. In other words, citizens were not as active as they should have been in the resistance movement. Therefore the task of prosegregation advocates can best be described as reinforcing existing beliefs and opinions rather than changing them.

The distinction is important. Discourse that reinforces existing beliefs and attitudes can effectively use techniques that go beyond traditional forms of argument. By *argument* is usually meant the introduction of evidence and reasoning to support a position. However, if the speaker can assume a basic agreement by listeners with his fundamental premises, then he can use, without "proving" them, the premises in a variety of ways. A highly connotative word or a single dramatic example can carry the speaker's point, though those supporting materials would fail the test of rigorous argumentation. This concept is useful in both understanding and evaluating the strategies of Council rhetoric.

Six strategies characterize the segregationists' discourse. First, the speakers tried to eliminate negative attitudes about the new organization. Second, they sought to advance the basic doctrine of white supremacy. Third, they defended the right of states to maintain segregated schools. Fourth, they attempted to legitimize segregation by appeals to religion and revered historical figures. Fifth, they employed techniques that praised defenders of segregation while attacking the character of the integrationists. This

---

10. Earl Black, *Southern Governors and Civil Rights* (Cambridge, Mass., 1976), *passim*.

aroused the emotions of their listeners. And sixth, the speakers promoted the Councils' stand outside the South.

John B. Martin asserted that the Councils had "a terrible yearning for respectability." On one hand, the leaders apparently felt that success depended on the support of the white middle class. In this assumption they were undoubtedly correct, for most historians agree that the Council failed in the peripheral South, and even in Georgia, because it could not enlist large-scale middle-class support.[11] On the other hand, organizers were anxious to avoid the stigma of racial hatred and other excesses identified with more radical movements such as the Ku Klux Klan. The two objectives were interrelated, since identification with the radicals would undoubtedly have cost the Council substantial white middle-class support.

To achieve these goals, Council leaders carefully planned organizational meetings and rallies to promote respectability. As noted earlier, organizers were urged to gain support from community leaders such as physicians, lawyers, prominent businessmen (especially bankers), and clergy. Such leaders appeared on the platform at organizational meetings and rallies in the hope that their presence would help create the image of an organization devoted to preserving traditional, conservative values by peaceful, legal means. To further the aura of respectability, organizers chose to meet in schools, city halls, or churches.

Continuing the efforts to build respectability, segregation speakers insisted they were not acting out of race hatred. On the contrary, they claimed the South had shown deep concern for blacks. Judge Tom Brady told his audiences that the South had shown "a great deal of genuine affection and understanding between the races." He asserted that the region had cared for, provided for, and educated the black man, who, though paying only 12 percent of the taxes, shared equally in the benefits provided by taxation. He concluded that blacks have become wealthy and well educated in the South, and "it is only in the social sphere that the barrier is raised."[12]

11. Martin, *The Deep South Says "Never,"* 15; McMillen, *The Citizens' Council,* 85–115.

12. Thomas Pickens Brady, "Segregation and the South," in Ernest Wrage and Barnett Baskerville (eds.), *Contemporary Forum* (New York, 1962), 335.

To reinforce further the respectability of the movement, speakers tried to dissociate the Council from more radical resisters, especially the Ku Klux Klan. Judge Brady told a Mississippi audience, "None of you men look like Ku Kluxers to me. I wouldn't join a Ku Klux—I didn't join it—because they hid their faces; because they did things you and I wouldn't approve of." Stressing the commitment of the Council to nonviolent, legal means of resistance, the same speaker informed another audience: "We have no Ku Klux Klan in Mississippi, and we want none. The Klan is negligible in the South."[13]

Whether in fact the Council maintained this separation from the Klan is open to question. There is reason to believe that some, like Brady, were sincere in their protestations. However, some Councilors, such as Ace Carter in Alabama, had been leaders in the Klan prior to their involvement in the Councils, and at the local level some individuals undoubtedly maintained membership in both organizations. On occasion, Klan-type literature was distributed at Council rallies. Although the Council disclaimed responsibility, people at the Montgomery rally received a racist leaflet. The obscene language illustrates the mixture of coarse ridicule and anger that characterized the attitudes and responses of some whites:

> When in the course of human events it becomes necessary to abolish the Negro race, proper methods should be used. Among these are guns, bows and arrows, slingshots and knives. We hold these truths to be self-evident, that all whites are created with certain rights; among these are life, liberty and the pursuit of dead niggers. In every state of the bus boycott we have been oppressed and degraded because of black, slimy, juicy, unbearable stinking niggers. The conduct should not be dwelt upon them because they have an ancestral background of Pigmies, head hunters and snot suckers. My friends it is time we wised up to these black devils. I tell you they are a group of two-legged agitators who persist in walking up and down our streets protruding their black lips. If we don't stop helping these African flesh eaters, we will soon wake up and find Rev. King in the White House. LET'S GET ON THE BALL, WHITE CITIZENS.[14]

13. Thomas Pickens Brady, *A Review of Black Monday* (Winona, Miss., 1954), 14; Brady, "Segregation and the South," in Wrage and Baskerville (eds.), *Contemporary Forum*, 339.

14. Martin, *The Deep South Says "Never,"* 39–40.

Nevertheless, white middle-class support depended on the Councils' rejection of extremist positions, and the speakers continued to emphasize the organization's disapproval of violent means of protest.

A second strategy of speakers was to reinforce the basic doctrine of white supremacy that formed the cornerstone of the segregationists' position. Reduced to its simplest terms, this doctrine held that any mixing of the races was impossible because the white man is inherently superior to the black man. According to Council discourse, the inferiority of the black man was the product of racial differences that were deep and ineradicable. To support this claim of white supremacy, Council speakers offered several lines of argument. Segregationists turned to the evidence of history, alleging that all great civilizations had been the product of races other than the black. Indeed, speakers said, the black man in Africa had not produced one accomplishment to rank alongside the glories of Europe and Asia.[15]

To explain that failure, segregationists fashioned an amalgam of anthropology and sociology to argue that the black man is incapable of accomplishments to match other races. The black race, they asserted, possesses certain physical traits that set it apart from the white race. Some of these traits related to physical appearance, such as the hair, the nose, and the lips. Other differences included the claim that the Negro's brain pan seals and hardens quicker than the white man's, that the Negro has elliptical blood cells that cause disease, and that his skull is one-eighth thicker than the white man's. According to Council rhetoric, these differences carry an evaluative dimension. Not only do they mark the black man as different from the white man; they also indicate his inferiority. Perhaps the most original rhetorical contribution of the movement came at this point in the form of "scientific racism," whose foremost exponent was Carleton Putnam. His speeches and writings became the definitive statement of this theory. Putnam interpreted the Negro's physiological differences as evidence of racial inferiority. According to Putnam, modern psychologists support the view that the black man's smaller brain and skull size means that his intelligence is inherently lower than the

15. Brady, *A Review of Black Monday*, 3, 4.

white man's. Supporting Council claims that changing the black man's environment will not correct these deficiencies, Putnam argued first that topography has little correlation with mental capabilities; the black man had improved no faster in America than in his native Africa. Second, the former airline executive insisted that if any modification had been produced in the black man by virtue of his environment, such changes had taken over thirty thousand years to develop. Therefore, Putnam concluded, simply changing the Negro's environment by placing him in free association with the white man, as the integrationists proposed to do, would not change his inferiority.[16]

The inability of the black man to rise above limits imposed on him by heredity rendered any significant degree of free association between whites and blacks unthinkable, according to the speakers. Repeatedly, segregationists asserted that intermingling of whites and blacks would inevitably lead to intermarriage, which Councilors alleged to be the ultimate goal of integrationists. And invariably, when blacks interbreed with any race, speakers contended, the black characteristics become dominant. In Council rhetoric, the decline of great civilizations in the past could in each instance be traced to the introduction of Negro blood. Obviously, then, racial purity must be maintained at all costs, according to segregationists. The only guarantee, they insisted, that white and black blood would remain unmixed was to continue segregation.[17]

Having argued the necessity of segregation on the principle of white supremacy, segregationists defended the legal right of states to maintain separate schools. The right of states to control education policy rested, they claimed, on a strict interpretation of the Constitution. Suggesting what was to become a standard line of segregationist reasoning, Senator Eastland insisted that states' rights are inherent in American government, citing the Tenth Amendment to the Constitution as evidence. Among the rights granted to the federal government is nothing that authorizes school integration; therefore, the power to establish and control

16. *Ibid.*, 3, 16; Carleton Putnam, *Race and Reason* (Washington, D.C., 1961), 40–41, 45–46.
17. Brady, *A Review of Black Monday*, 3, 4; Ross Barnett, "Mississippi Still Says 'Never'!" *Citizen*, September, 1962, p. 8.

public schools resides with the individual states. On September 13, 1962, in a television and radio address carried throughout Mississippi, Governor Ross Barnett summed up the governmental rationale expressed in segregationist rhetoric. Issuing a proclamation, he declared:

> Whereas, the United States of America consists of fifty Sovereign States bound together basically for their common welfare; and Whereas, the Constitution of the United States of America provides that each State is sovereign with respect to certain rights and powers; and Whereas, pursuant to the Tenth Amendment to the Constitution of the United States, the powers not specifically delegated to the Federal government are reserved to the several States; and Whereas, the operation of the public school system is one of the powers which was not delegated to the Federal government but which was reserved to the respective States pursuant to the terms of the Tenth Amendment; . . . we are face to face with the direct usurpation of this power by the Federal government.[18]

Furthermore, the spokesmen claimed that Court-ordered desegregation rested on the due process clause of the Fourteenth Amendment, which they insisted had been illegally adopted. Their argument ran as follows. In 1866, Congress submitted to the states the Thirteenth, Fourteenth, and Fifteenth amendments to the Constitution. The Thirteenth and Fifteenth promptly passed, including approval by the all-white electorates and legislatures of the South. The Fourteenth Amendment failed to receive the approval of three-fourths of the states, with Tennessee the only southern state to approve it. Only after Congress had instituted military rule in the South, disfranchising whites and creating legislatures composed of carpetbaggers and scalawags, was the Fourteenth Amendment finally passed. In Council rhetoric, that ratification process was represented as illegal; as one speaker expressed it, the amendment "has never been of moral force in the South." Therefore, the Supreme Court decision ordering desegregation of public schools was illegal and nonbinding on the states.[19]

Employing a fourth rhetorical strategy, segregationists invoked

18. James O. Eastland, *We've Reached Era of Judicial Tyranny* (Greenwood, Miss., 1955), 8–9; Barnett, "Mississippi Still Says 'Never'!," 8–9.
19. Brady, "Segregation and the South," in Wrage and Baskerville (eds.), *Contemporary Forum*, 335; *Congressional Record*, 85th Cong., 1st Sess., 4340.

the sanctions of religion and revered historical figures. In the heavily Protestant, religiously conservative Bible Belt of the Deep South, the claim that Holy Writ approved of segregation was a strong argument against integration. Prosegregation ministers aided the Council in developing the biblical arguments. Drawing upon both the Old and New Testaments, speakers concluded that from beginning to end, from the patriarch Abraham through Jesus and his disciples, including the apostle Paul, Judaism and Christianity alike explicitly approved of segregation.[20]

Council speakers also claimed that three much-admired figures from the American past advocated segregation. The first was Thomas Jefferson. Although Jefferson urged emancipation, he believed so strongly in the separation of the races that he argued for repatriation of blacks at government expense. Perhaps most surprising, speakers cited Abraham Lincoln to support their cause. Contending that Lincoln favored colonization of blacks in Africa or the West Indies, Dr. G. T. Gillespie offered Lincoln's own words to prove the point. Quoting Lincoln's speech at Charleston, Illinois, on September 18, 1858, the minister noted Lincoln's position:

> I will say then, that I am not now, nor ever have been, in favor of bringing about in any way the social and political equality of the white and black races . . . that I am not now, nor ever have been, in favor of making voters or jurors of negroes, nor of qualifying them to hold office, nor to intermarry with white people; and I will say, in addition to this, that there is a physical difference between the white and black races which I believe will forever forbid the two races living together on terms of social and political equality.

In a second quotation, Gillespie drew from Lincoln's remarks to black freedmen at the White House, August 14, 1862: "You and we are different races. We have between us a broader difference than exists between any other two races. Whether it is right or wrong I need not discuss, but this physical difference is a great disadvantage to us both. . . . If this is admitted, it affords a reason at least, why we should be separated." The third figure cited as approving segregation was Booker T. Washington, whose Atlanta Exposition address in 1895 was offered as affirming from the black man's side the principle of segregation.[21]

20. G. T. Gillespie, *A Christian View of Segregation* (Jackson, Miss., 1954), 8–13.
21. *Ibid.*, 14–15.

To these arguments in support of segregation, speakers added custom. Even with the Fourteenth Amendment, speakers argued, the courts had approved southern racial practices right up to the time of the *Brown* decision in 1954. Why, then, the sudden reversal? Most Council speakers placed the major blame on the NAACP. This organization, which segregationists traced in origin to northern blacks unfamiliar with real conditions in the South, was held primarily responsible for the Supreme Court abandoning its separate but equal stance.[22]

However, the NAACP was not the only scapegoat identified by Council members. Speakers asserted that it was backed by large organizations determined to brainwash Americans into accepting integration. Foremost among these groups was the Communist party; indeed, Council spokesmen identified worldwide communism as the major cause of the integration movement, with the NAACP serving mainly as an agent for Communists. According to segregationists' analysis, Communists at one time planned the violent overthrow of the southern states by blacks, and the 1954 integration crusade followed suggestions on black rights expressed by the Communist party.[23]

Close behind the Communist party as an instigator of racial unrest was organized labor, which some Council orators suggested had been heavily infiltrated by Communists. In addition, speakers implicated "the almost equally red . . . National Council of Churches of Christ in the U.S.A."[24] Furthermore, numerous philanthropic foundations were alleged to support integration, including the Marshall Field Foundation, the Rosenwald Fund, the Rockefeller Foundation, and the Dorothy and Louis Rosenteil Foundation. Orators singled out the Ford Foundation and the Carnegie Foundation for special attention. The Ford Foundation was attacked because of its contributions to the Southern Regional Council, the National Council of Churches, and the Legal and Educational Fund of the NAACP. The Carnegie Foundation was criticized because it financed the work of Dr. Gunnar Myrdal, which the Supreme Court used to defend its racial decisions, and

22. Eastland, *We've Reached Era of Judicial Tyranny,* 5.
23. Brady, "Segregation and the South," in Wrage and Baskerville (eds.), *Contemporary Forum,* 334–35.
24. Eastland, *We've Reached Era of Judicial Tyranny,* 5.

because the foundation made heavy contributions to the National Urban League. In addition to these groups, segregationist rhetoric blamed several individuals for promoting integration. Chief among these people were Dr. Martin Luther King, Jr., John F. Kennedy, Robert Kennedy, and Hubert Humphrey.

A final source of pro-integration sentiment, according to speakers, was an ill-defined group known collectively as "outside agitators." The term occurs frequently in Council rhetoric. Perhaps the closest statement to a definition was supplied by Mississippi Governor Ross Barnett, who told his audience that his state was being invaded by "professional agitators, an unfriendly liberal press and other troublemakers," including "paid propagandists."[25] Other passages in his speeches indicate that Barnett included in this group the student volunteers, trained on northern college campuses, who came South to assist blacks in protest marches and voter registration.

However, undoubtedly the largest segment of "outside agitators" was the mass media, both broadcast and print journalism. Barnett, Wallace, Eastland, and other speakers made journalists a particular object of their ire, placing on the news media the responsibility both for encouraging racial unrest in the South and for promoting an unfavorable image of the South outside the region.

Speakers added impact to their claims by invoking myths still potent in the South. Most frequent were references to the Lost Cause, to which speakers appealed in several ways. Occasionally, speakers triggered the Lost Cause myth by mention of historic southerners such as Robert E. Lee, Stonewall Jackson, and Jefferson Davis. At other times, they inserted direct references to the Civil War. Graphically describing the horrors of Reconstruction, speakers used those conditions as an analogy for the Second Reconstruction, which resulted from the *Brown* decision, suggesting that implementation of Court-ordered integration would inevitably lead to conditions as bad for the South as were those during Reconstruction.

Two powerful symbols were used in Council discourse to conjure up a spectrum of myths. One was the Confederate flag, prominently displayed at almost all Citizens' Council rallies. In

25. Barnett, "Mississippi Still Says 'Never'!," 6.

fact, reverence paid the Confederate flag aroused such criticism from pro-integration forces that segregationists occasionally felt compelled to defend the practice.[26] The second was the song "Dixie," often played during rallies. Council rhetoricians worked references to both flag and song into their presentations, thereby promoting identification among their audiences with the southern cause.

For further emotional impact, speakers used epithets to add connotative values to their language. Some of these epithets were positive and were intended to evoke favorable evaluations. Segregationists' goals were described as supporting "the southern way of life," "constitutional government," "freedom of choice," "states' rights," "neighborhood schools," and "race purity." In the same vein, spokesmen for the cause were labeled "defenders of State sovereignty," "Southern gentlemen," "true sons of the South," and even "rebels," a favorable designation because of its link with the Lost Cause. By contrast, the opposition was given negative labels. The goals of integration were "mongrelization," "socialism," "Communism," "moral degradation," "naked and arbitrary power," and "illegal usurpation." Pro-integrationists were "Marxian Christians," "Neo-Socialists," "bearded beatniks," "wandering minstrels of racial friction," "travelling agitators," "liberals," "left-wingers," "un-American pressure groups," and "scum of the earth."

When the Council took its message outside the South, segregationists faced a somewhat different rhetorical challenge from the one they encountered in their own region. Here were audiences to be convinced, that is, with beliefs and attitudes that had to be changed in order to win support for the southern cause. As early as the mid-1950s, spokesmen began to address audiences in the Midwest and the West. In part, speakers attempted to organize Citizens' Councils in areas outside the South. However, they also presented their case before other audiences. Their eagerness to speak wherever invited reflected a growing realization by Council leaders that if the South had any hope of resisting integration, support of other regions was essential.

Three speakers illustrate the approach taken before audiences in other parts of the nation. On October 4, 1957, Judge Tom Brady

26. George C. Wallace, " 'We Shall Continue to Resist!' Gov. Wallace Tells White Monday Rally," *Citizen*, June, 1963, pp. 15–16.

addressed the Commonwealth Club of California. Defining his purpose as "to present the case for the South," Brady told his audience that southerners practiced segregation not only by choice, as "a precious and sacred custom, . . . one of our dearest and most treasured possessions," but also out of necessity. "Segregation," the judge continued, "exists not simply because we prefer it, but because we must maintain it. . . . Self-preservation, the first law of life, has required that we do so." Adapting to his audience, Brady gave his argument a somewhat different emphasis than he did when speaking to southern groups. Downplaying the usual argument of racial inferiority, Brady suggested two aspects of the alleged differences between blacks and whites that made segregation essential. One difference, the intellectual inferiority of blacks, Brady touched on only briefly. He chose instead to emphasize the moral inferiority of blacks, devoting a substantial part of his speech to his claim that blacks subscribed to a moral code far below that of white men. Pointing to the excesses of Reconstruction and to widely publicized acts of black youths in the North in the 1950s, Brady concluded that the only way to prevent such outrages in the South was to preserve segregation, especially in schools. In the remainder of his speech, Brady placed blame for the situation on Communist-inspired groups that, he alleged, were pushing integration as part of a master plan to seize control of the United States. He concluded with a glowing description of the Citizens' Councils that, he said, were composed of middle-class southerners dedicated to using peaceful, legal means to prevent the triumph of integration—and communism.[27]

A second example of a southerner speaking outside the region occurred on February 3, 1958, when William Simmons addressed the Farmers-Merchants Annual Banquet in Oakland, Iowa, a rural community in the southwest corner of the state. Even more than Brady, Simmons virtually ignored the usual white supremacy arguments. He spoke only briefly of the differences between the ratio of blacks to whites in the Deep South and the Midwest, noting that in Mississippi 45.28 percent of the population was black while in Iowa 0.75 percent was black. Much more succinctly than Brady, Simmons mentioned the origin of the South's problems during Radical Reconstruction and insisted that in the eighty

27. Brady, "Segregation and the South," in Wrage and Baskerville (eds.), *Contemporary Forum*, 335–36.

years since the Civil War, the South had developed a biracial system that was pleasing to whites and blacks alike and that had permitted the two races to live in peace.

Simmons covered this exposition in approximately one page out of the fifteen pages of the printed text. He then devoted the remainder of the speech to one major theme: states' rights. The integration movement, he urged, must be viewed with alarm as an opening assault by "liberals" in the federal government whose aim is the eventual destruction of any meaningful power of the states to manage their own affairs. Even in placing blame for integration sentiment, Simmons carefully avoided racist claims, insisting that even such groups as the NAACP were in reality the tools of Communists. Thus "the radical pro-integration movement which brought about the Supreme Court decision is not primarily a Negro movement. It is especially not of Negro origin." The situation was portrayed as the product of years of work by "inter-related pressure groups," skillfully employing "revolutionary techniques" to achieve their objective of establishing a totalitarian state in Washington. In the final one-fourth of the speech, Simmons tried to present the Citizens' Councils in a favorable light. Like Brady in California, Simmons disavowed any association with radical groups such as the KKK. He painted the Councils as organizations of southerners of all faiths—Protestant, Catholic, and Jewish—banded together to prevent "the steady march toward an all powerful centralized government."[28]

A third speech by a southern figure to a California audience is worth noting for the sake of comparison. On November 17, 1965, George Wallace addressed the Comstock Club in Sacramento. The speech is notable for the complete absence of white supremacy arguments. In fact, Wallace began with an extended presentation of statistical evidence to show that 8 percent of the black voters in Alabama supported his wife, Lurleen, in her successful bid for the governorship. Rather than discussing race, Wallace chose instead to use the entire speech to attack the encroachments of the federal government in states' affairs. In short, the speech emphasized states' rights.[29]

28. William J. Simmons, *The Mid-West Hears the South's Story* (Greenwood, Miss., 1958).
29. George C. Wallace, address to Comstock Club, Sacramento, Calif., recorded November 17, 1965.

Reports of other southern speakers before audiences outside the region suggest that most followed the pattern set by these men. They chose to emphasize the Council as the defender of states' rights, racial integration being only one manifestation of the growing threat of an all-powerful central government.

IV

Several conclusions emerge from this survey of segregationist rhetoric. Most notable was the failure of segregationists to offer an effective plan of action. Speakers made their greatest impact in delineating the problem facing southerners. They were less effective when they turned to solutions. Few speakers offered any concrete proposals. Probably the most impressive suggestion was made by Senator James Eastland. To be successful, he insisted, any plan of action must work through the federal government, with the state government taking the initiative. Individual districts or counties, he asserted, "are sitting ducks and will be picked off one by one." Specifically, he urged state governments to "segregate under the police powers, to promote the public health, raise academic standards, protect the psychological welfare of the child, prevent violence [and] promote peaceful and harmonious relations." Segregation on these principles would not be based on race, and therefore would not be subject to the Fourteenth Amendment, on which the Court had based its desegregation order. Offering further suggestions, Eastland urged such tactics as having the state abolish school districts and create new ones. This maneuver would destroy the basis of existing suits (aimed at specific school districts) and require new suits to be initiated. The resulting litigation could be stretched out for years. Also, he suggested that states could change their laws and create new policies that would have to be challenged in court, thereby bringing about indefinite delays. Essential to his plan was the need for the states to offer a policy or program aimed at preserving segregation. As evidence of the workability of his plan, Eastland cited the case of Virginia, where a "strong governor" and strong state leadership had forestalled integration; by contrast, Arkansas, he noted, had witnessed early integration of schools because it lacked a statewide program.[30]

30. Eastland, *We've Reached Era of Judicial Tyranny*, 12.

No other speaker offered a plan as concrete or specific as East-land's. Brady proposed an organization of southern states to be called a federation of states, whose function he never clearly defined. Ross Barnett attempted interposition in Mississippi. However, by and large most speakers simply concluded with an appeal for southern unity against desegregation, urging south-erners to stick together; exactly how that action would prevent in-tegration was not made clear.

In the long run, failure of southerners to see any effective re-sults from the antidesegregation movement undoubtedly led to disillusionment on the part of the masses. The disillusionment deepened as, one by one, attempted maneuvers were struck down by the courts.

Another strong impression produced by segregationists' speeches is the absence of originality in their content. There is a striking homogeneity among the speeches in that they repeat ar-guments. Perhaps the closest to innovation was Putnam's scien-tific racism; however, even that line of reasoning had its anteced-ents in the doctrines of George Fitzhugh and others before the Civil War. This absence of originality has one other dimension. Not only were the speeches homogeneous in thought among themselves, they also repeated stock southern racial arguments that had been in existence since before the Civil War. Previous studies of southern oratory have documented how states' rights and white supremacy arguments developed in defense of slavery and have found use in every period of southern history since then.[31] The lines of argument, and even the supporting evidence, for the most part repeat timeworn pronouncements by genera-tions of southern orators. Already subjected to the adjudication of court and battlefield, the arguments had lost in both arenas. Even the charismatic personalities of some of the advocates could not make them prevail in the mid-twentieth century.

31. George Fitzhugh, *Cannibals All! or Slaves Without Masters* (Richmond, 1857). See Waldo W. Braden (ed.), *Oratory in the Old South, 1828–1860* (Baton Rouge, 1970); Waldo W. Braden (ed.), *Oratory in the New South* (Baton Rouge, 1979); Cal M. Logue and Howard Dorgan (eds.), *The Oratory of Southern Demagogues* (Baton Rouge, 1981).

The Speaking of the Governors of the Deep South, 1970–1980

Waldo W. Braden

In 1971 when new governors were inaugurated in Georgia and South Carolina, Tom Wicker of the New York *Times* wrote that Jimmy Carter and John West "described themselves as products of a particular time and mood in the South, rather than as creators of a movement. As they see it, the people of most of the southern states are not only tired of the struggle to maintain old racial customs but are convinced the battle is irrevocably lost." Sensing these changes, John D. Saxon in 1975 suggested that "essentially the rhetoric of contemporary 'New South' Southerners is optimistic" and that contemporary southern oratory of the early 1970s showed "a spirit of renewal, of change, of departure from the past, a recognition that the South will no longer frustrate itself with lost or negative causes." He based his conclusions upon addresses delivered during a three-year period (from 1970 to 1973) by Dale Bumpers of Arkansas, Jimmy Carter of Georgia, Linwood Holton of Virginia, Terry Sanford of North Carolina, and William Winter of Mississippi to the L. Q. C. Lamar Society or to NBC's "Meet the Press." Except for Carter and Winter, his cited speakers came from the "peripheral South," where a more liberal racial tradition has prevailed and agitation has been less rabid than in the Deep South.[1]

1. John D. Saxon, "Contemporary Southern Oratory: A Rhetoric of Hope, Not

This essay proposes to revisit Saxon's subject and to extend his analysis to include the gubernatorial speaking during the entire decade and to concentrate upon the five Deep South states of Alabama, Georgia, Louisiana, Mississippi, and South Carolina, where traditionally white supremacy has become almost a religion; defiance of racial integration has been most extreme; and the governors have received the most coverage for their outbursts against blacks. The study considers 15 campaigns that involved at least 120 politicians as well as 15 governors and their inaugural addresses. Most attention is given to candidates who received 10 percent or more of the vote. The concentration upon campaigns for governor provides an opportunity not only to look at statewide canvasses in which competing politicians had to woo voters with diverse attitudes and interests including both urban and rural black and white voters but also to view the chief executives who frequently have become central figures in racial reform.

I

The "particular time and mood" of the Deep South states between 1970 and 1980 offer a marked contrast to events of the preceding twenty years when the struggle to avoid or to slow down integration was most intense. With the *Brown* decision, southern politicians became defiant, violent, and demagogic about racial purity and concurred with Governor George C. Wallace, who dramatically declared in his 1963 inaugural address: "Segregation now, segregation tomorrow, segregation forever." They vied with one another over who could proclaim most loudly and vehemently adherence to the southern way of life, abhorrence of racial mixing, and disgust with the federal courts. It was a time when the slightest hint of liberality toward blacks or willingness to cooperate with federal officials brought character assassination,

---

Desperation," *Southern Speech Communication Journal*, XL (1975), 268. Earl Black divides the South into two subregions: the Deep South (Alabama, Georgia, Louisiana, Mississippi, and South Carolina) and the Peripheral South (Arkansas, Florida, North Carolina, Tennessee, Texas, and Virginia). He concludes that the Deep South states "exhibited a greater preoccupation with the segregation issue than the states of the Peripheral South" and that the strong (militant) segregationists dominated the policies of the lower South. *Southern Governors and Civil Rights* (Cambridge, Mass., 1976), 52.

rabble-rousing, and in extreme instances harassment and mob violence. Basing a survey on "the campaign stances of gubernatorial candidates" who polled 10 percent or more of the popular vote for the twenty years after 1950, Earl Black determined that of seventy-eight persons who sought the highest office in the five states, thirty-seven were militant segregationists, thirty-seven were moderate segregationists, and only four were nonsegregationists. In Georgia and Mississippi, militant segregationists won four of five elections. In Alabama the militants, including George Wallace and Lurleen Wallace, triumphed three of five times. In South Carolina, two out of five were militants. But the exception was Louisiana, where moderate segregationists always won. In the sixteen years after the *Brown* decision, thirteen of the twenty governors were strong segregationists.[2]

The particular mood of the 1970s was shown most dramatically by the persons who sought governorships, in their campaign strategies, and by those who were elected. Among the fifty politicians who won 10 percent or more of the vote in one or more elections in the five Deep South states or who were in the general elections were many new spokesmen who dared to urge social and economic reform. Of the fifty, only five had served terms as governor prior to 1970. Six others had lost races for that office, and a few were familiar because they had previously sought or served in state or national offices. The majority had attended college (78 percent, or 39) and were lawyers (26). At least 30 percent were businessmen. Four were radio or television personalities or country singers. One who posed as a "peanut farmer" was a graduate of the U.S. Naval Academy and later president of the United States. Among the Mississippians were independent black mayor Charles Evers and Evelyn Gandy, who had made her start as an aide to Senator Theodore Bilbo.[3]

2. Throughout this essay, I use Black's classification and terminology. Having carefully read campaign speeches, candidate profiles, and their political literature for some six weeks before the first primary through the general election, he classifies those candidates as (1) militant, (2) moderate, or (3) nonsegregationist (Black, *Southern Governors and Civil Rights*, 10–16).

3. Evers, the first black to run for governor, received about 28 percent of the vote. Jason Berry, *Amazing Grace: With Charles Evers in Mississippi* (New York, 1973). Edythe Evelyn Gandy, known in Mississippi as "Miss Evelyn," was a member of

II

The fifteen gubernatorial elections during the decade from 1970 to 1980 show that the great majority of the leading vote-getters steered clear of the race issue. In fact, in none of the five Deep South states except Alabama in 1970 with George Wallace did racial rhetoric prove to be advantageous in winning the highest state office. Out of the fifty leading contenders, only five or six could be classed as moderate or militant segregationists. Instead, politicians sought the support of blacks, who constituted in the various states 17 to 26 percent of the electorate.[4]

A brief review of what happened to those who attempted to capitalize on the race problem supports this conclusion. In 1974 after four years as lieutenant governor of Georgia, Lester Maddox tried for a second term, singing gospel songs, riding his star-spangled bicycle backwards, playing the harmonica, selling his symbolic ax handles in his Atlanta gift shop, and mouthing his tired old racial slurs, expressions of the good ole-time religion, and tributes to "the little people." Facing Maddox were moderate George Busbee and "Machine Gun" Ronnie Thompson, well known as a former television performer–rock composer–singer–pianist, who symbolized his stand for law and order by wearing a gold-plated lapel pin shaped like a machine gun. Thompson attracted attention for his pronouncement about how he intended to clean up crime, particularly in Atlanta, and for his obvious racial bias. Maddox at first worked actively for black support in Georgia. A day or so before the first primary, declaring his true feelings, he confirmed what every voter in Georgia already suspected: "I term myself a segregationist, not a racist. I think a racist is a black or white person without any racial pride, who does not care what happens to his or her race. I believe a segregationist

---

the state legislature from Forrest County (1948–52), assistant attorney general (1959), commissioner of public welfare (1964–67), state treasurer (1960–64, 1968–72), commissioner of insurance (1972–76), and lieutenant governor (1976–80). *Who's Who of American Women, 1981–82* (Chicago, 1981), 267.

4. In 1976, blacks constituted 17 percent of the registered voters in Alabama; 25 percent in Georgia; 26 percent in Louisiana; 25 percent in Mississippi; and 26 percent in South Carolina. *Statistical Abstract of the United States, 1979* (Washington, D.C., 1979), 512.

is a black or white person who loves his race and other races . . . and cares what happens to them." After polling a disappointing 36 percent of the first primary vote, Maddox stepped up his racial rhetoric in the second primary. To slur Busbee, Maddox associated him with Julian Bond, speaking of "two B's—Busbee and Bond." He suggested that he opposed Bond's radicalism, meaning his antiwar stand. But neither the simplistic Maddox nor the blustering Thompson could defeat the quieter, more moderate George Busbee. Dismissing the Maddox ploy, Georgians gave former governor Maddox only about 40 percent of the second primary vote. In the same election, J. B. Stoner, one of the South's militant segregationists and racists and the Klan's candidate, polled only 10 percent for the lieutenant governorship. In 1978, Busbee had no difficulty winning reelection, and in the first primary, Stoner was limited to about 5 percent.[5]

In 1970 the South Carolina voters demonstrated a clear choice on the racial issue in a contest between Lieutenant Governor John C. West, a Democratic moderate, and two conservative racists— U.S. Congressman Albert W. Watson, a Republican, who symbolized his racial views by wearing a white tie; and state representative A. W. ("Red") Bethea, the candidate of the segregationist South Carolina Independent party. In spite of help for Watson from the Richard Nixon administration and his own vigorous efforts, the South Carolinians gave West 52 percent of the vote, compared to 46 percent for Watson and 2 percent for Bethea. A 7 percent margin of victory certainly did not indicate a strong shift toward integration, but West in his inaugural address declared an end to racism in the state.[6]

In Mississippi since 1970 the militant segregationists have had difficulty in making a significant showing. In 1970, country singer

5. Howell Raines, Atlanta *Constitution*, August 4, 1974; Atlanta *Constitution*, August 4, 12, 14, 15, November 6, 1974; Wayne King, New York *Times*, August 4, 30, 1974; John Dillin, *Christian Science Monitor*, September 5, 1974; Miami (Fla.) *Herald*, August 15, 1974; *Congressional Quarterly*, August 4, 1974, pp. 2035–36, August 12, 1978, pp. 2114–15.

6. Black classified Watson as a militant segregationist. New York *Times*, October 4, 24, 30, 1970; *Congressional Quarterly*, October 23, 1970, pp. 2596–97, November 6, 1970, p. 2777; John C. West, inaugural address, January 19, 1971, reprinted in Ernest M. Landers, Jr., and Robert K. Ackerman (eds.), *Perspectives in South Carolina History: The First 300 Years* (Columbia, S.C., 1973), 408–14.

Jimmy Swan, a militant racist, traveled about the state in a red, white, and blue bus with "Save the Children" painted on the side and refused to appear on the same platform with black mayor Charles Evers, who was also seeking the governorship. Making clear his racism, Swan said, "It even makes me sick to call his name [Evers]. . . . I love the image of Mississippi the old stronghold of the Confederacy." With all his dramatics, Swan was limited to 16 percent of the vote in this second try. A second self-announced segregationist, Marshall Perry, polled about 3 percent. In the general election William Waller defeated Evers, with a coalition of black and blue-collar voters. In 1975, John Arthur Eaves tried as a white supremacist, driving a white Cadillac and wearing a white three-piece suit in the style of James Vardaman, but he won about 6 percent of the vote. Seeing the futility of a racial campaign, Eaves changed his image in the next election (1979), secured the endorsement of Charles Evers, sought other black support, parked his white Cadillac, discarded his white suits, and put his children in public schools. In the first primary, however, he garnered about 19 percent of the vote.[7]

In Louisiana no major candidate espoused a racial bias in the campaigns during the ten years. Here the racial song was ended, but the melody lingered on in two cases of old-timers, well known for their past stands for segregation. In 1971, Jimmie Davis, twice governor before and a militant in the early 1960s when he attempted to block school integration, confined his efforts to a plea for "peace and harmony." Knowledge of his earlier militancy was of little help, for he came in a poor fourth in the first primary, with about 12 percent of the votes. In 1975 another old-timer, Wade O. Martin, Jr., an official in state government for more than thirty years and known for his strong racial stands, could only garner 12 percent. In both elections A. Roswell Thompson, a militant racist, received less than 1 percent.[8]

Alabama was a special case. Of course during the 1960s, George

7. *Congressional Quarterly*, August 6, 1971, p. 1675; Black, *Southern Governors and Civil Rights*, 65–66; Jackson *Daily News*, July 30, 31, 1975; Jo Ann Klein, Jackson *Clarion Ledger*, July 11, June 24, 1979; Bill Minor, *Capital Reporter* (Jackson), July 5, 1979.

8. Black classified Davis as a moderate segregationist in the 1971 campaign. *Congressional Quarterly*, November 13, 1971, p. 2367, November 8, 1975, p. 2378.

C. Wallace established himself among southerners as being first for his militant racial pronouncements and showmanship. The 1970 campaigns did not completely neglect the flimflam of the past. To attract the voters, Albert Brewer and George Wallace brought to Alabama "well-known and high-priced country musicians," and George Wallace, Jr., playing along in some of his father's groups, was an added attraction. In the first primary the two leaders had said little about racial matters, but Asa Carter, a strong segregationist, ran third, receiving less than 2 percent of the vote. In the second primary, Wallace returned to racial insinuation and suggested in newspaper ads and on billboards that "Blacks Back Brewer Against Wallace." To reheat old fears, Wallace warned that "if the black vote controls the run offs, it is going to control politics for the next 50 years in Alabama. I know you won't let that happen." His helpers circulated photographs showing the Brewer family associating with blacks, but holier-than-thou Wallace denied that he had encouraged these tactics. Four years later, Wallace modified his tune. At this time he was in a wheelchair, put there by a would-be assassin's bullet, but still looking toward another try for the presidency (1976). He made peace with his opposition, including business and labor, commenced to mollify the black voters, too many to be ignored any longer (about 17 percent of the total electorate, but concentrated in some districts).[9]

The changing times and moods were quite evident in the men who became governors in the five states. George Wallace was the only holdover from the 1960s. None of them except Wallace won by the flamboyance that characterized the earlier popular leaders. Instead, voters across the Deep South opted for more conservative and businesslike approaches, refusing to respond to gimmicks and showmanship. For the first time in the century, two Republicans, arch-conservatives, won governorships: James B. Edwards of South Carolina (1975) and David Treen of Louisiana (1979). Wallace and Cliff Finch of Mississippi, at the other extreme, made the most pronounced pleas to capture the blue-collar votes. The other eight, urbane, sober, and often mild in mien,

9. George Wallace, Jr., and James Gregory, The Wallaces of Alabama (Chicago, 1975), 140; Marshall Frady, Wallace (New York, 1976), 266; Wayne Greenhaw, Watch Out For George Wallace (Englewood Cliffs, N.J., 1976), 215–16; Congressional Quarterly, April 24, 1970, p. 1121, April 27, 1974, p. 1037.

were moderates or progressive-conservatives. Forrest James, a newcomer to politics, won the governorship of Alabama on his first try, touring the state for eighteen months in a yellow school bus. None of them attempted to fit the good ole boy stereotype.[10]

The fifteen spent considerably more than did past politicians in getting elected. All fifteen made more use of radio and television and the other mass media and called upon large staffs and public relations advisers, many from outside their states, for assistance. In 1979, for example, the five contenders in Louisiana spent more than $20 million. The leading contenders in a given election were often not widely diverse in their platforms and were likely to quarrel about minor issues. With the exception of the two Republicans and Wallace in 1971, the other twelve and Wallace in 1975 actively solicited and received substantial black support.

III

The character of the changing political scene and moods in the Deep South became more evident on inaugural days. Knowing that they had won in most instances by decisive majorities and had eliminated racists and many old-timers in state politics, they felt free to go their own ways. With the support of a cross section of voters, these new men exuded confidence and optimism. They expressed the changes in direction in three ways: their neo-populist programs, their declarations to end discrimination, and their expressions of good will toward all (and they did use the word *all*) citizens including white and black, young and old, rich and poor, and urban and rural.

As a group, the fifteen inaugural addresses are like many other speeches: they are pedestrian and filled with the customary platitudes, *i.e.*, "I pledge my full efforts"; "This is the most important day of my life"; "My prayerful pledge is that the program of my administration will please a Higher Power"; "Let us . . . continue bravely to seek happiness"; "I say what is in my heart"; "My pledge is to work with you." Perhaps their distinctiveness comes

10. Edwards (1974) won with about 51 percent of the vote in the general election (B. Drummond Ayres, Jr., New York *Times*, November 6, 1974); Treen (1979) won with 50.3 percent over Lambert (49.7 percent), or less than 10,000 votes (*Congressional Quarterly*, December 1, 1979, pp. 2722–23, December 15, 1979, p. 2831).

from what was omitted rather than from what was said. Gone were the usual paranoia, appeals to myth, attacks upon federal authority, and racial bigotry. They largely concentrated upon internal problems and attempted to be optimistic about the future. Most of the addresses had neo-populist overtones in their advocacy of improved education, better care for the handicapped and the aged, improved health care, protection of the environment, equalization of taxes, more efficiency in government, building of better highways and waterways, and promotion of industries for more jobs. Wallace's 1971 speech and Finch's 1976 speech put the greatest emphasis upon neo-populism. Wallace vowed to reduce "the daily cost of living of all Alabamians especially working men and women," "to work toward more adequate medical services" and toward a "voluntary health insurance program," and to "equalize the tax burden." He resolved to "revamp and revise a system which allows multi-billion dollar foundations . . . and multi-millionaire property holders to escape taxation while the low and middle level wage-earner pays and pays and pays."[11]

In 1976, Finch, a former legislator and former district attorney from Batesville, Mississippi, styled himself "the working man's candidate." To dramatize his stand, one day a week he donned khakis and worked with his hands, driving bulldozers, mixing cement, pumping gas, repairing cars, bagging groceries, and doing other manual jobs. In his inaugural address, Finch again made clear his "partnership" with "working men and women."

> This is a mission to be proud of—for here we are rendering service to those who have served—and saved—Mississippi and America.
>
> Some refer to working people as "average" Americans and infer that they are small men and women. The truth is they are the giants of modern history. No people of any nation have matched their courage or their contributions to mankind. They may be silent Americans—but their deeds will bless them until the end of time.
>
> These men and women—the farmers—the wage earners—the small businessmen—have placed their trust in their leaders of our government. They deserve and they will have our help.[12]

11. George C. Wallace, inaugural address, January 19, 1971, published in Montgomery *Advertiser*, January 19, 1971.
12. Cliff Finch, inaugural address, January 20, 1976.

Perhaps under the influence of the imminent Bicentennial, several of the governors spoke of the decade as "a time of reawakening . . . of new awareness . . . a new understanding . . . a new era of achievement" (West, 1971) or "a new beginning" (James, 1979) or "a new spirit . . . among us" (Edwin Edwards, 1972). Others expressed the same thoughts in slightly different words. In 1975, after being his typical cantankerous self, even George Wallace, now from his wheelchair, told Alabamians in his third inaugural, "Admittedly, many things have changed. . . . We cannot become lost in the daydreams of the past or the satisfaction of the present. To realize our greatness we must always march forward to meet the challenge of the future." [13]

In comparison to his earlier two, Wallace's third inaugural address (January 20, 1975) was indeed mild and innocuous. The subdued governor omitted racial code words and appeals to myth. Nor did he mention integration or the transgressions of the federal government, the liberals, or the intellectuals. He seemed more like other southern governors because of his omissions, his mildness, and his inserting the word *all* throughout his address. With blacks sitting on the platform, Wallace wanted to demonstrate that his constituency now included blacks as well as organized labor and business leaders. The pugilist without the sneer on his lips and the chip on his shoulder had become a conciliator seemingly eager to insult no one, to appear cooperative and helpful. With the cooling of the old fire, Wallace definitely tended toward a rhetoric of optimism, but he could not quite bring himself to state openly his new attitudes. [14]

One other signal of the "new beginnings" was the attempt of the several governors to give assurance of an end to racial bias and bigotry. In 1971, Jimmy Carter "quite frankly" told Georgians that "the time for racial discrimination is over." In neighboring South Carolina, John C. West announced that in the next four years his administration would eliminate from "government, any vestige of discrimination because of race, creed, sex, religion or any other

13. George C. Wallace, inaugural address, January 20, 1975 (pamphlet published by the governor's office).
14. *Congressional Quarterly*, April 27, 1974, p. 1037; Howell Raines, New York *Times*, February 7, 1979; George C. Wallace, inaugural address, January 20, 1975.

barrier to fairness for all citizens." In closing, he stated that "the politics of race and divisiveness have been soundly repudiated in South Carolina." In 1972, Edwin Edwards of Louisiana pledged "to black Louisianians . . . that the outdated, artificial barriers which have kept black people from most policy making positions and job opportunities at all levels of state government are going to come tumbling down. The old imaginary barriers no longer exist. My election has destroyed the old myths, and a new spirit is with us." [15]

After defeating two moderate segregationists in 1974, George Busbee of Georgia, who had received black support, declared that "the politics of race has gone with the wind." With a second overwhelming victory in 1979, Busbee reiterated that "state government stands for equal opportunity for all citizens and that it will be a vigilant influence in the battle against insidious forms of discrimination, bigotry and fear." [16]

William Winter told Mississippians in 1980 that his administration would have "no place for bias or prejudice based on sectionalism or class or race or religion or anything else." Richard W. Riley assured South Carolinians:

> We have passed laws, adopted policies, created agencies and built programs to abolish the evils of prejudice and discrimination. But it is the duty of all of us now—as individual citizens in the great democracy of ours to translate those documents of public will into real progress—economic progress, educational progress, human progress. For black South Carolinians, for women, for the elderly, for the handicapped, for the disabled and the disadvantaged, this is not the time to make more promises. This is the time to make good on promises long overdue. This is a long-standing duty which we all share. [17]

Alabamian Forrest James made his 1979 inauguration a simple but meaningful occasion. By nonverbal symbols he communicated more than by what he said. One observer confirmed "that sym-

15. Jimmy Carter, inaugural address, January 12, 1971, in Waldo W. Braden (ed.), *Representative American Speeches, 1970–1971* (New York, 1971), 142–46; West, inaugural address, January 19, 1971, in Landers and Ackerman (eds.), *Perspectives in South Carolina History,* 408–14; Edwin Edwards, inaugural address, May 9, 1972.

16. George Busbee, inaugural address, January 14, 1975, inaugural address, January 9, 1979 (copy supplied by governor's office).

17. William Winter, inaugural address, January 22, 1980, in *Congressional Rec-*

bolism . . . seemed to discredit the racial policies of the Wallace era." Onlookers must have noticed, for example, that Wallace in the company of the new governor "was obliged to ride to the reviewing stand" in a yellow school bus, James's campaign vehicle. Here was irony, for the bus stood for what Wallace had devoted so much time to lambasting—integration. Another sign telegraphed a second message to Alabamians. The Confederate battle flag, "which flew from the top-most staff of the capitol dome" at four Wallace inaugurals was now dropped below the national and state flags. If anyone missed these symbolic gestures, Governor James made it most clear that during his term he would end racial animosity: "On this, the birthday of Martin Luther King, Jr., I claim for all Alabamians a New Beginning free from racism and discrimination. Let us bury forever the negative prejudices of the past. The same standards of justice, responsibility, and reward are for one and all. I stand on this commitment without equivocation. So be it." [18]

This brief speech echoed what other progressive southern governors said. What Wallace had seemed to hint at four years earlier (1975), James now brought into the open. And surprisingly, Wallace in an interview thought that James had made "a good speech" and endorsed change. Hoping that he would not be remembered as "a racist" but as "a populist crusader," the former governor admitted, "It's good that it's a racial situation being changed. It's good that the civil rights bill has passed. It hasn't been the evil that we thought." [19]

In all fifteen inaugural addresses, the newly elected governors made strong pleas for unity among *all* citizens. In contrast to some of their predecessors who stirred class hatred and bigotry or silenced opposition with threats, these governors sought to develop consubstantiality and assured citizens regardless of status of their good will and eagerness for cooperation. As rhetoricians, they stressed similarity of purposes and interests instead of differences.

---

ord, 96th Cong., 2nd Sess., 473–74; Richard Riley, inaugural address, January 10, 1979, in *Congressional Record*, 96th Cong., 1st Sess., 970–71.

18. Howell Raines, New York *Times*, January 21, 1979; Forrest James, inaugural address, January 15, 1979 (copy supplied by governor's office).

19. Wallace quoted in Howell Raines, New York *Times*, January 7, 21, 1979.

In 1971, George Wallace said, "Our state government is for all so let us join together, for Alabama belongs to all of us—black and white, young and old, rich and poor alike." Four years later he reaffirmed this plea: "We find in our state today a determination on the part of all our people to work untiringly and in unison for the betterment of Alabama." Perhaps Wallace was a little self-conscious about speaking of black and white together, after having put so much rhetorical effort into driving them apart. In 1979, with Wallace listening on the platform, Forrest James stood forth boldly to ask for "unselfishness": "I believe if Robert E. Lee and Martin Luther King, Jr., were here today, their cry to us—their prayer to God—would call for 'The Politics of Unselfishness'—a people together—determined to climb the highest plateau of greatness." In linking Lee and King, he demonstrated rhetorically how far Alabama had come since the time when Wallace blocked an entrance to a schoolhouse.[20]

The three governors inaugurated in South Carolina likewise promoted consubstantiality. In the close of his 1971 address, Governor West eloquently asked that citizens "work together": "The achievement of these goals can become a reality if the people of this state unite . . . putting aside differences of race, politics, generation, or other. Two thousand years ago, the greatest philosopher and teacher who ever lived said: 'And if a Kingdom be divided against itself, that Kingdom cannot stand, and if a house be divided against itself, that house cannot stand.' The politics of race and divisiveness have been soundly repudiated in South Carolina." Four years later his Republican successor James B. Edwards, echoing the same sentiment, suggested, "South Carolina to me is 2.8 million great people—black, white, rich and poor, all standing tall, and ready to do whatever is necessary to overcome any hardships that can be ahead." Richard W. Riley assured his listeners on January 10, 1979, that his inaugural belonged to "young people impatient for change and reform . . . to older citizens looking for human dignity and financial security . . . to newcomers . . . and South Carolinians whose roots stretch back through . . . hard times and hard earned victories."[21]

20. Wallace, inaugural address, January 19, 1971, inaugural address, January 20, 1975; James, inaugural address, January 15, 1979.

21. West, inaugural address, January 19, 1971, in Landers and Ackerman (eds.),

In 1971, Jimmy Carter of Georgia suggested that "we cannot afford to waste the talent and ability given by God of one single Georgian." He offered himself as a representative "of Georgians, north and south, rural and urban, liberal and conservative." The following governor, George Busbee, declared on January 14, 1975, that Georgia was "no longer a provincial state with conflicting rural and urban interests": "Each part of Georgia must now accept the other, take pride in its achievements and understand its special problems. Any effort to pit one section of the state against another, or in any way to seek political profits from the problems of any section or city or county, will do injury to all of Georgia." Four years later, at his second inauguration, he "called for unity" and asked that Georgians "put aside bickering and squabbling and political clatter . . . and work together."[22]

The same change in direction was evident in Mississippi in Waller's inaugural address of January 18, 1972. Obviously he wanted to recognize the support that had come from the black community. In speaking of his many advantages, he mentioned "a cooperative public basically at peace with each other." A little later he expressed his concern about needy citizens: "I will not stand aside and idly observe the God-given talents of one single Mississippian wasted. Every adult illiterate, every school drop-out, and every untrained retarded child is an indictment of us all." He too made a strong appeal for a united Democratic party that had been split over the segregationist issue. He suggested that Mississippi "must have a state party representing all two million people." Calling attention to forthcoming precinct meetings, he urged, "Every Mississippian is invited to participate." His emphasis upon "every" Mississippian suggested he was extending the olive branch to blacks as well as whites, inviting them to participate in the party.[23]

Cliff Finch's inaugural address, delivered January 20, 1976, offers another good example of striving for what Kenneth Burke has

Perspectives in South Carolina History, 408–14; James B. Edwards, inaugural address, January 15, 1975, in Congressional Record, 94th Cong., 1st Sess., 565–66.

22. Carter, inaugural address, January 12, 1971, in Braden (ed.), Representative American Speeches, 142–46; George Busbee, inaugural address, January 14, 1975, inaugural address, January 9, 1979.

23. William Waller, inaugural address, January 18, 1972.

termed "consubstantiality." Playing upon the Bicentennial theme, he touted togetherness: "Our 82 counties—our cities and towns—are more united by beliefs than divided by boundaries—and we are one state, our 50 states are bound together—not by mere physical proximity in the same section of this planet—but by faith in the greatest system of government ever devised—and we are one nation." In light of Mississippians' fondness for speaking about "the sovereign state," states' rights, and the tyrannical federal government, Finch rejected past stereotypes and appealed to American tradition, not that of the southern way of life, the Lost Cause, or the Old South.[24]

Of the three Mississippi inaugural addresses of the 1970s, the speech that William Winter delivered on January 22, 1980, best represents what Saxon called a "rhetoric of optimism." Waller and Finch hinted at their desire to depart from the rancor of the 1960s, but each, a little self-conscious, was careful about how he reflected the new spirit. A better wordsmith, Winter skillfully blended tradition with optimism about the future. Reflecting the spirit of change in mood, Leontyne Price, prominent black concert and opera singer whose birthplace was Laurel, sang "The Star-Spangled Banner" to open the ceremony. Not missing the significance, Winter declared "how pleased" he was that she "would honor them by coming home for this occasion and singing so beautifully our national anthem." Winter made her appearance a symbolic expression of the new spirit. He adroitly shifted from the past to the future without jarring deep-seated traditional sensitivities: "But there have been so many years that the locusts have eaten, when we still pitted ourselves against each other, white against black, rich against poor, businessman against farmer, the Delta against the Hills. . . . We have wasted too much time. . . . We have spent too many of our years, too much of our energy being against things we did not understand, being afraid of change, being suspicious of the intellectual, and being oblivious to our image and our reputation." In sentiments reminiscent of those John F. Kennedy (whom Winter had backed in 1960) had expressed in his 1961 famous inaugural address, Winter asked that "bitterness" be put aside, "where people do not ask 'Where did

24. Finch, inaugural address, January 20, 1976.

he come from?' or 'What club does he belong to?' or 'What color is his skin?' The question they ask is 'What can he do?' "Winter demonstrated rhetorical strength in how he set forth his pleas for tolerance and unity by presenting them in a historical context.[25]

Like other southern inaugural speakers of the decade, Edwin Edwards of Louisiana in 1972 appealed for unity and optimism and extended a hand to people who had moved away from the state: "Come home, the barriers are gone and a new spirit is with us." In his second inaugural address (1976), he expressed his gratitude for being reelected. He reminisced about his twenty-two years in politics and expressed satisfaction that he had moved from a "share-cropper's farm to the Mansion in Baton Rouge." He directed this appeal at the poor, black and white, who were struggling to move upward. He expressed great pleasure in bringing "people together." In this portion, quoted almost in full in the newspapers, he said: "I chose to bring people together, appealing to their similarities, not to their differences; I chose to put away the sad part of factional strife and bury forever yesterday's bitterness. Let it be said that I concern myself with the larger task of improving the lives of those of you who have entrusted me with your lives and ideals."[26]

IV

During the 1970s the gubernatorial speaking in the Deep South states seems to support Saxon's contention that public address reflected "a spirit of renewal, of change, of departure from the past." New faces appeared, and strategies were planned to accommodate an expanded electorate, namely, blacks, women, blue-collar workers. The frequent appearance of Republican opposition assured a two-party system. Noticeably absent were flamboyant electioneering, class appeals, racial code phrases, overworked popular myths, talk about states' rights, and attacks upon federal authority. James Eastland, Gene and Herman Talmadge, and Strom Thurmond lost their fiefdoms.

25. Winter, inaugural address, January 22, 1980, in *Congressional Record*, 96th Cong., 2nd Sess., 473–74.
26. Edwin Edwards, inaugural address, May 10, 1976 (copy supplied by Edwards). See excerpt in Crowley (La.) *Post Signal*, May 11, 1976.

Seldom dramatic, the leading politicians were in the middle of the economic spectrum. Almost all of them except the Republicans advocated mild neo-populist programs, suggesting improvement of education, better health care, equalization of taxes, and responsiveness to human needs. Differences between candidates were often relatively minor. The voters refused to respond to the racism or showmanship of the past. The campaigns were often orchestrated by public relations men who knew how to put to full use the mass media.

The central motivation of the fifteen inaugural addresses was consubstantiality, seeking to unify the various factions in a common purpose. Aware that black voters had become important, most of the new governors by action and word declared an end to discrimination and racial antagonism. They frequently spoke in terms of "all" citizens, asking for cooperation in the pursuit of equal rights. Another important rhetorical strategy was to stress the state's relationship to the national tradition instead of promoting regionalism and paranoia.

What does the future hold? This study has considered only the speaking of governors. Had it examined the contests for the U.S. House or the state legislatures, the findings might have been different. The question arises as to whether the speaking of the 1970s represents the beginning of a continuing trend toward a rhetoric of optimism or whether it will fade and southern politicians will resume an exploitation of racism. The American Civil Liberties Union has accused the Deep South states of continuing to discriminate against the black voters through at-large elections, majority votes to force black-white runoffs, gerrymandering, and annexations to dilute black voting strength.[27] The racial code words, in more subtle forms, still creep into some politicians' vocabularies. The Klan still finds willing listeners in rural areas and continues to harass its critics. Other threatening signs are the rise of ultraconservatives, especially in the South, the reluctance of the Ronald Reagan administration to pursue vigorously civil rights, the antibusing legislation in Congress, the eagerness of budget cutters to discontinue programs that benefit blacks the most, and the talk of a "New Federalism" that is another name for states'

27. New York *Times*, February 14, 1982.

rights. Is the rhetoric of optimism to be as fickle as the on-again, off-again slogans of "the New South" that have a way of appearing when politicians want to impress outsiders or quiet the restless natives? Only time will tell.

Jimmy Carter's Rhetoric of Idealism
From Southern Justice to Human Rights

John H. Patton

The moral direction that great leaders provide is based on some deeper appreciation of the requirements of justice in their time, along with an ability to tap the emotions and the interest of the people to win their support for this larger vision. The sad thing for Jimmy Carter, and maybe for America as a whole, is that for all his high ambition, he does not understand this."[1] With these words, Betty Glad concludes her insightful volume on Jimmy Carter. I want to begin where she leaves off. Glad's comment supplies a critical lens through which to view the rhetoric of Jimmy Carter. In particular, it allows us to see how Carter responded to the question of the "requirements of justice" through an attempted rhetoric of idealism. My purpose is to describe, interpret, and analyze the discourse of President Carter in an effort to illuminate the nature and quality, successes and failures, of the moral directions he brought to politics largely from roots and experience in the South.

Portions of the research for this essay were made possible by funds from the Speech Communication Association's Karl R. Wallace Memorial Award for Scholarship in Rhetoric and Public Address, December, 1977. The author extends special gratitude to the Trustees of the Wallace Award Fund.
    1. Betty Glad, *Jimmy Carter: In Search of the Great White House* (New York, 1980), 507.

From the standpoint of a rhetorical critic, there are two basic questions I wish to raise about the discourse of Carter: first, what did he view as the "requirements of justice," that is, what does his use of discourse tell us about his basic conceptions of justice, and second, how did his rhetoric explain, interpret, and justify his conceptions of justice to the public? My examination centers on Carter's public discourse, along with related rhetorical documents such as interviews, books, and the comments of expert observers and key members of his administration.

An evolving sense of justice and the desire to supply a moral dimension to public policy are basic characteristics of Jimmy Carter. Justice, however, was not a simple matter for Carter, or a uniform one, and at least three key stages in his conception of justice are observable: an early stage characteristic of his pre-presidential days; a formulation stage, which culminated in the concept and policy of human rights; and a later fragmentation stage, in which the initial urgency and power of the idea of justice became diffused and deflected.

Early Justice

"It is a long way from Plains to Atlanta" he said in 1971 in his inaugural address as governor of Georgia. Carter used the occasion to speak about his "feelings about Georgia," noting that this was a "time for truth and frankness." Part of that candor included a reminder that "our country was founded on the premise that government continually derives its power from independent and free men. If it is to survive, confident and courageous citizens must be willing to assume responsibility for the quality of our government at any particular time in history." This is a revealing statement in light of what we would later learn of Carter's reliance on "the people" as the source of moral direction for government. His immediate pronouncements were declarations of moral intention. Thus, referring to illiteracy, school dropouts, and the lack of training for retarded children, Carter declares that "it is time to end this waste." Then, in a statement that startled many of his supporters, Carter affirms that "based on [my] knowledge of Georgians, north and south, rural and urban, liberal and conservative, I say to you quite frankly that the time for racial discrimination is over." The emerging notion of justice here is not only doing the right thing but doing it because of who we are, that is, knowing about citizens north and south, rural and urban, provides a moral superstructure on which to act. Justice and the inner qualities of the people are deeply connected, even at this early time.

The speech continues with a series of goals emphasizing honesty, active government in behalf of the people, and confidence in governmental leadership. Such objectives are quickly followed with a characteristic stratagem that appears consistently over the years in Carter's discourse: locating a problem's solution in the mind and actions of the audience. He raises the rhetorical question, "What officials can solve the problems of crime, welfare, illiteracy, disease, injustice, pollution, and waste? This control rests in *your* hands, the people of Georgia." This locating device is immediately followed by the statement that "in a democracy, no government can be stronger, or wiser, or more just than its people."[2]

The rhetorical structure of this speech is quite remarkable. Here was a southern governor speaking to southerners, doubtless trying to instill pride and inspire as befits the occasion of an inaugural. Yet, there is something else happening here. The tone of the language reveals a resolve to tackle long-standing problems, even though it means stirring things up, to the displeasure of many in the audience. This determination is admirable and suggests a strong, decisive, independent form of leadership. Nonetheless, it is precisely at this point that the logic shifts and the moral momentum created by Carter's call for "the utmost in dedication and unselfishness" becomes blurred and, if not reversed, rather thoroughly confused. The governor and his administration have the responsibility, the argument goes; the people, however, have the control. Exactly how governmental responsibility and popular control—by virtue of moral capacity—mingle and work in a series of mutual actions and programs is the critical question. It arises naturally from the logic of Carter's own speech. Significantly, in 1971 in Atlanta, and throughout most of his presidency, Carter provided no definite, or perhaps it is better to say no satisfying, answers to this controlling question. This stage points to

2. Jimmy Carter, inaugural address, January 12, 1971, pp. 1, 3; John H. Patton, "A Government As Good As Its People: Jimmy Carter and the Restoration of Transcendence to Politics," *Quarterly Journal of Speech*, LXIII (1977), 249–58.

Carter's tendency to use justice as an abstract term of moral intensity, left incomplete in relation to his audience.

How can we account for this rhetorical strategy—abstract moral intensity about goals and means that moves in two conflicting directions? One way to begin to answer such a question is to examine the person himself in relation to the structure of discourse. Rhetorical critics have long been concerned with ethos, or those dimensions of a speaker's character that make him credible. This notion needs to be enlarged with the realization that communication is always partly the product of a person's self-concept and the way that self is shared with others. Discourse and the articulation of the self are interdependent in that basic sense, and the patterns of thought and speech are influenced by the critical factors that shape and structure self-concepts over the years. In Carter's case, significant parts of his childhood, family experience, and cultural context are extremely useful in helping us grasp the role of the self in his discourse.

Carter is consistently described as isolated and introverted. Bruce Mazlish and Edwin Diamond, for example, observe that Carter grew up in a subcommunity of Plains, Georgia, called Archery, "a collection of houses about two miles from Plains." Moreover, his family was "one of only two white families surrounded by about twenty black families." Within that cultural context, it also is true that Carter's family was elite. Laurence Shoup, in a book sharply critical of Carter, stresses that he "was born into one of those local gentry families, historically conservative and racist, yet having a paternalistic, 'noblesse oblige' feeling towards those they had in control in their local area." Part of this isolation created a sense of determination and independence. Another part led to a sense of almost infallible rightness because of that very isolation. The most influential force on Carter in that respect was doubtless the example of his mother, Lillian. Mazlish and Diamond note that Lillian described herself as "a lone person," which sounds at first ironic in light of her activist reputation. A deeper clue as to what she meant is found in her reaction to public criticism: "One value I taught my children is never—Do the best you can with what you have and don't worry about criticism." It has been argued that Carter carried this approach over directly to his governmental style. According to Mazlish and Diamond, "as President, Jimmy Carter could echo his mother and say, 'This is not an office which can be conducted on the basis of looking for approbation.' Like her, he felt secure in his superiority, even when his abilities came under attack."

Clearly, the most formative events in shaping Carter's self-concept were his contacts with blacks. Carter was a numerical minority, but a political and economic majority—a virtual mirror image of the plantation system of the Old South. For Carter, however, this was not a "balanced" situation reflecting the proper order of things. The imbalance existed at some deeper, probably intuitive, moral level, and it became a genuine rhetorical exigence to which a great deal of his public discourse was directed. Unlike other experiences, black-white relations were not matters of abstraction. We are told that Carter's best friend until age fourteen was A. B. Davis, a black youth, and that "the sort of segregation that occurs in cities and small towns, even in Plains, where whites and blacks live apart, was unknown in Archery. The boys could be close, but had to be separate: Jimmy had to go first, to be the pitcher, to lead—'to star' in Davis' own words."[3] The pattern of interaction established here made it possible, indeed necessary, for Carter to strike a balance between personal closeness constrained by cultural distance.

Precisely this feature of his self-development is singled out by Lloyd deMause and H. Ebel. They observe that "growing up as a white Southern boy in a densely populated black neighborhood meant that Jimmy had to learn to combine distance and intimacy along racial lines. In childhood, blacks were the common people to Jimmy and they took on a special meaning as representatives of his repressed desires." One result of the need to "combine distance and intimacy" for Carter was a rhetorical style that seemed terribly personal and distinctly detached at the same time. Paul Elovitz comments about Carter's discourse after a field study of Plains that "the hallmark of Carter as a politician has been the *image* of intimacy. He has literally touched millions of people, which he confuses with actually getting to know them. To say, 'I love

3. Bruce Mazlish and Edwin Diamond, *Jimmy Carter: An Interpretive Biography* (New York, 1979), 22, 54; Laurence H. Shoup, *The Carter Presidency and Beyond: Power and Politics in the 1980's* (Palo Alto, 1980), 22.

you' to factory workers on the 5:00 a.m. shift reveals what little depth he attaches to the concept of love."[4] That last is too harsh a verdict, but it certainly can be said that comments of the "I love you" type in a campaign are frequently viewed by audience members as shallow or naïve.

The "image of intimacy" reflects both Carter's prime rhetorical asset and liability. One can almost see the internal logic chaining its way out in the attitudes and actions of this young, landowning, white youth: "If A. B. Davis and I can play together and have a friendship, then no other differences matter. If such a friendship can work in Archery, why not in the larger society in Georgia, in the United States, in the world at large?" The original intimacy was surely genuine, as was Carter's desire to model larger social structures along those lines. The problem was that while Carter understood the workings of individual intimacy on a very selective basis, he did not discover ways of creating or awakening that intimacy in the larger, seemingly impersonal, structures of the social world. He falsely assumed that it was sufficient to testify about his own individual intimacy and that his own experience would be automatically generalizable. Carter's background and early experience help us to see that at an early stage his conception of justice was primarily an individual one, filled with moral energy, essentially private, and not directed toward the perceptions and values of a wider public.

The Rhetoric of Human Rights

Not long after gaining the presidency, Carter reintroduced the issue of moral quality into the role of government, much as he had attempted to do in Georgia. The focal point of this effort became his policy on human rights. As a rhetorical concept, human rights contained a powerful cluster of positive values, entirely consistent with Carter's personal commitment to moral order and his basically fundamentalist religious beliefs, which he explicitly stated by this time. Moreover, human rights had the potential for

4. Lloyd deMause and H. Ebel (eds.), *Jimmy Carter and American Fantasy* (New York, 1977), 56; Paul H. Elovitz, "Three Days in Plains," *Journal of Psychohistory*, V (Fall, 1977), 198.

becoming a legitimate transformative symbol, one that could provide public audiences with a structure for reshaping politics and even the social order. But moral terms of this magnitude also create correspondingly high expectations, and they require specific pragmatic direction if they are not to dissolve in the heat of their own effervescence. Carter experienced the promise and the problems of the concept of human rights from the beginning.

His early interest in the concept of human rights appears in his remarks at a press conference on March 16, 1977: "I want to see our country set a standard of morality. I feel very deeply that when people are put in prison without trials and tortured and deprived of basic human rights, that the President of the United States ought to have a right to express displeasure and to do something about it."[5] Notice the pattern of appeal that immediately emerges. "Our country" as a repository of moral goodness is the starting point, just as the good people of Georgia were to be the initiators of moral action in that state. The movement is always from a set of interior values and beliefs to the external world. That development, in itself, is clear and characteristic of almost any reform movement.

On the next day, Carter addressed the General Assembly of the United Nations. He argued that "the search for peace and justice also means respect for human dignity. All the signatories of the U. N. Charter have pledged themselves to observe and to respect basic human rights."[6] Here human rights as a concept is linked with the universally positive notions of peace and justice. Indeed, Carter is saying to an international audience that respect for the human rights of others is central to the definition of justice and a condition of peace. Ironically, though his statement sounds forceful and direct, the concept of basic human rights was left vague and abstract. Moral intensity coupled with sheer generality again marked Carter's rhetoric.

Despite its vagueness, the concept itself was powerful, and once introduced into the public vocabulary, especially media vo-

5. Jimmy Carter, "Opening Remarks at Clinton, Massachusetts Town Meeting," March 16, 1977, in *Public Papers of the Presidents of the United States, Jimmy Carter, 1977*, I, 385.
6. Carter, "Address Before General Assembly of the United Nations," March 17, 1977, *ibid.*, I, 449.

cabulary, the concept of human rights seemed to invite additional development. Some of Carter's best rhetorical moments were his major addresses at the University of Notre Dame on May 22, 1977, and in celebration of the Universal Declaration of Human Rights on December 6, 1978. The former provides a representative example for analysis.

One senses from the beginning that the Notre Dame speech will be more than an ordinary commencement address. Carter opens with a relatively rare reference to southern pride, saying that "in the minds of many people in our country, for the first time in almost 150 years, there is no accent [in the White House]." He quickly invokes the names of several bishops and cardinals who share a common condition: "Quite often, brave men like these are castigated and sometimes punished, sometimes even put to death, because they enter the realm where human rights is a struggle." Carter skillfully accomplishes several things here. He establishes a virtual trinity—Catholic leaders, human rights, and himself—without having to say that he is chief advocate of human rights. Further, human rights is identified as part of historic, moral struggles to rectify living conditions and protect the oppressed. Similarly, the authority of religion, and in this case the moral force of Catholicism as an institution, is wedded to the cause of human rights, which is no minor achievement for a Southern Baptist from rural Georgia. Finally, Carter in effect recasts the role of president in distinctly religious terms, making the president a type of pastoral reformer rather than political bargainer or administrator.

Carter's purpose, he explains, is to discuss "the strands that connect our action overseas with our essential character as a nation." The words "essential character" stand out as the dominant symbols suggesting an identifiable core of values and beliefs. He does not explicate the content of that essential character by example or illustration. Rather, he adopts a strategy of what may be called argument by antithesis, indicating that to realize the potential of our essential character in foreign policy would require a reversal of the standard mode of policy actions. To make this point, Carter employs an intriguing pattern that functions metaphorically to reveal the operation of his moral logic: "For too many years, we've been willing to adopt the flawed and erroneous principles and tactics of our adversaries, sometimes abandoning our own values for theirs." This is the initial part of the pattern. The metaphoric theme evident here is the pull of expediency and the image of policy making by imitation, a gradual surrender to external standards of "the others." The act of definition, Carter seems to be saying, has come from outside the self, and thus the "essence" of the national character has not operated in policy decisions.

He introduces a specific metaphor to stress the point: "We've fought fire with fire, never thinking that fire is better quenched with water." Several things are noteworthy about this imagery. Carter is arguing that the very way we make foreign policy decisions is incendiary. The force of his "fire with fire" reference is that it clearly places us on the same level as our presumed adversaries, thus yielding no advantage of principle or moral virtue to the United States; and it actually worsens and complicates already inflamed situations and problems. For evidence of this negative result, Carter cites Vietnam, "the best example of its [the method of foreign policy decision making] intellectual and moral poverty."

The last stage of Carter's logic of morality here evokes a metaphor of learning through, indeed because of, failure. He pronounces a notion of restoration: "But through failure we have found our way back to our own principles and values, and we have regained our lost confidence." The pattern is that of a large circle finally completed by turning back upon itself. In sum, Carter has presented an encompassing framework. Policy decisions (the rhetoric that guides the state) have erroneously been forms of reaction rather than action, falling victim to the mode of imitating our adversaries. For that reason, the basic premises for policy decisions have been located away from our essential character, the internal values and beliefs that identify us as a people. The practical results have been disastrous; yet, out of those disasters comes a renewed awareness of our inner identity. The language suggests not only a critique of past policy but a radically different way of making governmental decisions.

This part of the speech in key respects overshadows the "thematic statements" that follow. As a critic, I regard the metaphoric pattern as especially crucial because it discloses the assumptions Carter brings to the discourse and to the rhetorical situation he faces. The speech does contain five specific policy elements, but the pattern of an overarching moral logic controls their presentation. Four policy statements follow from the first, which is Carter's reaffirmation of "America's commitment to human rights." They include efforts "to reinforce the bonds among our democracies," to "engage the Soviet Union in a joint effort to halt the strategic arms race," to work toward "lasting peace in the Middle East," and to "reduce the danger of nuclear proliferation and the worldwide spread of conventional weapons." Significantly, all these relatively particular aims are derived from and are to be pursued within the perspective of a general moral abstraction, the concept of human rights.

Carter elaborates the policy of human rights as a moral principle. In an important passage he remarks, "No common mystique of blood or soil unites us. What draws us together, perhaps more than anything else, is a belief in human freedom. We want the world to know that our nation stands for more than financial prosperity." By naming "human freedom," Carter articulates an emotive and positive value, though it is equally abstract and general. More interesting, he locates "human rights" in the non-material world and suggests that there is a spiritual dimension to our basic values that sets them apart from such tangible phenomena as blood, soil, or wealth.

What we need to see about Carter at this point is that he operates at the level of metaphysics. Human rights is a nonmaterial, ordering premise that is not bound to the ebb and flow of finite physical and historical conditions. Rather, it pushes beyond the physical to provide a pattern of interpretation and meaning for all sets of those conditions as they develop. In short, Carter's articulation of a world view provides a metaphysical structure for the complex and tangible arena of politics.

With all its ambiguities, this speech nonetheless marks the high point of Carter's rhetoric as president. It stood as his most complete articulation of the moral logic that undergirded his approach to power. He concludes by outlining a definitive hierarchy of values: "Our policy is rooted in our moral values, *which never change. Our policy is reinforced* by our material wealth and by our military power. Our policy is *designed to serve* mankind [emphasis added]." Moreover, here as nowhere else, President Carter seemed to grasp the suasory significance of his language and office. For a moment, albeit fleeting, he knows that the concept of human rights as a symbolic form is indeed a way of acting upon the minds and hearts of audiences. Thus, he bids the audience not "to undervalue the power of words and [the power] of the ideas that words embody," citing Thomas Paine and Martin Luther King, Jr., as his examples. He then links society and the human spirit through the medium of language: "In the life of the human spirit, words *are* action."[7] Within this positive perspective about the power of language to affect life, the concept of human rights was initially articulated as Carter's compelling response to the requirements of justice in his time.

The Administration of Justice

The trouble with moral principles is that they must be applied, a process that immediately involves levels of interpretation and definition. One avenue of application is the development of a uniform moral ideology to comfort and support the "true believers" and to ostracize those who are not. But the United States has not been particularly excited about ideological systems as such, and Carter in any case displayed little of the ideologue's persona and zealous fire. But if the path of ideology is not chosen, then there must be some other set of intelligible frameworks or patterns by which to translate the effects of moral principle into daily life, or else risk the "generic calcification," to borrow Kathleen Jamieson's term, of the principle itself.[8] The rest of Carter's administration was largely the story of inadequate and incomplete definitions and interpretations of the central theme of human rights.

Both before and after the Notre Dame speech, the theme of human rights was interpreted as a major step in reorienting foreign policy. James Reston notes that the Russians sneered at the idea "as if it were a dreary Sunday School lesson out of Plains, Georgia," but he stresses that this was an obvious undersight. He reports that "Mr. Carter is touching something much deeper in the American

7. Carter, "Address at Commencement Exercises, University of Notre Dame," May 22, 1977, *ibid.*, I, 954–56, 958–59, 961–62.
8. See Kathleen Jamieson, "Antecedent Genre As Rhetorical Constraint," *Quarterly Journal of Speech*, LXI (1975), 406–15, and "Generic Constraints and the Rhetorical Situation," *Philosophy & Rhetoric*, VI (1973), 162–70.

character," namely, the revival "of the old biblical notion of the human family, that national boundaries do not forbid concerns for human decency and pity, and that there must be what H. G. Wells once called an 'open conspiracy' to pull the world together in a common collective consciousness or awakening toward a different world."[9] Reston's words tell us much about the perceived impact of Carter's theme. The idea of the "human family" is particularly revealing, for it suggests the efficacy of human rights to generate similar metaphors of moral value and at the same time indicates how helpful a pattern of such metaphoric themes would have been in explaining the concept to audiences over time.

In a related fashion, C. L. Sulzberger underscored the positive appeal of the human rights theme. Noting in particular Carter's letter to Soviet dissident Andrei Sakharov, Sulzberger comments that "the firm, fresh attitude of President Carter has given new leadership to internal movements for freedom and human rights in a whole series of lands governed by one or another form of autocracy." Significantly, however, he goes on to raise a series of pragmatic questions related to human rights, questions about modification of immigration laws for the discontented and persecuted abroad; questions about "the continued jamming of broadcasts by Radio Liberty and Radio Free Europe"; questions about the nature of America's future response to another crisis in Eastern Europe involving the Soviets.[10] Such issues are but a small portion of the extensive variety of specific and pragmatic problems that would presumably come under the directive moral logic of human rights. Indeed, the concept of human rights would be developed in terms of clearly definable implications for a vast array of specific policy issues. What is left unstated is that the connection between human rights as moral principle and human rights as operational policy is not self-evident within the statement of the principle itself. An act of translation is yet required.

Reston makes a similar point in observing that Carter "has put together a Cabinet of pragmatists, of businessmen and lawyers, who are accustomed to dealing with one problem at a time, but have no real philosophy of where we are and where we are go-

9. James Reston, "The Open Conspiracy," New York *Times*, March 6, 1977.

10. C. L. Sulzberger, "Where Do We Go Now?" New York *Times*, February 20, 1977.

ing."[11] While this apparently lays the foundation for an almost perfect match of Carter's moral logic and his advisers' pragmatic directions, it also alerts us that unless such harmony is created, neither a viable philosophy nor an effective strategy would likely result.

The rhetorical problem hence became interpreting the concept of human rights so that a coherent, if not entirely consistent, set of applications could be developed. It remains a telling mark on the Carter legacy that a coherent interpretation never fully emerged. Instead, the specifics of policy application began to crop up everywhere and soon dominated the scene. Indeed, specific problems shifted the emphasis from moral principle to seemingly case-by-case pragmatics. For example, leading Soviet dissidents hailed human rights, but the reception in Latin America was noticeably different. Juan de Onis writes that in Brazil, Argentina, Chile, and Uruguay, "authorities have denounced his criticism of what they see as their internal affairs and spurned any further United States military aid." The issue quickly arises, exactly what does human rights mean in those "developing" countries where struggles, even wars, for "liberation" are occurring? Does it commit the United States to support existing governments or the efforts of an interesting combination of leftists and worker-clerics who frequently are at the core of revolts and resistance movements?

Without doubt, the sheer moral force of the symbol "human rights" as Carter used it shaped a rhetorical exigence in the form of aroused expectations that awaited further completion. Especially for those who shared the common trait of being outside the system, whether in Poland, the Soviet Union, or Latin America, a genuine sense of anticipation resulted from Carter's affirmation of human rights. For the most part, however, the expectation dissolved, unfulfilled. As de Onis puts it, "The confusion that exists centers on Mr. Carter's motives and on his degree of commitment to follow up his admonitions with tougher measures. To many South Americans, it is not clear if he is moralizing for the benefit of a domestic constituency, or whether he is needling the Russians, or whether he is really interested in helping to restore democratic

---

11. Reston, "The Open Conspiracy."

government in the hemisphere." [12] The label "moralizing" juts out here like a dangerously raw, sharp edge. As a symbolic form, moralizing is the polar opposite of a genuinely positive rhetorical concept. It connotes the essentially sophistic move that would reduce Carter's discourse to nothing more than an attempt "to make the worse appear the better case." What quickly and thoroughly undermines a moral principle is its being widely perceived not as principle, but as moralizing.

The tension between rhetoric as moral principle and rhetoric as moralizing remained a major problem for Carter and contributed to public perceptions about his leadership and competence. The challenge itself was created by Carter's moral rhetoric and, having been created, became an issue to be addressed in his discourse. The rhetorical challenge involved was put aptly by Hugh Sidey, who described Carter's human rights theme as a "hazardous course" and drew a close parallel with the presidency of Woodrow Wilson. Sidey, citing John Morton Blum's book on Wilson, remarks that "Wilson, in the judgment of his chronicler, was at once the keeper of a rigid conscience and the creature of a political system that worked only when he bent that conscience to conform. Wilson found that the power of his office could only carry him so far. Then . . . the President either had to combine influence with compromise or, defending virtue, lose his way. Carter, 'the missionary,' travels a hazardous course." [13]

The comparison between Carter and Wilson reveals a remarkable similarity in moral emphases and rhetorical strategies. Because Wilson drank as deeply of the waters of southern religion, especially the southern streams of Calvinism, he provides a virtual prototype of Carter's moral rhetoric. After somewhat shaky beginnings, Wilson developed a firm set of religious principles that served as the center of his views on education, politics, and leadership itself. As John Mulder observes in his insightful discussion of Wilson's early years, he had sharpened his religious views by his sophomore year in college:

> Wilson at this time saw the relationship of the Christian faith to political life as primarily one of relating morals to action, principles to

12. Juan de Onis, "Latin View on Rights Is That Carter Doesn't Understand," New York *Times*, March 13, 1977.

13. Hugh Sidey, "Hazardous Course for Carter," *Time*, June 27, 1977, p. 9.

deeds; ignorant of the nature of actual political life, he showed no appreciation of the moral ambiguity inherent in most political decisions,
indeed in most areas of life. For Wilson, the problem of being a Christian was not being able to do good or even determining what was
good. Rather, confident of the truth revealed in "the Bible's standard,"
assured of his own duty and ability to obey that standard, Wilson
maintained that the Christian life, inside or outside of politics, was essentially the disciplined and faithful performance of one's duty.

Wilson's conception of duty as a direct, uncomplicated moral imperative contained many of the same assumptions reflected in
Carter's idea of human rights. Chief among them were a reliance
on the power of the individual and a tendency to regard statesmanship articulated in moral terms as a panacea. Mulder observes that "the continuous stress on individualism and morality
made Wilson appear conservative, but his rhetoric had the sound
of a zealous reformer."[14] This description aptly characterized the
tenor of Carter's rhetoric on human rights as well. Yet, the basis of
reform was largely a matter of transforming the individual, and
exactly how that process could be extended to complex policies
and systems remained problematic for both Wilson and Carter.

While there is not space here to treat extensively the parallels in
the rhetoric of Wilson and Carter, one critical example requires
mention. Having succeeded in 1905 as president of Princeton University in developing the preceptorial system of instruction, which
has been called "an almost unsurpassed example of educational
innovation," Wilson proposed another reform in 1906. Drawing
from southern Calvinism and moral principle, he argued for the
"quad plan," which would restructure residential arrangements
along the lines of democratic colleges and in sharp contrast to the
divisive campus clubs that had become dominant. Although the
trustees approved the plan in principle, John M. Cooper, Jr.,
notes that this was actually "the biggest blunder of his educational or political career." Students, alumni, and some previously
committed faculty reacted negatively, and Wilson was publicly
humiliated. Significantly, Cooper comments that there was a series of strategic errors: "Wilson's self-confidence formed the source
of both his failures and his successes, his weakness and strength.

14. John M. Mulder, *Woodrow Wilson: The Years of Preparation* (Princeton, 1978),
50, 244.

His most glaring failure with the quad plan lay in not consulting others and in not preparing for it. The faculty and trustees had heard little about the plan before Wilson broached it, which meant that important details had not been discussed and the president had not lined up support in advance."[15] This suggests a feature common to both Wilson and Carter: The strength and rightness of moral principles, like those on which the quad plan and human rights rested, were taken as sufficient unto themselves. The development of, indeed even the need for, a persuasive strategy to communicate the workings of such principles seems to have been largely ignored or discovered too late. This tendency to resist—in Sidey's words, to "combine influence with compromise"—set the stage for considerable difficulties in developing the concept of human rights.

The hazards of Carter's course centered on the need for definition. Carter's response to that need contained three essential dimensions: he chose to leave the process to secondary sources of authority, chiefly to officials in the Department of State; by so doing, he reinforced the perception of human rights as primarily a dimension of foreign, not domestic, policy; while continuing to use the language of moral principle, he did not develop a comprehensive method or pattern of relating moral inclination to specific problems and needs, despite serious pressure at home and abroad to do so.

Secretary of State Cyrus Vance became one of the first to speak about defining human rights. In a speech at the University of Georgia Law School, he presented three categories of human rights: "the right to be free from governmental violation of the integrity of the person, . . . the right to fulfillment of such vital needs as food, shelter, health care and education . . . the right to enjoy civil and political liberties." As Elizabeth Drew noted, these were incredibly sweeping definitions that did not develop the concept. Her questioning of State Department officials yielded little further illumination, and she reports that one such official simply said, "We still haven't worked out our tactics very well yet."[16]

15. John M. Cooper, Jr., *The Warrior and the Priest: Woodrow Wilson and Theodore Roosevelt* (Cambridge, Mass., 1983), 93, 96–97.

16. Elizabeth Drew, "A Reporter at Large: Human Rights," *New Yorker*, July 18, 1977, pp. 42, 44.

A somewhat better response came from Patricia Derian, assistant secretary of state for human rights. On "Face the Nation" on Christmas Day, 1977, she made several key points. First, the actual application of human rights policy means deciding "on a case by case basis," for "other interests must always be considered." Second, consistency is not necessarily the main issue in human rights—"you can do two things at one time." Third, there has been progress in human rights because "we have put human rights into international discussions; expectations have grown; we have made it an idea whose time has come." These comments are properly viewed as part of the extended pattern of Carter's moral rhetoric. The problem with the State Department responses was that they complicated and diminished the impact of Carter's moral logic. The State Department, given the task of defining and applying the concept, could apparently do neither. Statements by department officials could easily be perceived as an indication that they really did not know what the policy meant, or at the very least they were unable to explain it. Beyond that, portions of the State Department versions seemed considerably at odds with Carter's discourse of principle. An obvious tension existed between a "case by case" approach and the implication that "other interests" may equal the importance of the principle itself and the moral aspect of human rights. That tension remained unresolved.

Moreover, Carter himself did little to aid in creating a widely shared understanding of human rights. Indeed, the very decision that made human rights a policy area in the Department of State legitimized it as a branch of foreign policy. This was a powerful symbolic action in its own right, and one that seriously damaged the viability of the concept. By making human rights an official foreign policy area, Carter symbolically split foreign and domestic concerns. No similar placement of human rights was developed in the Department of Justice, for example, or in Health, Education and Welfare. This became increasingly crucial because almost from the time he spoke the words, American audiences began to focus on domestic problems as the most pressing areas for applying the moral logic of human rights. The key point is that while Carter and others struggled to speak in specific terms about the meaning of human rights, domestic audiences had no difficulty identifying a wide variety of concrete problems and issues that they now expected the Carter administration to address. Virtually every special-interest group in the country perceived the language of human rights as aimed directly at them: Minorities saw it as related to their needs; women's rights groups were certain it was meant for them; even coal miners then on strike thought Carter must have invented the term with them in mind. These groups tended to see their interests as exclusive, ends in themselves. No one, not Carter and certainly not the State Department, showed them how their interests related to those of other citizens under the concept of human rights, or even how human rights would provide direct relief for the problems they faced. Americans were left, then, with the ironic circumstance of a rhetorical dilemma: Having aroused the expectations of domestic audiences by allowing them to define their needs and wants in moral terms, Carter sought to make the concept of human rights operational in an area that bypassed domestic concerns in favor of foreign policy. In the concept of human rights, Carter had created a truly significant rhetorical form, but he had understood little about the psychology of the audiences who responded to that form. The words of Kenneth Burke come to mind: "Form is the creation of an appetite in the mind of the auditor, and the adequate satisfying of that appetite." [17] Carter's moral logic centered on the concept of human rights did much to create such appetites, especially in domestic audiences, but provided inadequate satisfaction.

This is not to say that Carter did not try to reach domestic audiences and infuse them with moral awareness and urgency. At Clinton, Massachusetts, in 1977 he observed, "I want our country to be the focal point for a deep concern about human beings all over the world." Note the direction of the moral logic here, from the internal experience of the United States to the world outside, a virtual parallel with the development of his own moral beliefs while growing up in rural Georgia. At the U.N. General Assembly, Carter envisioned a "hopeful world, a world dominated by increasing demands for basic freedoms, for fundamental rights, for higher standards of human existence." He then commented on the special role of the United States with respect to human rights: "I know perhaps as well as anyone that our own ideals in the area of human rights have not always been attained in the United States, but the American people have an abiding commitment to

17. Kenneth Burke, *Counter Statement* (Berkeley, 1968), 31.

the full realization of those ideals." This undoubtedly refers to race relations and civil rights and springs from Carter's background and experience in the South. He repeatedly said that the Civil Rights Act of 1964 was the best thing that had happened to the South in his lifetime, and it is clear that much of the moral intensity of human rights came from his personal beliefs about civil rights and black/white relationships. In retrospect, one wonders why the connection between civil rights and human rights was not developed more explicitly in Carter's rhetoric, for that would have provided domestic audiences with much greater grounds for identification.

Just when it appeared that Carter might find the key to open the concept of human rights fully, his discourse lapsed into vagueness that removed the concept from concrete experience. At Charleston, South Carolina, he used these terms to defend the concept: "Our policy is exactly what it appears to be: the positive and sincere expression of our deepest beliefs as a people. It's addressed not to any particular people or area of the world, but to all countries equally, yes, including our own country." One can almost hear different domestic audiences, not to mention officials at the Department of State, anxiously asking, "Mr. President, what does this mean?"

Late in Carter's presidency, the strategy for developing the moral logic of human rights was to link it with a series of parallel value terms. It was assumed that those terms would satisfy and motivate the American people. Hence, in the 1979 State of the Union Address, Carter stresses the cause of human rights by associating it with the founders of the country: "We are their heirs, and they are sending us a message across the centuries. The words they made so vivid are now growing faintly indistinct, because they are not heard often enough. They are words like 'justice,' 'equality,' 'unity,' 'truth,' 'sacrifice,' 'liberty,' 'faith,' and 'love.'" These terms constitute an arsenal of positive moral values that in Carter's perspective are useful to prompt the American people to overcome a powerful and threatening set of negative terms, "the threats of selfishness, cynicism, and apathy."[18]

18. Carter, "Opening Remarks at Clinton," and "Address Before General Assembly," both in Public Papers of the President, 1977, I, 385, 445, 450; Carter, "Remarks at the 31st Annual Meeting of the Southern Legislative Conference, July 21, 1977," ibid., II, 1314; Carter, "State of the Union Address," ibid., 1979, I, 108.

Precisely these same "devil terms," to borrow a phrase from Richard Weaver, became the basis for attack in Carter's noteworthy energy speech in July of 1979. In the striking opening to that speech, which many regard as his best effort since his grass-roots Law Day speech at the University of Georgia just prior to becoming a presidential candidate, Carter focused on "a fundamental threat to American democracy." That threat consisted of an erosion of confidence and loss of a sense of national purpose because "too many of us now tend to worship self-indulgence and consumption. Human identity is no longer defined by what one does, but by what one owns." [19] This speech reflects a remarkable turn in the logic of human rights. Human rights as a positive moral concept is not directly presented. Instead, the negative values that by their influence prevent the realization of the moral force of human rights are attacked, almost in the manner of a Puritan sermon. While this approach might have struck home earlier in Carter's administration, it came too late and was tied to an issue, energy policy, about which Americans were extremely uncertain in the first place. Although the speech was forceful, it was largely perceived as Carter's attempt to blame the public, to induce guilt without providing a way of redemption. Once again, Carter's moral logic fell into the pattern of appetite creation without corresponding satisfaction.

Conclusions

Carter clearly represents developments in the contemporary South. One finds evidence of a hard-driving reformist zeal characteristic of much of southern life and an intense degree of determination. At the same time, these are clothed in the vestments of reticence, loftiness bordering on aloofness, and a general sense of moral abstraction. Significantly, Carter at the end of his tenure indicated despair about his status as a southerner, depicting it as a burden never successfully overcome in the public mind. Ironically, the culture that conditioned him for public responsibility may also have stigmatized him to the point that it was difficult for the public to accept him in the roles for which he had trained.

19. Carter, "Energy and the National Goals," July 15, 1979, in Owen Peterson (ed.), *Representative American Speeches* (New York, 1980), 80–81.

Thus it seems appropriate to consider the relationship between Carter's rhetoric and the South, a relationship that is at least dualistic, if not more complex.

I agree with William Lee Miller's thoughtful description of Carter as a "Yankee from Georgia," basically nonrepresentative of southern tradition and experience. Even so, it can justifiably be said that Carter's experience in the South powerfully influenced him and that he made many of the choices reflected in his later rhetoric as a result of the shaping quality of that experience. The nature of this influence is noted in Miller's account of what he terms the particularly southern experience: "The very distinctiveness of the Southern experience—defeat, poverty, racism, tortured conscience, and Northern disapproval—that insulated the South from the rest of the nation, and that hobbled that sequence of modern industrial New Souths, provided also a crust under which the Puritan substratum of American culture was preserved. . . . It was preserved especially in parts of the South that were not included in 'Society'; in the Sunday School of the Plains Baptist Church more than in the Piedmont Driving Club." This indicates a pervasive sense of inferiority to which the characteristic response was a peculiar brand of pride and cultural cohesion. In addition to the general pressure of this essentially negative context, Carter also had to cope with a competing set of circumstances and demands. Carter confronted the necessity of having to bridge the gap between the security and relative power in his local situation and the insecurity and relative lack of prominence in any larger cultural context beyond the confines of Plains, and eventually beyond the bounds of the South. This obviously entailed critical choices for an aspiring public official, especially one who envisioned becoming a national figure.

Miller makes the insightful observation that the way Carter chose to respond to his southern experience was indeed unsouthern. Identifying southern regional identity and pride as "the 'collective egotism' and the defensive need to prove something," he remarks that "there are, though, two ways to do the proving. One is by way of the assertion of a superior code, or Southern ethic or way of life that is better than the busy, materialistic, unromantic North. . . . Another way is to adopt the Yankees' code and beat them at their own game: to outYankee the Yankees. Mr. Carter's way is the latter." Evidence of this was found in the perceptions that Carter was not gregarious or good company, that he consistently behaved as a loner, and that he displayed a basic lack of style and eloquence in his speaking. Says Miller, who is especially credible on this point because of his own experience as a speechwriter for the late Adlai Stevenson, "His spontaneous talk is not eloquent. In a particularly un-Southern way, his speeches have no rhythm. Big words pop out in unexpected places. Complex formulations intrude when he is trying to be simple. Parallels don't parallel."[20]

Paradoxically, there was another sense in which Carter was very much a product of the newest of the New Souths. I refer here to what may be called the "Atlanta syndrome," that is, the emergence of Atlanta as the center of an economically prosperous and culturally vibrant modern southern culture. This was especially true in the 1960s. Anyone trying to win public office statewide, not to mention nationally, had to gain the approval of the powers in that central city. Shoup says it is no accident that in the 1970 governor's race in Georgia, Carter received overwhelming financial support from "Atlanta's corporate lawyers and their clients" and only "one large contribution—of $500—came from a labor union." Shoup probes this dimension of Carter's support by raising the revealing question, why would the wealthy and socially prominent of Atlanta invest their money in Carter? His answer is that "the corporate leaders of the Atlanta establishment look for candidates who can command a large populist following while remaining sympathetic to corporate interests. Jimmy Carter was a man who could convincingly speak the language of the mass of voters, yet represent business interests once in office."[21] This is not to suggest that Carter was in any sense intentionally deceptive; no direct evidence points to that. However, his rhetoric reflected a lingering unresolved tension between idealism and pragmatism characteristic both of politics and of the contemporary South.

Perhaps the most revealing view of Carter's conception of the

20. William Lee Miller, *Yankee From Georgia: The Emergence of Jimmy Carter* (New York, 1978), 38, 26–27, 31–32.
21. Shoup, *The Carter Presidency and Beyond,* 26.

South came in his response to a question from a housewife during a public meeting in Yazoo City, Mississippi. When she inquired, "What aspects of what you consider to be your southern heritage have led to your concern with human rights in this nation and abroad?" Carter named three key factors: a core of religious beliefs "which emphasize compassion, love, concern about downtrodden people, equality in the eyes of God, basic human freedoms, courage to stand up for one's convictions, and so forth"; a "spirit of independence" rooted in rural cultures; and a tradition of belief in the principle of equality grounded in inalienable rights, so much so that "human rights is part of the American consciousness." Later, in remarks at Emory University in Atlanta, he expressed with some eloquence the culmination of his concept of southern heritage in a composite picture of "the real meaning of America." Carter tried to articulate that meaning in terms of the relationship of the many to the one: "We must, of course, continue to cherish the many. . . . But in this time of crisis, both material and spiritual, we must learn to place greater emphasis on the 'one'—on the shared values and the shared interests that unite us. For in a varied nation like our own, those transcendent values and that concern for the common good are the sole and indispensable basis for harmony and social cohesion." [22] Here Carter is saying that the ultimate lesson to be gleaned from southern experience is that the bonds that hold human beings together for the good of all are more important than features that separate them. It is in this sense that Carter's South is a moral South, indeed a metaphysical South, and his understanding of it is fundamentally mythic. It is moral because it has undergone the fire and suffering of separation, racial tension, and war and, having "overcome" these demons, stands "redeemed." The internal dynamics of the redemptive process follow a thoroughly mythic pattern. [23]

Such an orientation is evident both in the nature of Carter's language—the very choice, for example, of "human rights" as his central political words—and in the manner of his appeal, especially to southern audiences. For example, Glad observes that

22. Carter, *Public Papers of the President*, 1977, II, 1328, and 1979, II, 1563–64.
23. Rather than contrived falsehood, "mythic" and "mythic pattern" refer here to a coherent system of thought and belief that structures meaning. See Ernst Cassirer, *Language and Myth*, trans. Susanne Langer (New York, 1946).

"Carter's appeal to blacks was less a matter of his past record and/ or concrete policy proposals than certain mythic accounts (a rich elaboration on the facts, mostly) of what he and his family had done—topped off with his ability to relate to black people on the campaign trail and to win the endorsements of black political leaders." She also cites as a typical utterance, " 'It is a great tribute to the South that we have been able to overcome this problem [segregation] and we are recognized throughout the world for the progress we have made.'" [24] Carter's optimistic belief in the South's progress functions as a major force in shaping his rhetorical themes. It, in fact, supplied the energy that generated the moral logic of the rhetoric of human rights.

In the final analysis, Carter saw the South as a microcosm of the nation and indeed of the world. What civil rights was to the South, recombining a potent mixture of religious conviction, racial relations, and regional pride, human rights was to be for the nation and for the world. If we consider Jimmy Carter exclusively in terms of pragmatic success or failure, we shall probably never discern the enormity of what he attempted. We would do well to remember the words of one of Carter's favorite authors, James MacGregor Burns, on the nature of reform leadership by American presidents: "The capacity of presidents to transcend their everyday role as bargainers and coalition builders and to confront the overriding moral and social issues facing the country gives rise not only to questions of principle, purpose, and ethics, but to considerations of sheer political effectiveness—of presidential impact on social change and causation." [25] Certainly the first part of the equation—principle, purpose, and ethics—was present throughout for Carter. The second part eluded him in many circumstances, but that is not the harshest verdict of history. By examining Carter's discourse as a response to "the requirements of justice," this essay has aimed at putting us in a better position to view the world from the standpoint of Carter's moral logic and southern perspective. If for a moment we look through Carter's eyes, then perhaps we also will see that the distance from Archery and Plains to Washington and America is neither physical nor very far.

24. Glad, *Jimmy Carter*, 323, 325.
25. James MacGregor Burns, *Leadership* (New York, 1978), 390.

Nature has given women so much power that
the law has very wisely given them little.
—*Samuel Johnson*

I don't believe in women's rights; I believe in chivalry.
—*Phyllis Schlafly, 1974*

Women have been stepped on, crept upon and slept
upon too long.
—*Liz Carpenter, 1973*

On a Tupperware Pedestal
The ERA and the Southern Experience

Martha Solomon

In 1972, with strong majority votes in both the House and the Senate, the Equal Rights Amendment seemed certain of quick and easy ratification. Only hours after the Senate vote, Hawaii rushed to be the first state to ratify the amendment. The next day the state legislatures of Delaware, Nebraska, and New Hampshire enthusiastically gave their approval. The strong vote for ratification by the Texas Legislature suggested that support extended from coast to coast, through the heartland, and into the South. In the first year, twenty-two states endorsed the amendment, and by late 1973 it needed approval by only eight more states to gain the majority required for ratification. Then progress halted. In the next four years, only five more states ratified it and four states, which had been on the initial bandwagon, rescinded their approval. In 1978, with the early momentum gone, supporters requested a three-year extension of the ratification deadline (to

My special thanks to Richard Shelton and Yvonne Kozlowski of the Ralph B. Draughon Library at Auburn University and Teresa Ceravolo of the Birmingham Public Library, who provided valuable research help. Gregg Phifer at Florida State University and James Pence at University of North Carolina at Chapel Hill provided materials that were crucial in the preparation of the manuscript. Miller Solomon was invaluable in editing the manuscript. The phrase in the title is from Ron Hartung, "ERA's Threat to the Family," Tallahassee *Democrat*, April 10, 1977.

June 30, 1982). But even this successful move failed to rejuvenate the amendment. Although thirty-five states representing 72 percent of the population supported it and although polls even in nonratifying states showed a majority approving it, the ERA finally failed.[1]

The major stumbling block for the amendment was the South, where only Texas and Tennessee approved it. Before a House judiciary subcommittee in 1978, one observer argued that in the South "a handful of willful and mischievous men—two in Florida, two in North Carolina, five in South Carolina, seldom more than a dozen anywhere" were using political "fun and games" to block the ERA, deciding that justice toward women was an "expendable issue which can be used to barter for political mischief."[2] Although this appraisal of motivation may be biased, it is clear now, a few years after the failure of the amendment, that the widespread refusal of southern legislatures to ratify the ERA was the crucial factor in its defeat and merits fuller and more dispassionate examination. Although observers have offered various reasons for the amendment's failure in the South, none has examined closely the rhetorical factors that influenced the outcome. This essay explores those factors. First, it traces briefly the legislative course of the ERA in the South; second, it examines the strategies and issues that became salient in southern debates on the amendment; finally, it probes the interaction between those features of the debate and those characteristics of southern culture that led to the amendment's defeat there.

1. *Congressional Quarterly*, October 28, 1972, p. 280; United States Commission on Civil Rights, *Statement on the Equal Rights Amendment* (Washington, D.C., 1978), reports the House vote totals differently (p. 2); Janet K. Boles, *The Politics of the Equal Rights Amendment* (New York, 1979), 2–3. For discussion of rescission, see William H. Heckman, Jr., "Ratification of a Constitutional Amendment: Can a State Change Its Mind?" *Connecticut Law Review*, VI (1973), 28–35; Raymond M. Planell, "The Equal Rights Amendment: Will States Be Allowed to Change Their Minds?" *Notre Dame Lawyer*, LXIX (1974), 657–70; Ruth Ginsburg, "Ratification of the Equal Rights Amendment: A Question of Time," *Texas Law Review*, LVII (1979), 919. *Congressional Quarterly*, June 22, 1978, p. 1852; United States Commission on Civil Rights, *The Equal Rights Amendment: Guaranteeing Equal Rights for Women Under the Constitution* (Washington, D.C., 1981), 2.

2. John Herbers, "The Battle Over the Equal Rights Amendment: Emotional Tactics, Confused Issues," New York *Times*, May 28, 1978.

The ERA in Southern Legislatures

The ERA initially followed the pattern of quick ratification typical of successful amendments. Six states ratified within two days of congressional approval. Of the thirty-two state legislatures in session later that year, twenty-one approved it, sometimes suspending rules to avoid the delay of committee consideration. For example, on March 28, 1972, the Texas Senate, following this pattern, sent the amendment to the Committee on Transportation, the only committee in session, which immediately endorsed it. The Texas House's referral to its Committee on Constitutional Amendments also took only a single day. Tennessee also rapidly ratified on April 4, 1972. But elsewhere in the South the amendment was stymied. However, southern legislative struggles over its passage varied from state to state both in intensity and in the closeness of the final outcome. For example, in Mississippi the amendment never emerged from committee, though the 1976 senate committee vote was only four to three against. In North Carolina after an initial defeat by the house in 1975, the ERA was approved in 1977 and sent to the senate, which rejected it by two votes. Similarly, the Florida House approved the ERA in 1975 while the senate rejected it by only a few votes. In 1977 the Florida Senate voted again, and again narrowly withheld approval. In Virginia, which had added an equal rights amendment to its state constitution in 1971, the senate twice failed by a single vote out of forty to muster the majority needed to ratify, though supporters on both occasions had more votes than did the opposition. The Virginia House Committee on Privileges and Elections kept the ERA from floor consideration for seven consecutive years, often resorting to closed meetings and once permitting no speeches on either side. Opponents in the South Carolina House tabled it by a narrow margin. They called for a surprise vote minutes after the lunch recess when many members had not returned.[3]

The attitudes of individual southern governors, which ranged from warm support to strong opposition, were not tied to legis-

3. Boles, *Politics*, 61, 149; Riane Tennenhaus Eisler, *The Equal Rights Handbook* (New York, 1978), 91–92; New York *Times*, January 22, 1977, February 3, 1979, February 14, 1980; "Rights Amendment Seems Dead for '75 After New Setback," New York *Times*, March 27, 1975.

lative outcomes. For example, in Virginia the ousting of a governor who opposed the ERA and the election of an ERA supporter did not secure passage. Jimmy Carter's support in Georgia did not gain adoption; instead, the folksy anti-ERA testimony of a former Georgia governor, Marvin Griffin, set the tone of the legislative debate. Although Florida governor Reubin Askew volunteered to call a special session of the legislature to consider ratification and although South Carolina governor James B. Edwards actively lobbied for the amendment, both states rejected it.[4]

Strategies: Color, Chaos, and Competence

Despite the variety of legislative tactics used to defeat the ERA from state to state, similar strategies emerged throughout the region. Because the ratification process involved state legislatures, both supporters and opponents of the amendment lobbied representatives intensely. The pressures applied by the anti-ERA forces are well illustrated in a Tennessee legislator's explanation of his vote to rescind: Rescission "won't be legal; Tennessee will still be in the ratified column, but it will get those hysterical women off my back." The "hysterical women" were members of Phyllis Schlafly's "housewife corps"; but a similar vehemence animated both sides. A Georgia legislator testified: "We're more afraid of some of these women's groups than we are of men's groups because they can really build up an organization against you and really tear you apart in the Capitol. It's hard to get around some of these women's organizations."[5]

The lobbying efforts on both sides were varied and sometimes colorful. Opponents often sported red stop-sign buttons with "STOP ERA" on them while supporters wore green buttons with "ERA YES." Florida opponents of the ERA wore buttons with two nude children and the legend "There is a difference." Banners

4. Ben A. Franklin, "Loser in Virginia Governor Election Declines to Felicitate G.O.P. Victor," New York *Times*, November 10, 1977; "Georgia Turns Down Equality for Women: Idea Called Communistic," Los Angeles *Times*, January 29, 1974; Marjorie Hunter, "Lobbyists for Equal Rights Amendment Focus on 4 States," New York *Times*, November 27, 1978; Eisler, *The Equal Rights Handbook*, 77.

5. Lisa Cronin Wohl, "White Gloves and Combat Boots: The Fight for ERA," *Civil Liberties Review*, I (1974), 83; Boles, *Politics*, 113.

and signs summarizing the issues were also plentiful: "Send the libbers to Siberia—We'll stay home and keep the Beds Warm," "Motherhood is not a DIRTY word," and "ERA is ANTI-Women, Anti-Motherhood, ANTI-Family. ERA SCARES ME!" Since women opponents identified themselves as "feminine" rather than "feminist," they often dressed to convey the desired image. During the rescission debate in Texas, scores of women in pink dresses crowded the legislative chambers. Red dresses, floppy hats, and red-checked aprons were symbolic attire for opponents in Florida, where they also carried red roses to give to legislators voting against the amendment. To counter accusations that they were unfeminine, supporters of the measure sometimes deliberately chose to lobby in traditional female clothing, eschewing blue jeans or slacks. Even food became a symbolic weapon in the struggle. AWARE (American Women Are Richly Endowed), an opposition group in Tennessee, offered legislators homemade bread; in Arkansas the loaves were accompanied with a note, "From the Bread Makers to the Bread Winners." Georgia opponents in checked aprons provided homemade cookies while supporters prepared a meal of baked chicken, creamed corn, and peach cobbler. On the first anniversary of house passage, North Carolina supporters sent birthday cakes to legislators who supported the amendment. Opponents received only infant pacifiers with the note "NOW will not be pacified till the ERA is ratified."[6]

Although both sides used many identical strategies, three distinctive features of the opponents' campaign became great assets. First, in contrast to supporters of the amendment, who relied on established women's organizations with disparate purposes composed largely of professionals, opponents developed an effective grass-roots group of many housewives with a single unifying goal—defeat of the ERA. Second, this large grass-roots structure allowed strategists to initiate a letter-writing campaign that literally inundated legislators. Finally, opponents "witnessed" their allegiance to shared values and beliefs. Although such public avowals often did not address the substantive issues, they injected a moral and theological tone into the debate and, thereby, served effectively as ethical and emotional proof.

6. Boles, *Politics*, 114–15, 124, 180; Carol Ashkinase, "ERA Proponents Treat Ga. Legislators," Atlanta *Constitution*, January 20, 1981.

Early in the struggle the organizational structure of the two sides became a major strategic difference. To disseminate pro-ERA information, supporters initially relied on local chapters of national women's organizations that endorsed passage, such as the American Association of University Women (AAUW), the League of Women Voters (LWV), and the National Federation of Business and Professional Women's Clubs (BPW). Until 1975, the national coalition of such groups was loose and poorly coordinated. Only when the momentum for ratification ebbed in 1974 did the BPW take independent, decisive action in mapping a concerted legislative strategy; and it was January of 1976 before a more dynamic coalition was formed as ERAmerica. Even with cooperation at the national level, local groups were still loosely coordinated and sometimes even competitive. Often the ERA's supporters had difficulty unifying groups with disparate temperaments and interests. Coalitions disintegrated in debates over lobbying strategies, over the attempt to mesh conservative and radical elements, over the selection of speakers from outside the region, and even over the best attire to wear in lobbying efforts. As one supporter lamented: "We have become the dispersed silent majority."[7] Ironically, the political diversity of the ERA supporters proved to be an organizational liability.

Initially opponents also had no single national focus. But after devoting the February, 1972, issue of the *Phyllis Schlafly Report* to attacking the ERA, Schlafly established the National Committee to Stop ERA and castigated the measure in almost every subsequent issue. Unlike supporters' groups that had other, often different and even opposite goals, her national organization established state and local chapters with a single purpose: blocking passage of the ERA. The answer of an active Stop ERA member to my question about the history of the movement in Alabama suggests how groups developed. After being alerted to the dangers of the amendment by a friend of Schlafly's, the woman felt that those working against the measure were ineffective. Concerned about its impact, she organized a local Stop ERA chapter and served as its chair. Supporters throughout the country envied the tight, personally

7. Boles, *Politics*, 28, 62–65. Similar intragroup conflict emerged in Louisiana. Patricia Beyea, "ERA's Last Mile," *Civil Liberties Review*, IV (1977), 49. Wohl, "White Gloves and Combat Boots," 82.

dedicated organization of Stop ERA. Patricia Beyea, noting the group's success in Florida, asserted: "ERA opponents have waged a very astute, tightly organized campaign. The STOP ERA effort has shown discipline and single purpose to defeat the Evil Rights Amendment, as it is called by the Conservative Caucus." David Brady and Kent Tedin traced the loss of momentum for ratification to "the emergence of an organized coalition of women who are vocally opposed to ratification . . . and who have been very active in lobbying state legislatures." *Newsweek* agreed: "When the feminists did go after the votes, they sometimes did it badly. . . . ERA supporters collected big name endorsements (from Betty Ford and Rosalynn Carter), only to find themselves out-maneuvered at the grass roots level by ERA opponents who skillfully lobbied state legislators."[8]

Often using these grass-roots groups, strategists organized a two-pronged letter-writing campaign. First, organized groups outside the region mailed letters to voters in key states, berating the amendment and urging them to take action. Second, voters then wrote directly to their representatives. The Washington-based Conservative Caucus (TCC) wrote to 90,000 voters in North Carolina and 150,000 in Florida. Howard Phillips, TCC's national director, credited his mailings with defeating the ERA in those states, claiming that legislators were heavily influenced by calls and letters from constituents that "flooded them on the eve of voting." Although the letters were sometimes identical, they did have an impact. An anti-ERA pamphlet reported of the North Carolina mailings: "We are told tens of thousands of postcards were sent to members of the North Carolina Senate as a result of the TCC mailing, which is credited with a decisive role in the outcome." The two-level letter-writing campaign was effective both in increasing awareness of the issues urged by the opponents and in providing an opportunity for direct lobbying by grass-roots sympathizers. As Janet Boles contends: "Letter writing is particularly appropriate and effective for the opposition movement," since it can be done at home, at one's discretion, "ideal condi-

8. Boles, *Politics*, 68; Stop ERA member to the author, September 8, 1977; Beyea, "ERA's Last Mile," 46; David W. Brady and Kent L. Tedin, "Ladies in Pink: Religion and Political Ideology in the Anti-ERA Movement," *Social Science Quarterly*, LVI (1976), 564; Susan Fraker, "Women vs. Women," *Newsweek*, July 25, 1977, p. 38.

tions for the housewife antagonistic to the ERA who wants to do something."[9]

The ERA's opponents also frequently used a version of the witnessing that is part of fundamentalist religions. Witnessing, in this sense, is a public affirmation of personal beliefs and values, in the presence of nonbelievers and skeptics as well as supporters. Usually, these public affirmations were only tangentially related to the economic, political, and social issues raised by supporters. Instead, they were emotional appeals to traditional, shared values. For example, one woman appealed to her representative: "Please keep our home, family, marriage, and children the way they should be."[10] The implication was, of course, that supporters of the amendment did not share these values and that the ERA was antithetical to them. Frequently, opponents brought small children with them to lobby as a concrete demonstration of their values, commitments, and priorities.

Proponents of the ERA castigated such testimony and behavior as irrational emotionalism. But such charges, though logically sound, underestimated the power of witnessing in developing emotional and ethical proof. The obvious sincerity of these people and the fact that the values they espoused were widely held made their public witnessing rhetorically powerful. Moreover, their appeal to traditional values introduced a moral note into the debates. In fact, this witnessing, growing out of a theological tradition, carried religious as well as moral associations. Thus, whether the result was rationally justified or not, legislators who did not join the opposition risked alienating a major religious constituency.

In essence, then, while both groups shared many lobbying strategies, the opponents' single focus and their tighter grassroots organizations, developed in response to a perceived crisis, became assets in the extensive, often prolonged lobbying. Schlafly became an effective, nationally recognized spokesperson for the opposition, and her frequent public appearances throughout the South enhanced the group's image as an effective, coordinated,

9. Boles, *Politics*, 125, 7, 131; Herbers, "The Battle Over the Equal Rights Amendment"; Eisler, *The Equal Rights Handbook*, 136.

10. Kaye Northcutt, "Fighting the ERA: The Ladies Mobilize," *Texas Observer*, November 15, 1974, p. 1.

consistent lobby. In contrast, many national supporters, like Bella Abzug and Gloria Steinem, were less effective as advocates in the South because their personalities and backgrounds differed too dramatically from the constituency they needed to court. Problems in uniting disparate sympathetic groups and in coordinating lobbying activities further hampered supporters' attempts to educate and persuade. Moreover, opponents had a particularly well developed, intense letter-writing campaign. Finally, the witnessing of opponents undoubtedly had a strong emotional impact on legislators.

Emergent Issues

The ERA as a Trojan Horse

Advocating change in a traditionally conservative area, the ERA supporters faced formidable but predictable rhetorical obstacles. While their strategies often paralleled those of the opposition, their approach to the issues surrounding the passage of the ERA was too often dictated by the opposition's skillful campaign. In effect, supporters of the ERA were constantly on the defensive, reacting to charges that their cause was invidiously destructive of traditional southern culture, morality, and religion. One widely distributed pamphlet, *The Equal Rights Amendment: A Trojan Horse,* neatly summarized the opponents' depiction of the ERA. Beginning with a picture of the amendment as a Trojan horse with an attractive woman's head on a base strewn with flowers, the pamphlet uses cartoons to suggest the losses women will suffer with the ERA: the adverse impact on working women; the threat of women being drafted; the encroachments of the federal government on schools and domestic-relations law; the danger of abortion on demand; the legitimization of homosexual marriage (the stomach of the Trojan horse is shown disgorging a homosexual couple with a puzzled baby asking, "Mama?"); and the misuse of federal funds to finance "women's lib." The final page shows the ERA Trojan horse with a malevolent look, trampling a frightened and fleeing family.[11] This view of the ERA as a deceptive, destruc-

11. Vic Lockman, *The Equal Rights Amendment: A Trojan Horse* (Alton, 1976).

tive measure permeated the ratification debates in the South, thus allowing opponents to dictate the focus of public discussion. Opponents pictured the ERA as a measure that would undermine society and religion by despoiling women's special privileges and status, intrude into private matters and states' rights, and oppress women with extra responsibilities and "mandated equality." Their rhetorical vision was of a struggle to maintain societal values against a legislative Trojan horse concealing federal bureaucrats, women's libbers, and homosexuals. In a public hearing before the Alabama Women's Commission, one opponent vividly articulated this theme: "As a jurist, a mother and a grandmother, I find the provisions and possibilities of the so-called Equal Rights Amendment a vicious threat to the very foundation of our country. This nation, based upon the family unit, has survived nearly two hundred years. But should the stability, the security and the morality of a solid family basis be eliminated, this nation will surely fall. Just as the Tutwiler Hotel was recently imploded with dynamite, detonated from bottom to top, the structure collapsed beginning at the foundation. So will this nation go down in ruins—not from outside forces—but from within." [12] Testifying before a legislative committee in North Carolina, another opponent labeled the ERA a "Pandora's box" and connected women's agitation for it with Eve's temptation of Adam to sin against God's order. An opponent in the same hearings, inebriated with metaphor, asserted: "ERA is an invisible asset [acid?] eating away at the moral anchorlines in North Carolina society. You are asked to cast us adrift into the plunging currents of egalitarian nihilism. The ERA drive is a rodent cut[ting] through the cupboard that houses the cream of all systems of human government of all time." [13] In Florida a letter to the Tallahassee *Democrat* highlighted this threat: "Let me say that we have a war on our hands, a war is

12. Ms. Glea H. Tutwiler, Testimony in the Public Hearings on the Status of Women for the Seventh Congressional District before the Alabama Women's Commission, March 2, 1974, hereinafter cited as Alabama Hearings. Pagination in the transcripts is inconsistent; thus, no page numbers are noted. Transcripts were typed phonetically as the testimony was delivered; spelling errors have been corrected. Grammatical errors and questionable transcriptions are noted.

13. Mrs. Jane Fondeal, Testimony before the North Carolina House of Representatives Constitutional Amendments Committee, January 26, 1977, pp. 18–19, hereinafter cited as North Carolina Hearings. Obvious spelling errors are cor-

being waged against our families, and against the constitutional principle of states rights. The Equal Rights Amendment is the weapon being used to destroy us."[14]

The rights women would allegedly lose included the right to be supported by their husbands, to have a home provided for them, and to receive homemakers' Social Security upon the husband's retirement. Opponents argued that the loss of these rights would evict women from their homes and push them into the work force, since they would be equally responsible for supporting the family. Deprived of the privilege of caring for their own children, they would be required to place the children in state-run nurseries and schools. "The Women's Lib Movement has, as a direct goal," one opponent argued, "the establishment of training schools for children of all ages to take away the training of children from the home and put it in the power of the state. I can only imagine, in my most horrible dreams, of this bright new country and what it would be if people like this were to train our children for a generation or two." One Alabama opponent prophesied the end of freedom for women in America: "I submit to you all women would be literally enslaved upon passage of the Equal Rights Amendment. . . . The alternative to protecting women is to force them by law to struggle, to fight on their own for survival in the market place, which would disrupt the natural evolution of human behavior. . . . The real issue at stake is freedom. Today women have the freedom to choose between staying at home or going to work. In essence, women currently have the right to reject or accept their cultural heritage as women. The Equal Rights Amendment will take away this freedom." Schlafly, associating passage of the ERA with "Women's lib," concluded, "The Women's lib movement is *not* an honest effort to secure better jobs for women who want or need to work outside the home. This is just the superficial sweet talk to win support for a radical 'movement.' Women's lib is a total assault on the role of the American woman as wife and mother, and on the family as the basic unit of society."[15]

rected, with grammatical errors and questionable transcriptions noted. E. R. Isley, North Carolina Hearings, 33–34.

14. Tallahassee *Democrat*, April 10, 1977.

15. Ron Brotherton, *ERA—Women's Lib: What Effect Will It Have on Your Life?* (West Monroe, La., 1975), 11; Phyllis Schlafly, "The Precious Rights ERA Will Take

Not only would the ERA threaten the family by forcing women to work outside the home, opponents insisted, but the amendment would also permit homosexual marriages—perhaps such couples might adopt children—and would thus undermine morality and affront God. Schlafly listed "the homosexuals and the lesbians" together with "the abortionists" as groups profiting from the ERA. A young lobbyist in Florida argued: "Homosexuals—they could get married and adopt children. And if all the inequalities between men and women were wiped out, I'd have to marry my roommate if I wanted to live with her." In Florida, where homosexuality became a key issue, many expressed similar fears: "Homosexuals cannot reproduce, they can only recruit—that's a known fact. The ERA would open the door to legalizing their lifestyle and allow them to approach young children openly."[16]

In addition to harming society by undermining the family, the ERA would violate the sexual roles mandated by the Bible, opponents argued. Contrasting the Bible with a National Organization for Women pamphlet that urged restructuring of sex roles, one North Carolinian characterized the ERA as "a direct rebuke of God's roles for women as he ordained us. . . . If this amendment is passed we'd better put away the Bible as our highest symbol of truth, because we will be making a mockery of God's order for men and women and we will have condoned all that is the antithesis of finding truth [sic] liberation according to God's law." During floor debate in Florida, Representative Alan Trask, having read aloud passages from the Bible, opposed the ERA by insisting that "we should never pass anything contrary to the teachings of God." A Georgia minister was even more impassioned: "God clearly created male and female as different and distinct, though both are equally human. Thus, to deny the difference is to deny reality, but, more than that, to deny the word of God. . . . I would

Away from Wives," *Phyllis Schlafly Report*, August, 1973; Brenda Carson, Alabama Hearings, March 2, 1974; Schlafly, "What's Wrong With 'Equal Rights' for Women?" *Phyllis Schlafly Report*, February, 1972.

16. Schlafly, "The Hypocrisy of ERA Proponents," *Phyllis Schlafly Report*, July, 1975; Nora Leto, "The ERA Will Never Go Away," Tallahassee *Democrat*, April 14, 1977; Gina Biggar quoted in Roger M. Williams, "Women Against Women: The Clamor Over Equal Rights," *Saturday Review*, June 25, 1977, p. 11.

242 Contemporary Southern Rhetoric

point out here that I believe this is the essence of ERA. It is a denial of God, both as to his person and to his program and purposes for mankind."[17]

Opponents' insistence that the ERA would intrude into individual lives was equally emotional. One opponent asked, "Do most citizens realize the authority over the individual's personal life which would be placed in the hands of the judicial system? . . . Whose moral and national standards will this government in control be promoting? How will our children, torn from the loving arms of their mothers to be raised by strangers, be affected?" In print and on the stump, Schlafly argued that the ERA would force all single-sex schools to integrate and would compel churches to ordain women. A pamphlet distributed by the Jefferson County, Alabama, Committee to Stop ERA alleged that it would force integration of boys' and girls' gym classes and would prohibit single-sex organizations such as the Girl Scouts, Mortar Board, YMCA, and sororities. In his federal minority report on the ERA, which was widely distributed by Stop ERA groups, Senator Sam Ervin argued that dormitories, prisons, and bathrooms would be integrated if the ERA passed. An opponent in the North Carolina hearings linked the amendment to the Department of Health, Education and Welfare's activities in enforcing federal legislation in schools and concluded: "It is obvious that the powers that be are determined to completely take over our lives."[18]

Supporters of the ERA faced two tasks: demonstrating the need for the amendment and answering opponents' charges against it. As Boles observed, opponents did not need to prove its adverse impact: "They only needed to generate doubt in the minds of the general public."[19] After the opposition mobilized, ERA proponents were on the defensive. Often they were drawn into arguing

17. Marilyn DeBrees, North Carolina Hearings, 11; Trask quoted in Williams, "Women Against Women," 46; Bob Spencer, "Equal Rights for Women," in *God's Truth for Today* (Atlanta, 1973), 56, quoted in Boles, *Politics*, 109.

18. Millie Hobbs, Alabama Hearings, May 11, 1974; Schlafly, "How ERA Will Affect Churches and Private Schools," *Phyllis Schlafly Report*, March, 1975; *STOP the Equal Rights Amendment* (Pamphlet/newsletter distributed by Jefferson County, Alabama, Committee to Stop ERA, n.d.); Senator Sam J. Ervin, Jr., *Equal Rights Amendment: Excerpts from the Minority Views of Sen. Sam J. Ervin, Jr.* (Pamphlet distributed by Stop ERA, n.d.); Mrs. D. L. Anderson, North Carolina Hearings, 29.

19. Boles, *Politics*, 108.

against the "straw men and red herrings" of their opponents rather than justifying the need for the measure in their own terms. In response to opponents' depiction of the ERA as malevolent, pernicious, and deceptive, southern proponents took three major tacks: they urged the need for the amendment; they explained its ramifications, often concentrating on refuting charges by the opposition; and they described it as a "human rights" measure intended to aid men as well as women. These approaches usually drew their force from logical argument and evidence rather than from vivid rhetorical depictions.

To establish the need for the ERA, proponents pointed to legal inequities and identified the amendment as a crucial step in guaranteeing full citizenship to women. For example, the report entitled *The Legal Status of Homemakers in Georgia* followed one hypothetical female resident, Jane Smith, through marriage and divorce to illustrate the problems in current domestic law. The report concluded that Georgia law did not offer women much real protection and even penalized them in dealing with their spouses. ERA advocates cited reports by the Commission on the Status of Women that reached similar conclusions about most southern states.[20]

Supporters also stressed the lower wages of women and their problems in getting credit. A typical supporter at the hearings in North Carolina, citing the differences in pay between male and female professionals, technicians, and administrators, asserted that women "have been denied compensations and employment that have been enjoyed by men. Too long they have been passed over for promotion because of discrimination against the sex." In Louisiana, Mrs. Gillis W. Long noted: "A dead man can get more credit than an alive woman." A southern representative of the League of Women Voters explained the ERA's benefits for poor and minority working women: "Through our studies, we have realized that ERA will help most the disadvantaged women who must work and who now lack education and an opportunity to obtain decently paying jobs. It would help them and their daughters by opening more educational programs through the schools, voca-

20. Lucy S. McGough, *The Legal Status of Homemakers in Georgia* (Homemaker's Committee of the National Commission on the Observance of International Women's Year, 1977), 1, 13. Commission reports are available from the Government Printing Office.

tional programs and armed forces benefits for which they are not now eligible. . . . It is easy for those of us who are advantaged to say we want to stay on our pedestal, but for many women, the laws which are supposed to keep them on a pedestal, put them not on a pedestal at all, but in a cage."[21]

To refute the charge that the ERA would destroy women's rights to financial support and would hurt them in obtaining fair divorce settlements, supporters noted that the current laws were not as favorable as opponents contended. One Alabama proponent quoted the *Report on Alimony and Child Support* by the Citizens Advisory Committee on the Status of Women: "The rights of women and children are much more limited than is generally known and enforcement is very inaccurate. A married woman living with her husband can, in practice, get only what he chooses to give her. . . . Alimony is granted in only a small percentage of cases. . . . Alimony and child support awards are very, very difficult to collect." Reacting to arguments that women would lose the protection they had, Georgia representative Cathy Steinberg argued: "What protection? . . . It is unfortunate that these folks don't know the law in Georgia. Let me state some facts. Women in Georgia have little, if any, legal protection." One male in North Carolina attacked the chauvinism in the desire of male legislators to protect women from the ERA: "Could it be that we southern men take pride in taking care of women? Just as we took care of our blacks?"[22]

Because they were supporting a change in the legal system, proponents were also compelled to predict the ramifications of the amendment. Often relying on materials developed by national organizations, state pro-ERA groups issued fact sheets and pamphlets that outlined the amendment's impact. One such pamphlet, issued by the Georgia Association of Educators and entitled *The Equal Rights Amendment: What it does and does not do*, reports: "ERA will assure that the rights of Americans, established in the Constitution, shall apply equally to all Americans

21. Robert Blackburn, North Carolina Hearings, 64; "Equal Rights Amendment Backers Hear Ms. Long," New Orleans *Times-Picayune*, May 5, 1974; Janet Richards, Alabama Hearings, March 2, 1974.
22. Pat Boyd, Alabama Hearings, March 2, 1974; Cathy Steinberg, Speech to the American Association of University Women, Savannah, September 15, 1979, p. 3; Charles Petty, North Carolina Hearings, 72.

without regard to gender. ERA does not: say men and women are the same; . . . affect personal relationships; force wives to work outside the home; interfere with the family or family relationships; create or require unisex restrooms; legalize same sex marriages; eliminate a husband's legal obligation to support his family; affect abortion laws in any way; change homemakers' rights to social security coverage through their husbands' qualifications; interfere with states' rights—ERA must be ratified by the states in order to become part of the Constitution of our country, therefore the states have the final say, and that's what states' rights under the Constitution is all about."[23] This pamphlet is indicative of the extent to which opponents determined the rhetorical stance of ERA advocates. Repeatedly, pro-amendment forces were forced to deny the allegations of the opposition. They were required to state what the ERA "does not do."

The opposition's religious appeals for traditional family roles were countered by alternate interpretations of and attitudes toward biblical injunctions. In testimony, one ERA supporter pointed to Christ's actions as a model for a new religious view of women: "The New Testament reveals countless ways in which women are an integral part of Jesus's ministry. He gave them new respect and new dignity. He forsook the old tradition of his day—he talked to women in public—he visited in their homes—and it's little wonder . . . that women were the last ones at the cross. They were the first ones at the Resurrection, too. . . . Jesus vigorously promoted the dignity and equality of women in a very male dominated society." Similarly, Dr. Charles Petty, director of the Christian Life Council of the Baptist State Convention, answered arguments against the ERA with close attention to Christian teachings about family life. He concluded: "Like the Pied Piper, those who advocate the simplistic solutions, who contend that all would be right in family life if the ERA would be defeated, that women would just be submissive, who promote female obedience to a man rather than to the lordship of Jesus Christ, lead us down a yellow brick road, not to happiness, but over a cliff."[24]

Some opposition charges about the amendment's dire con-

23. Georgia Association of Educators, *The Equal Rights Amendment: What it does and does not do* (Pamphlet distributed by the Georgia League of Women Voters, n.d.).
24. Marse Hunt (chairman of the Baptist State Convention of North Carolina), North Carolina Hearings, 59; Petty, North Carolina Hearings, 73–76.

sequences were ridiculed by supporters. "Unisex" toilets they labeled the "potty" issue, noting that the right to privacy was protected constitutionally. A supporter in Alabama termed that objection "gibberish" while another offered a bizarre non sequitur: "I hope no one takes seriously the argument that public restrooms would no longer be segregated by sex. I ask you, would Mrs. Gerald Ford [who supported the ERA] use a men's room." They also asserted that the amendment would not keep states from prohibiting homosexual marriages as long as the statute applied equally to male and female couples. They rejected firmly the argument that passage of the ERA would undermine the family, noting that it would not compel any woman to join the work force or mandate any change in personal relationships. As one representative of the American Association of University Women in Alabama argued: "The ERA will not break down the family unit, but will strengthen it; women will still be able to choose being a full-time homemaker as a way of life; marriage will be truly a partnership, and this does not mean that the woman will have to go to work outside of the home to contribute to the income. Her contribution as a homemaker is as valuable, if not more valuable, than a paycheck." Another legislative witness was more concise: "The Equal Rights Amendment can't make you work; it will just protect you if you decide to do so."[25]

The stance of supporters of the ERA was usually defensive and the resultant tone was sometimes condescendingly pedantic. For example, one handout that explained the amendment's provisions was entitled *The Equal Rights Amendment: Cool Facts for the Hot-Headed Opposition*. A frustrated supporter in Georgia acknowledged the power of the opponents' allegations against the amendment: "It was misinformation which defeated the ERA in Georgia." To counter misinformation, Virginia supporters equipped a caravan that was painted red, white, and blue to tour the state, spreading the "truth" about the ERA.[26] Supporters assumed that presenting the "facts" about the ERA would allay fears

25. Judy Wilson, Alabama Hearings, September 24, 1974; Dorothy Moser, Alabama Hearings, March 2, 1974; Marguerite Dollar, Alabama Hearings, March 1, 1975.

26. Georgia League of Women Voters, *The Equal Rights Amendment: Cool Facts for the Hot-Headed Opposition* (N.p., n.d.); Boles, *Politics*, 104; Susan Braudy and Mary Thom, "ERA: On the Move in Virginia," *MS.*, February, 1978, p. 19.

and persuade doubters; they believed that by refuting inaccurate assertions about the amendment with argument and evidence, they could neutralize what they viewed as the emotional tactics of the opposition.

The ERA as the Extra Responsibilities Amendment

In addition to showing the ERA as a despoiler of women's special status and of societal values, opponents characterized it as an oppressor of women. One issue of the *Phyllis Schlafly Report* termed the ERA the "Extra Responsibilities Amendment." Another issue depicted the plight of the factory worker "who stands on her feet all day in front of a machine, whose work may be sweaty or exhausting, and who is eager to go home to take care of her children." Such women, Schlafly argued, are now exempt from mandatory overtime and certain physically demanding jobs and appreciate the special rest rooms with couches where they "can escape a few moments rest each day from the drudgery of a manual labor job." By terminating such special treatment, the ERA would unfairly oppress these women. One pamphlet, *The Real World of the Working Woman*, bore illustrations of a woman straining to lift a seventy-five-pound box while another, looking dismayed, is jolted mercilessly by a jackhammer. A letter on the back cover from Naomi McDaniel, president of Women of Industry, avers: "ERA should be called the TWERP Amendment: Terminate Women's Extra Rights and Privileges." The pamphlet characterizing the ERA as a Trojan horse argued: "The ERA will *wipe out* existing laws that protect women from being . . . *Beasts of Burden and Midnight Oil-Burners.* . . . ERA is called 'the liftin' and 'totin' bill."[27]

The ERA's impact on the draft was a prominent issue everywhere. Observers in Georgia and Florida thought it was crucial in debates over the amendment. An editorial in the Biloxi, Mississippi, *Daily Herald* quoted Ervin's statement that the ERA was like "using an atomic bomb to exterminate a few mice." "Although we retreat from Mr. Ervin's extravagant language," the *Daily Her-*

27. Schlafly, "How ERA Will Hurt Divorced Women," *Phyllis Schlafly Report*, May, 1974; Schlafly, "Women in Industry Oppose Equal Rights Amendment," *Phyllis Schlafly Report*, July, 1973; Naomi McDaniel, *The Real World of the Working Woman* (Alton, n.d.); Lockman, *A Trojan Horse*, 4.

ald said, "we feel as he does that it is not proper to draft women into the army and 'have their fair forms blasted into fragments by the bombs and shells of the enemy.' . . . We may be a bit old-fashioned, but to paraphrase an old pacifist song, 'We didn't raise our daughter to be a soldier.'" One Georgia legislator described a family's upheaval under the ERA: "If a mother's draft number comes up, can you imagine the men staying home scrubbing floors and watching the war news while the child learns a new version of 'Momma comes Marching Home again.'" In a pink pamphlet entitled *Ladies! Have You Heard?* an organization called Women Who Want to Be Women asked: "Do you want to lose your rights not to be drafted? . . . Men, do you want wives and daughters living in barracks with men? Going into combat with them?" In legislative testimony, one Alabamian clearly expressed her repulsion at the idea: "If you want your daughters to be drafted and see them on the afternoon news maimed and bleeding then I am afraid that you are just different, your nature is different from mine. If they had been drafted before and made prisoners of war—Can't you imagine the women made prisoners of war in the hands of these fanatics like our young men were? I am not going into that. I am going to leave what would have happened to these young ladies to your own imagination." One opponent's testimony in North Carolina focused graphically on the realities of war and women's unsuitability for it: "Being inducted is anything but glamorous. Months of boot training is degrading and a dog's life. Weeks of war games and maneuvers is uncivilized and degrading. Combat is a stinking, dirty, living hell where young men act like brave fools, cry like babies, bleed like stuck pigs, and die like yellow dogs. . . . All of the good things that ERA is supposed to bring is undoubtedly obscured by the very dark life that hangs over every young woman . . . if they are to be drafted and probably and undoubtedly fight in mortal combat." Retired brigadier general Gatts argued that even if women could master military skills, they were psychologically and physically unsuited for the job and would weaken national combat effectiveness, thereby creating a threat to national security.[28]

28. Boles, *Politics,* 170; Williams, "Women Against Women," 10; "Editorial," Biloxi *Daily Herald,* February 12, 1973; "Georgia Turns Down Equality for Women: Idea Called Communistic," Los Angeles *Times,* January 27, 1974; Women Who

Since total sexual equality was allegedly characteristic of communistic society, the purported "mandated equality" stemming from the amendment was used to conjure up images of a Communist conspiracy to overthrow the United States. Placards at a Stop ERA rally in Florida read: "Send the ERA back to Russia"; and an opponent in Florida declared, "If this amendment passed, the first step in Khrushchev's plan to take over the United States without firing a shot will have been taken." Similarly, Georgia representative Dorsey Matthews exclaimed that the amendment was "so stinking of Communism it's just pitiful to think of doing something like this to America."[29]

In part, supporters' explanations of the need for the ERA served to answer the arguments that it would bring new responsibilities to women. Supporters' responses to the charges that women would be drafted and that such action might endanger national security were more complex. One young woman in Alabama responded: "First of all I would like to say that if our country went to a war that my conscience could agree with, I would be glad to be drafted in the service of my country." More generally, supporters noted that Congress could draft women, regardless of the ERA: "Ladies, Congress could draft you any day of the week. They don't need the Equal Rights Amendment to do so. They already have that power." Steinberg, a strong supporter of the ERA in Georgia, noted that although Congress could already draft women, the consequences were not dire or unfair:

All women wouldn't serve in combat any more than all men do. In 1971 only 5% of the eligible men were drafted, and 1% of them were in combat. Physical requirements would continue to be a basis for draft classification. In addition, for many women today, the Armed Services is the only way to obtain an education or a skill. Because of different requirements, women often have been denied this opportunity. On a moral basis I would like to add that I'm sure we'd all prefer that none of our children, regardless of sex, would have to go to war. But as a mother of

---

Want to Be Women, *Ladies! Have You Heard?* (N.p., n.d.); Mabel Mize, Alabama Hearings, May 11, 1974; former representative Kitchin Josey, North Carolina Hearings, 20–21; General Gatts, North Carolina Hearings, 5–6.

29. Beyea, "ERA's Last Mile," 46; John W. Baldwin, "Louisiana Defeats ERA," *Progressive*, XXXVIII (September 1, 1974), 37; "Georgia Turns Down Equality for Women," 12.

two daughters, should I be exempt from the risk of either of my children going to war, but you, the parent of a son or sons, risk the loss of your children because they are male?

Having acknowledged that he would doubt the wisdom of the ERA if it mandated equal use of women in combat without regard to skill, William Van Alstyn, professor of constitutional law at Duke University, observed: "My own appreciation of this amendment and its legislative history and the manner in which the Supreme Court of the United States has treated other parts of the Bill of Rights in war-time circumstances professionally reassures me that the amendment would not be applied in a combat situation . . . to tie the hands of Congress to make it ineffective in waging war."[30] Typically, again, the tack of supporters was pragmatic and argumentative, responding specifically to the substance of the opponents' points and ignoring their "irrational" emotional appeals.

The ERA as a Federal Grab for Power

Opponents contended that the ERA's second section, the clause that granted Congress the power to enforce the amendment when it was ratified, would produce a dangerous shift in power from the states to the federal government. Arguing that laws such as those regulating divorce should be changed by state legislatures rather than by the federal government, one opponent in Louisiana temperately remarked: "These things would be better decided closer to home." Others were more outspoken. A state senator in Florida, having supported the amendment in 1972 but opposing it in 1977, explained his shift: "Can Congress write the laws that would be needed to enforce ERA adequately without massive encroachment upon individual liberties? . . . I have become more dissatisfied with and fearful of giving Congress any more power than it has." Ervin, labeling America "the most law-ridden land on earth," predicted: "If it is ratified, the Equal Rights Amendment will transfer from the States to the Federal Government vast governmental powers which have been reserved to the States

30. Nancy Trent, Alabama Hearings, May 11, 1974; Marguerite Dollar, Alabama Hearings, March 1, 1975; Steinberg, Speech, 9; William Van Alstyn, North Carolina Hearings, 81.

throughout our history. By so doing, the Amendment will substantially thwart the purpose of the Constitution to create 'an indestructible union composed of indestructible States' and reduce the States in large measure to powerless zeroes on the nation's map." Another witness at the hearings in North Carolina saw Section 2 as a "sweeping transfer of power from state legislatures to the federal government" and concluded that it "does in fact deliberately ambush our state legislatures and grabs their power for the federal government."[31]

Throughout the South the specter of the ERA as an infringement on states' rights and a federal "grab for power" became an extremely important and emotional issue. The straightforward answers of supporters, relying on rational argument, did not match the intensity of opponents' rhetorical depictions. First, supporters noted that the second section of the ERA was a standard clause in constitutional amendments. Van Alstyn pointed out: "The section . . . simply says Congress shall have the power to enforce the provisions of this article by . . . legislation. The origin of the phrase is not obscure. There are, as others have noted, six other portions of the Constitution that are accompanied by the same clause. . . . In short, the presence of the provision really means only as much as it says. . . . It contemplates a limited authority to prescribe remedies for violations. It does not enlarge the subject matter jurisdiction of Congress."[32] Further, supporters said that the third section, which would have provided a two-year delay before the amendment took effect, was designed to allow states to take action on their own to comply with the first provision without federal interference.

Proponents also urged the necessity of constitutional assurances of women's equality. In Alabama, Marilyn Williams, organizer of the Jefferson County Citizens for the ERA, argued: "Opponents say the 14th Amendment and recent legislation protect women against discrimination but these laws are piece-meal and apply to specific situations. If the 14th Amendment had applied to

31. "Women's Rights Backed by ERA Opposition Unit," New Orleans *Times-Picayune*, May 8, 1974; "Vote Switch Leaves ERA in Doubt," Tallahassee *Democrat*, April 5, 1977; Senator Sam Ervin, in *Congressional Digest* (June–July, 1977), 171; Mrs. John L. Matthews, Jr., North Carolina Hearings, 35.
32. Van Alstyn, North Carolina Hearings, 83–84.

women, they wouldn't have needed the 19th Amendment to vote. Without the ERA, the burden is on each woman to prove her case which means going to court, case by case, an expensive and time-consuming procedure." A North Carolinian supporter observed: "The intent of the amendment is to write women into the Constitution of the United States to give them the basic rights guaranteed in the Constitution of the United States to men. The U.S. Constitution takes no notice of women or their rights. The U.S. Constitution opens declaring all men are born free and equal, all amendments refer to men, people, party, and male citizen." Referring to the closing lines of "The Star-Spangled Banner," she concluded: "If the ERA is not in the national Constitution we will know that for the men only it is the land of the free and for women it is the home of the brave." In an editorial in the Columbus *Ledger*, Carroll Dadisman scoffed at states' efforts, without federal pressure, to correct abuses. The protest against federal interference, he wrote, "sounds a lot like the protests of Georgia legislators in the 1950's, who cried states rights and said they would take care of equality for blacks at the state level, in their own time and way. Blacks have a pretty good idea how long it would have taken Georgia to grant them legal equality had it not been for the 1954 Supreme Court decision and the 1965 Voting Rights Act. Women have a pretty good idea, too, how long it would take Georgia to change voluntarily all of the several hundred laws that discriminate for or against women. After all, it was 1970—yes, 1970— before the Georgia legislature got around to ratifying the 19th Amendment which gave women the right to vote." [33]

Finally, supporters frequently labeled the amendment a human rights measure rather than simply a women's issue. A teacher in Arkansas argued that the passage of the ERA "isn't a women's lib issue, it's a people's issue." In discussing the inequities men face with Social Security, an Alabamian concluded: "All men and all women will be assured the right to be free from discrimination on sex. . . . We are not re-defining social relationships. We are re-affirming the constitutional principle of equality under the law. I

33. Cheryl Blackerly, "ERA Advocate Dispels 'Myths,'" Birmingham *Post-Herald*, March 26, 1975; Gladys Tillett, North Carolina Hearings, 61–63; Carroll Dadisman, "Land's ERA Stand Has Hollow Ring," Columbus *Ledger*, February 11, 1979.

urge you to support ratification of the Equal Rights Amendment, not for women and not for men, but for all of us, we, the people of these United States."[34]

The issues raised in the debates over the ERA in the South illustrate the concerns and strategies of both sides. Since supporters were put on the defensive by well-organized opponents, their rhetoric was often reactive: They felt compelled to respond to the opposition's charges. Opponents, appealing to the shared fears and values of the audience, constructed a vivid rhetorical picture of the amendment as a deceptive Trojan horse filled with dangers to traditional southern culture, morals, and religion. They used public forums to witness, often emotionally, to their allegiance to traditional views and values. In contrast, hoping to persuade through education, supporters relied heavily on an argumentative approach, offering facts and explanations to allay the doubts aroused by opponents. Their tone was frequently dispassionate and deliberately pedagogical. They were lecturing to the unenlightened. However, the differences in approaches were not absolute. Sometimes opponents used expert testimony and cogent reasoning to support their views while supporters were guilty of fallacious reasoning and emotionalism. An examination of pamphlets, editorials, materials distributed by both sides, and testimony before legislative committees and hearings, however, supports the contention that the two sides had generally different rhetorical stances.

Derailing the ERA Bandwagon: Off the Track in Dixie

Many reasons have been offered for the ERA's failure in the South: conflicts over strategy among supporters, advocates' lack of political expertise, poor choice of sponsors in state assemblies, and skillful legislative maneuvering by opponents. However, opponents faced the same problems in many cases. Opponents claimed that the weight of "informed" public opinion and the amendment's inherent flaws doomed it. Yet, clearly, the reasons for its failure are complex. The South's almost total refusal to ratify it,

34. Georgia League of Women Voters, *The Equal Rights Amendment*, 1; Mike Trimble, "Panel Again Delays Action in ERA," *Arkansas Gazette*, January 27, 1977, Sec. A, p. 2; Vi Pitts, Alabama Hearings, October 26, 1974.

despite the initial national momentum and widespread public support, suggests that its legislative failure there had deep roots. I contend that the rhetorical approach of the opposition was a vitally important factor in defeating the amendment in the South. The persuasiveness of opponents' depictions of the ERA stems from their close correspondence to two deeply held southern attitudes: a protectionist view of women, and a suspicion of externally promoted political or social change. The South's view of the social role of women draws strong support from the fundamentalist religious groups that are predominant in the region and from a traditional romantic mythology about "southern women." The suspicion of political change promoted by "outsiders" emerges, historically perhaps, from the South's sense of alienation and its constitutional conservatism. This attitude was reinforced by struggles over civil rights in the 1960s and earlier. Rejection of the ERA became, thus, a symbolic reaffirmation of widely accepted religious beliefs and romantic myths and an assertion of sometimes frustrated political views.

Religious opposition to the ERA in the South came primarily from fundamentalist groups that accepted the inerrancy of the biblical dictates of a subordinate role for women. The ERA, when misconstrued as an attempt to produce absolute sexual equality, contradicted these injunctions. Many religious fundamentalists, perceiving the ERA as a repudiation of biblical truth, agreed with the analysis by a member of the Church of Christ: "To reject the Lord's message is to reject the Lord. We must make the same choice men have always had to make. Will we follow the wisdom of God or the wisdom of man?" The groups in the South holding this view are both numerous and vital. For example, in his comprehensive study of the sociology of the South, John Shelton Reed reported that 42 percent of all southern Protestants "are convinced a person cannot be a good Christian without literal belief in the New Testament." Charles Roland, whose data confirmed Reed's, commented not only on the predominance of fundamentalists in the South but also on their vitality: "Observers agreed that southerners continued to practice their religion in distinctive ways and with an intensity that exceeded that of other regions."[35]

35. Brotherton, *ERA—Women's Lib*, 20–21; John Shelton Reed, *The Enduring South: Subcultural Persistence in Mass Society* (New York, 1972), 61, 63–69; Charles P. Roland, *The Improbable Era: The South Since World War II* (Lexington, Ky., 1975), 119.

Furthermore, these groups put more importance on religion and attended church more regularly. Thus, opposition to the ERA in the South came from numerically dominant groups that were also more religiously active than were most denominations.

The role of these groups in the political process was often clear. Roger M. Williams, in analyzing the defeat of the ERA in Florida in 1977, pointed out: "Observers agree that churches, from the hierarchy down to the parish, were a critical element in organizing this year's Florida opposition. Although the fundamentalist churches took the lead, many other denominations were active also. Pastors excoriated the ERA from their pulpits, in newsletters, and at congregation meetings, focusing on such concerns as homosexuality and the ordination of women." The leadership of fundamentalist groups was apparent in Brady and Tedin's survey of demonstrators supporting rescission. Two-thirds of their sample were members of the denominations they termed fundamentalist (Churches of Christ, Assemblies of God, and Pentecostals); only 5 percent were Catholic and none were Jews, atheists, or agnostics. In contrast, throughout Texas, which ratified the amendment, fundamentalists were only 8 percent of the population while Catholics constituted 25 percent. Even there, however, fundamentalists were very active. One Texas legislator, for example, was deluged by identical letters opposing the ERA. The source was a Sunday school class in a fundamentalist church.[36]

In the South, the passage of the ERA became a theological issue. While the ERA stimulated many salient and central attitudes in the public, opposition deepened and solidified as many people saw it as a threat to their religious convictions. The purely temporal connection between the amendment and such issues as gay rights, legalization of marijuana, and liberalization of abortion laws added further credibility to the depiction of the ERA as an erosion of moral values in a region that, surveys suggest, has a strong moral orientation.[37] Active opposition came to resemble the religious act of witnessing. In essence, the tenor and intensity of religious feeling in the South interacted violently with the substance of the ERA to produce sustained, intense, and vocal resis-

36. Williams, "Women Against Women," 10; Brady and Tedin, "Ladies in Pink," 574; conversation with Jean Waltman (former administrative assistant to Texas state representative Serfonia Thomson), Auburn, Ala., November, 1981.

37. Reed, *The Enduring South*, 69.

tance to its passage. Rhetorically, *equality* became a devil word to opponents who were religiously committed to a hierarchical relationship in which women were subordinate to men. In opposition literature, pro-ERA lobbyists became second Eves, seducing male legislators into rebellion against God's order.

For many southerners, this religious viewpoint was augmented by the romantic myths about women that persist in many aspects of southern culture. Hodding Carter's 1950 characterization of "Southern Chivalry Toward Womanhood" as a mythic contrast between "Beauty and Helplessness" guarded by the "Armed Knight" who offers "Gallantry, Admiration and Protection from Danger" is still an accurate delineation of an influential cultural stereotype. Reflecting more recently on the difficulties of the ERA in the South, Roy Reed, a longtime southern correspondent for the New York *Times*, pointed to "the South's historical fascination with the romantic ideal: men are meant to wield power, women are made to be protected and idealized." In Arkansas, one opponent associated religious beliefs and the romantic myth when he noted "a close correlation of the votes to take God out of the state Constitution and to make sex equal. . . . The ungodly were the ones voting for equality of sex." It seemed to him "natural that a man wants to protect woman" because of "the respect that every man has for his mother and the mother of his children." He urged women to write legislators on flowered, perfumed stationery, enclosing something lacy or frilly to show their femininity.[38]

Thus, the fundamentalist religious injunctions about sex roles, paralleled and augmented by traditional romantic myths about women, created a strong psychological underpinning for arguments against equality. Reinforced by religious beliefs, romanticized by societal myths, and accentuated by the South's notion of its own distinctiveness, these stereotypes of women were rhetorically powerful. Opponents visualized themselves as protecting religious faith, revitalizing traditional myths, and reinforcing the South's pride in its regional distinctiveness and superiority. Their opposition was, for them, a crusade.

38. Hodding Carter, *Southern Legacy* (Baton Rouge, 1950), 65; Roy Reed, "In the South the Road to Equal Rights is Rocky and Full of Detours," New York *Times*, March 20, 1975, Sec. 1, p. 51; Tish Talbot, "Adoption of ERA 'Will Kill Sex,' 'Destroy Home,' Citizens Councils Told: Talk Stresses Motherhood," *Arkansas Gazette*, January 26, 1975, Sec. A, p. 18.

Ironically, the legislative progress already made by women's groups worked in tandem with the stereotypes to thwart the amendment. Opponents have repeatedly pointed to affirmative action programs such as Title IX of the Education Amendment Act of 1972, Title VII of the Civil Rights Act of 1964 (the Equal Employment Opportunities section), and fair-credit legislation as evidence that women currently have equal financial and educational opportunities. These gains substantiated opponents' claims that women were not discriminated against in employment or education and indirectly reinforced opponents' perceptions of the ERA as an attempt to create a "unisex" society. If women already received fair treatment at work and in schools, the ERA was unnecessary. Had supporters of the ERA been less successful earlier in achieving piecemeal recognition and protection of women's rights, opponents' depiction of the amendment as an intrusion into private affairs would have been less credible. Opponents, aware of the current protections for women, could persuasively state that the ERA was unnecessary for economic and educational equality and could concentrate on hypothesizing disastrous repercussions should it be ratified. This, in turn, allowed them to question supporters' "hidden" motives for wanting to bring their Trojan horse inside the city walls. Furthermore, the fact that the ERA would invalidate statutes that offered protective measures to women (*e.g.*, limitations on overtime) added credibility to opponents' charges that it terminated the special privileges and status currently accorded them and was, therefore, counterproductive, if the ideal was protection of women's rights rather than absolute equality. And, of course, equality between the sexes, far from being a desideratum in the South, was a repudiation for many of core values and a violation of comforting myths.

Not only was the ERA a threat to religious and social values, it also reinforced southern political attitudes and fears. Frank A. Rose, former president of the University of Alabama, suggests that historical forces have made the South "a closed organization." Among the results of this attitude, he observes "a militant reaction against self-criticism from within the South, and a chauvinistic reaction against anything that hints of changing social structures, especially 'outsiders' and the federal government." Charles O. Lerche, focusing on the South's changing attitudes, notes an understandable tendency of some southerners to feel that "they are struggling against an open conspiracy and a totally hostile external environment and that they can never receive a fair hearing." Analogously, in an essay entitled "Southern Culture As Defense," Reed concludes that "many southerners seem to feel (as many, it appears, have always felt) that hundreds of thousands of 'meddlers' are conspiring to undermine the South's institutions and the 'southern way of life.'" Moreover, Reed, like Lerche, admits the validity of this perception, since "in a region which has had at least its share of the American experience of rapid social change, one constant has been that change has been imposed from the outside."[39]

Opponents' depiction of the ERA as an extension of federal power and as an attempt to mandate social change corresponded closely to these southern fears and perceptions. Furthermore, the argument that it would transfer powers from local authorities to the federal government was particularly cogent for an audience with strong local allegiances. The tone and punctuation in an Alabama Stop ERA pamphlet convey the intensity of this perception: "*There are two indisputable facts concerning ERA.* I. Under Section 2 ERA would positively TAKE AWAY FROM STATE LEGISLATORS THEIR PRIMARY AUTHORITY IN EVERYTHING THAT INVOLVES THE RIGHTS OF WOMEN. . . . ALL LAWS DIFFERENTIATING BETWEEN THE SEXES WOULD ULTIMATELY BE INTERPRETED BY THE U.S. SUPREME COURT!!!!!!!!! II. Section I is SO VAGUE that NOBODY CAN SAY WITH CERTAINTY WHAT ERA MEANS. ERA WILL MEAN WHATEVER THE SUPREME COURT SAYS."[40] This alleged transference of power from local legislators to the federal government, especially to the Supreme Court, was repugnant in an area that had reacted very strongly to earlier Court decisions on integration, abortion, and prayer in public schools. The Supreme Court, often criticized in the South as a purveyor of liberal social programs, seemed to many likely to use the ERA as an excuse for further intrusion into local affairs. Moreover, the South is historically hesitant about "rights" amendments to the Constitution. For example, the South initially rejected the Fourteenth Amendment, which guaranteed

39. Frank A. Rose, "Reflections on Southern Society," in H. Brandt Ayers and Thomas H. Naylor (eds.), *You Can't Eat Magnolias* (New York, 1972), 303; Charles O. Lerche, *The Uncertain South* (Chicago, 1964), 243; Reed, *The Enduring South*, 89.
40. Pamphlet distributed by Alabama Stop ERA Committee.

equality under law for all citizens, and for a long time delayed ratification of the Nineteenth Amendment, which enfranchised women.

In short, opponents' depictions of the ERA, many of which were used nationally, were particularly compelling for southern audiences because of their correspondence to salient, stable attitudes in the region. The form and substance of the ERA, coupled, ironically, with the recent legislative successes of women's groups, lent credibility to opponents' arguments. Another factor was also at work. Because the ratification process was by state legislatures rather than by national referendum, it conferred unusual power on these groups to influence national policy. Thus, legislative rejection in the South thwarted the ERA nationally, though the majority of citizens supported it. Symbolically, then, rejection of the ERA was an assertion of political power and a reaffirmation of states' rights. Moreover, since the ERA had been so actively opposed by religious groups that viewed it as a threat to biblical morality and traditional social structure, rejection of the ERA was an act of piety and social responsibility. One zealous woman in Florida embraced the leading legislative opponent after the ERA's defeat and exclaimed, "Praise the Lord for you, Senator."[41] To politicians who felt constrained by federal government guidelines and directives, the defeat of the ERA was an assertion of political power. The experiences of the South with federally mandated and supervised changes in civil rights on a unique scale perhaps left a residue of political bitterness. The ERA was characterized as representing the same "social drift" and awakened many of the same fears, perceptions, and myths. The substance, the form, and the timing of the ERA made strong southern opposition to it a certainty. Opponents' rhetorical depictions of it struck a sensitive, exposed nerve in the South.

41. Williams, "Women Against Women," 46.

Contributors

WALDO W. BRADEN is Boyd Professor Emeritus of Speech at Louisiana
State University. He has published widely in speech and history
journals. His latest book is *The Oral Tradition in the South* (1983).

HOWARD DORGAN is professor of communication arts at Appalachian
State University. He wrote one of the essays appearing in *Oratory in
the New South*, was both a contributor to and a coeditor of *The Oratory
of Southern Demagogues*, and is a past editor of the *Southern Speech
Communication Journal*. He is currently the executive secretary of the
Southern Speech Communication Association.

G. JACK GRAVLEE is professor and chair of the Department of Speech
Communication at Colorado State University. He wrote "The New
Deal" in *America in Controversy*, coedited *Pamphlets and the American
Revolution* and *The Whores Rhetorick (1683)*, wrote one of the essays in
The Oratory of Southern Demagogues, and has published articles on
American and British rhetorical studies.

CALVIN M. LOGUE is professor and head of Speech Communication at the
University of Georgia. He wrote one of the essays in *Oratory in the
New South*, coedited *The Oratory of Southern Demagogues*, edited *No
Place to Hide: The South and Human Rights* (works by Ralph McGill),
and has written on southern rhetoric for the *Quarterly Journal of
Speech* and *Communication Monographs*.

HAROLD D. MIXON is associate professor of speech at Louisiana State University. He is former book review editor of the *Southern Speech Communication Journal*. He has served as associate editor of the *Speech*

261

Teacher, Southern Speech Communication Journal, and *Bibliographic Annual.* He wrote essays in *Oratory in the New South* and *The Oratory of Southern Demagogues.*

JOHN H. PATTON is associate professor and chair of the Department of Communication, Newcomb College, Tulane University. He has served on the editorial boards of the *Quarterly Journal of Speech, Central States Speech Communication Journal,* and the *Southern Speech Communication Journal.* He conducts research on rhetorical theory and criticism and has published essays on political and religious communication and related topics.

MARTHA SOLOMON is associate professor of speech communication at Auburn University and is currently editor of the *Southern Speech Communication Journal.* She has recently completed a critical biography of Emma Goldman and has contributed several articles to journals in speech and rhetoric.

DAVID ZAREFSKY is professor of communication studies and associate dean of the School of Speech, Northwestern University. He is the author of *President Johnson's War on Poverty: Rhetoric and History* (1985), coauthor of textbooks on argumentation and debate, and author of several essays on American political rhetoric that have appeared in speech communication journals.

Index

Abernathy, Ralph, 78
American Civil Liberties Union (ACLU), 204
Anderson, Marian, 74
Antilynching laws, Ralph McGill on, 92, 98
"Arrogance of Power" (Fulbright), 121, 133, 137
Ashmore, Harry, 104
Askew, Reubin: as a progressive governor of Florida, 3; for moderation, 9; in support of ERA, 233
Atlanta Manifesto, 18

Baez, Joan, 74
Baldwin, James, 82
Barnett, Ross: criticized by Ralph McGill, 107; as voice for Citizens' Councils, 169, 171–72, 173; on state control of education, 179; on "outside agitators," 182; on the press, 182; attempts interposition in Mississippi, 185
Bilbo, Theodore, 190
Birmingham, Ala.: racial disturbances, 3; bombing of a black church in, 27
Black churches: as centers of minority protest, 8; place of, in civil rights

movement, 56–57; as training grounds, 83
Black education, 98–99
Black employment, 99–100
Black English, 66
Black militants, influence of, 96
Black ministers, and southern black society, 65–67
Black Monday, 166–67
Black music: African origins, 59; as signal songs during slavery era, 59; introduction of militant themes, 60–61; revision of earlier protest songs, 61–62
Black Panther party, 80–81
Black Power, 80
Black rhetoric, of the civil rights movement, 65–88 *passim*
Black separatism, as advocated by Malcolm X, 79
Black subjugation, commercial, 55
Blacks, southern, and the public forum, 7
Bob Jones University, 84
Boggs, Marion: sermon in response to Central High crisis, 28–29; mentioned, 48, 51
Bond, Julian, 192
Brady, Tom: a voice for Citizens'

263